COMMUNICATIONS

George Gerbner and Marsha Siefert, Editors
The Annenberg School of Communications
University of Pennsylvania, Philadelphia

UNESCO
AND THE
MEDIA

C. Anthony Giffard
University of Washington

Longman
New York & London

Unesco and the Media

Longman Inc., 95 Church Street, White Plains, N.Y. 10601

Associated companies:
Longman Group Ltd., London
Longman Cheshire Pty., Melbourne
Longman Paul Pty., Auckland
Copp Clark Pitman, Toronto
Pitman Publishing Inc., New York

Executive editor: Gordon T. R. Anderson
Production editor: Halley Gatenby
Production supervisor: Eduardo Castillo

*Hum
PN
4888
P6
G54
1989*

Library of Congress Cataloging-in-Publication Data
Giffard, C. Anthony.
    Unesco and the media/C. Anthony Giffard.
        p.   cm.—(Longman communication books)
    Includes index.
    ISBN 0-8013-0232-3
    1. Journalism—Political aspects—United States.   2. Unesco in the
press—United States.   3. Press—United States—Influence.
4. Freedom of the press—United States—History—20th century.
5. Press and politics—United States—History—20th century.
I. Title.   II. Series.
PN4888.P6G54   1988
070.4'49341767—dc19

ISBN 0-8013-0232-3

88 89 90 91 92 93 9 8 7 6 5 4 3 2 1

Contents

FOREWORD

Who Did In UNESCO?

Leonard R. Sussman

Anthony Giffard has made a valuable, perhaps a landmark contribution in devising and conducting this study of American press coverage of the U.S. withdrawal from Unesco. While important for understanding the Unesco controversy, the study has far greater significance. It tells something about the Reagan administration's attitude toward multilateralism and, in particular, the U.N. system. But perhaps of greatest significance is Giffard's study of the theory and procedures of American journalism, and, equally important, the successful manipulation of the news media by a few Washington officials. Whether one agrees or disagrees with the policy of withdrawal from Unesco—any president has the right to pursue and achieve his or her policy—this study asks whether the press was manipulated in pursuit of that policy. That question is a serious one for Americans, and for the press. But manipulation of the press was not the sole, perhaps not even the main reason for the withdrawal.[1] The other reasons, and the direct role of the press in supporting withdrawal, also deserve the serious attention, and the study systematically examines these issues.

Beginning with the Hutchins Commission report in 1947, there has been increasing need to examine the role of the mass media in American life. A great deal depends upon American journalism—more today than in 1947: domestic as well as foreign policy agendas, policy debates and policy fulfillment are largely influenced by mass media acts of commission or omission.

From 1969 to 1977 for Freedom House I supervised Peter Braes-

trup's study of the performance of the American mass media during the two-month Tet offensive initiated by the North Vietnamese in 1968.[2] In a two-volume analysis of the ultimate distortion of that event by American news media, Braestrup concluded that this was not a conspiratorial exercise, but rather an institutional or procedural failure. He said, moreover, that unless fundamental changes were made in the way the media organize themselves to cover major events, the same kind of distortion would occur again in either domestic or foreign news coverage. The decade-long reporting of the controversies at Unesco, I believe, has produced just such a distortion in the American news media coverage of Unesco, the organization, and Unesco, the crisis.

I have been a journalist, and I am a member of the board of the World Press Freedom Committee, which Giffard credits as the prime mover in the press coalition opposing the communications programs of Unesco. Freedom House called the first press conference in the United States in June 1976 to warn that serious challenges to Western modes of journalism and, indeed, press independence, would be made at the first Unesco regional meeting on the media in San José, Costa Rica, the following month. That conference alerted the press to focus on the controversies over Unesco communications issues.

I published the first book on the subject in 1977. Giffard extensively quotes my statements to congressional committees, and in newspaper and magazine articles opposing withdrawal. Because of his time frame he does not cite my extensive writing, speaking and participation in international meetings, beginning in 1977, in opposition to many Unesco programs in the field of communications. I regarded—and continue to regard—many of those programs as *potentially* detrimental to press freedom. But at the same time I tried to support the valid appeals from the Third World for technical facilities and better coverage.

I would, therefore, amplify one statement quoted in this study. I did, indeed, recommend early on that *if* Unesco approved certain press-control measures, the U.S. should withhold funding. I did not contemplate U.S. withdrawal from the organization. On the contrary, for more than a year in 1975 the U.S. had withheld all funding over another issue, and that question had been resolved in favor of the American position. Many countries in the U.N. system have followed the same procedure. It is, I believe, a tactic of last resort. Withdrawal, I have always felt, is not a tactic to be considered.

That brings me to several points in amplification of the Giffard study, points relating to the context in which the U.S. withdrawal was played out, and finally, the theory of journalism which, I believe, underlies the bleak coverage of Unesco by the U.S. media.

The press from the beginning missed the larger story because it was

taking its lead on the Unesco question mainly from the State Department spokesman, Gregory Newell. He was an unchangeable ideologue, a man with a mission that was established before the Reagan administration came into office and that encompassed the entire U.N. system. One could have read his message in large road signs in California 30 years earlier: 'Get the UN out of the U.S., and the U.S. out of the UN.' A generation of conservative ideologues had grown up on this slogan. Now, in 1981, the new administration could act on that slogan. The first Reagan draft budget eliminated all funds for Unesco, but they were restored. There was no clear public mandate for that policy. On the contrary, public opinion polls for decades had regularly shown majority support for the U.N., while indicating disapproval for certain policies and procedures of the organizations. To seek a major change, the administration would need to prepare domestic and foreign publics.

Unesco was clearly the weak link in the U.N. system. It had become a forum for social, political, economic, historic, cultural and other discussions; for points of view that were indeed alien to mainline American thinking, but were, nevertheless, reflections of views in the real world. Ideologues in Washington would naturally oppose many of these views, but as the press was later to do, they erroneously equated discussions with formal acts of influence. In all the years of acrimonious debates at Unesco, I believe, there was never a resolution or an official action that assaulted a basic American interest. Indeed, the greatest loss to American interests and credibility were incurred by the policy of withdrawal and by withdrawal itself.

I recall a private conversation in 1983, the week before the decision to withdraw was made. I was speaking to one of three persons most responsible for setting withdrawal in motion—not the secretary of state or the deputy secretary. Neither of them had been informed by Assistant Secretary Newell as he began the campaign to pull out. In fact, the campaign had moved far along without their knowledge. Newell, only recently plucked from the White House staff to manage the withdrawal, was supported by several key individuals. With one of them I tried to reason at the final hour. The answer I received was that the Unesco withdrawal would be "a shot across the bow of the whole UN system." And indeed it was. But the press missed that larger story. That story, had it been told then, I believe would have cast a far different light on the Unesco controversy as it was being orchestrated from Newell's office. A British newspaper first revealed Newell's plan to manage the news in favor of withdrawal. Where was American investigative reporting when it was needed?

Even if Unesco was as evil an organization as pictured by several manipulators at the Department of State, the American public—as this

study demonstrates—never received a fair chance to weigh the evidence pro and con. Such balanced evidence seldom appeared in print, and almost never coherently. Indeed, the case against Unesco was won not in 1984 or 1985, but in the years from 1976 to 1983 when Unesco programs critical of news flows were vilified regularly and made to appear to be the only program of the multifaceted organization.

In those seven years the self-interest of the news media was thoroughly mobilized. Unesco was increasingly and imprecisely described as the hotbed of anti–free press machinations. No distinction was made in the news media between the valid appeals from the Third World for communication facilities and training, and for improved coverage of Third World news by the Western media, as distinct from the demand of some ideologues in the Third World and, of course, the Soviet bloc, to alter the *content* of global news flows. Good reporting should have made that distinction clear.

To be sure, Unesco was not blameless. Its programs repeatedly reinforced the image that a new, undefined "information order" would somehow, some day be ordained. Not until 1983 did the organization officially begin to define the so-called order as a "continuous and evolving process." That, in effect, rejected the concept of the imposition of an "ordered" system. But by then the mind set had been established, and Unesco was perceived as having hidden agendas. The middle-level Secretariat, particularly in the free-flow division, was not restrained until it was too late. While it could be said that member states were responsible for programming, in reality the Secretariat played a major role at every stage. All the official denials of a hidden agenda by the director general could not undo the seven years of bitter controversy.

During these years, a dozen free-press troops from the media nongovernmental agencies marched up the Unesco hill, time after time, to fight what they regarded as code words for censorship and press control: "protection of journalists," "licensing," "press responsibility," "information sovereignty," and others perceived by the non-government organizations as part of the hidden agenda. I was a regular part of that assemblage.

Lost in the melee over these issues, however, were the valid claims of Third World countries for better communication facilities and improved coverage. And that loss is not all due to Western misperception, resistance to change, or fear of competition. The Third World leadership, along with the Unesco Secretariat, misjudged the impact being made on two principal players: first, the American press, and second, the American government. Without the mind set against Unesco that had evolved over seven years, I doubt whether the 1983 U.S. decision to withdraw could have been successful.

Why, then, did a free press act without adequate balance—almost exactly as free-press opponents would have predicted? That is an important question. The Giffard study notes the role of self-interest, which was, indeed, an important factor. But there was also a procedural element as there had been in the press distortion of the Tet offensive in 1968. Giffard notes the inverted pyramid as the journalistic style that enables the top of the story to gain the headlines and the bottom to disappear when cutting is needed.

But what determines which part of the story is most important? In American journalism, conflict, alleged corruption, and attacks on established authority draw sure-fire headlines. The assault is reported at the top of the story, the defense generally appears down below and can easily be ignored or eliminated. Repeated often, this attack with little or no defense forms a pattern. The pattern is reinforced by widespread computerization of news. Press a button for Unesco, and out comes a backgrounder repeating the older attacks for reuse as the newest charge is fed into the computer. The pattern is reinforced. Much American journalism is based upon conforming new reporting to an existing pattern, and going on from there.

It should be remembered that only 8 or 10 journalists covered the Unesco story for 200 million Americans over a long period. Those few men and women generally spent a day on each story, against demanding deadlines and competitive pressure. Some visited the scene of the story briefly and wrote the piece from interviews with government or non-government officials, all of whom—as the study shows—were committed antagonists. Few read the massive program outlines and papers. It has been argued that the U.S. government was the natural source for most stories because the government was the principal player in a game in which only governments can play. But this ignores the fact that hundreds of thousands of Americans were participants, directly or indirectly, in Unesco science, education and other programs. The U.S. Navy depended on Unesco oceanographic science; all Americans were served by Unesco's copyright responsibilities and countless other programs. The failure in the coverage was not that the challenges to Western journalistic systems were misreported. They were not misreported. There were and are and will always be such challenges. Indeed, there should be regular, serious critiquing of the press by its own practitioners and by others. The great failure was not to place those challenges in perspective.

First, who was making the challenges (it was some governments using Unesco)?

Second, what was the chance for the success of censorious resolutions at Unesco (very small, since program decisions were made by consensus and not majority vote)? There would be no commanded

change in Western news systems, though notably, through the years on their own initiative and probably as a result of challenges at Unesco, the major U.S. news services improved their coverage of the Third World.

Third, and most important, what was happening in scores of other Unesco programs—in education, science, heritage preservation, copyright protection, literacy—conducted successfully without a word of press coverage?

Finally, the press repeatedly covered Unesco as though it was about to install press censorship—an impossibility—and when that did not happen, time after time, the press troops marched back down the hill. But they did so with no banner headlines proclaiming that the threat had evaporated once again. So both sides lived to fight another day, and both helped gut Unesco. For when the State Department formally added politicization, financial extravagance and maladministration to the charges against Unesco, the American press was amply conditioned to believe only the negatives.

NOTES

1. The public was also manipulated. Hundreds of thousands of members of non-governmental organizations in science, education, culture and other fields were beneficiaries of Unesco programs. Their organizations did not support the U.S. withdrawal from Unesco. Nor did some 90 U.S. government agencies at home and abroad. Yet the brief summary placed before the secretary of state misleadingly reported the attitudes of those polled. The body that Congress created to advise the State Department on Unesco affairs—a 100-member group representing the U.S. public—had its staff removed and funds withheld. This undermining of public awareness reduced the possibilities for public expression, and that also affected press coverage. But the press itself could have uncovered the public-interest aspect of the Unesco question.
2. Peter Braestrup, *Big Story—How the American Press and Television Reported and Interpreted the Crisis of Tet-1968 in Vietnam and Washington* (Boulder, Colo.: Westview, 1977).

Preface

Few have been as critical of the United Nations Educational, Scientific and Cultural Organization as the Western Press. The editorials and broadcasts would fill volumes.

                          —*San Jose* (*California*) Mercury-News

This report is about how the world's largest free press system reacted to a challenge to its global interests. It is a story of how the American media led a campaign against attempts by the Soviet bloc and the world's developing nations to play a larger role in international communications. More specifically, it is an account of how the media initiated, encouraged and reported on the U.S. withdrawal from Unesco, the United Nations Educational, Scientific and Cultural Organization.

Analysis of this coverage is important for several reasons. It provides a case study of U.S. media coverage of a foreign policy issue. Given the belief that an informed public can better make or accept policy decisions than one that is misinformed or kept in the dark, one can ask whether Americans were given sufficient information about the withdrawal to make an informed judgment on the issue. A second reason is that the Unesco withdrawal was intimately linked to the dispute over the proposed New World Information Order, also known as the New International Information Order. The media and the Reagan administration cited Unesco's backing for this new order as a major reason for the pullout. But Unesco's communication policies have the virtually unani-

mous support of the developing countries, and those countries are the beneficiaries of most Unesco programs. They stood to lose the most if the United States stopped paying 25 percent of Unesco's budget. One of the complaints from proponents of a New International Information Order is that issues of importance to them are treated unsympathetically in the Western media. This analysis, then, is also a case study of the validity of their criticisms. Third, since American media organizations were not merely impartial observers, but had played an active role in opposing moves in Unesco to establish a new information order, one can ask whether the proclaimed Western journalistic tenets of objectivity, impartiality and balance were met.

Unesco was founded in London in 1946 to promote peace and international cooperation in education, science and culture. It has about 160 member states, each with one vote at the biennial General Conference that usually meets at Unesco's Paris headquarters. It is one of the largest U.N. agencies, with an annual budget at the time the United States withdrew of about $200 million. It also carries out programs funded by other agencies and donors.

Unesco's major program areas include education, natural science, social and human sciences, culture, and communication. Education is the largest sector, with an emphasis on combatting illiteracy in developing countries. The natural science programs strengthen the ability of member states to use science and technology, and provide a structure for international research projects. The social and human sciences sponsor the study of development, economics, human settlements, human rights and peace. The cultural programs promote the study of cultures, facilitate cultural development and artistic creation, and restore and preserve cultural monuments. Communications programs include studies of the development of communications systems, book promotion and international exchanges, and studies on the role of the media and the impact of mass communications. More recently, Unesco has been the main forum for debate over a New World Information Order.

It was support for the new information order, coupled with criticism of Israel, that first drew the attention of American media to Unesco. The media were concerned that proposals to extend government control over the press, to limit the activities of Western news agencies, and to license journalists—although never formally adopted by Unesco—would hamper their international operations. Unesco's programs to develop communications capabilities in the Third World, while part of U.S. government policy, were seen as also potentially creating competition for the Western agencies.

To defend their interests, media organizations resorted to a range of

tactics. They drew attention to the most controversial of Unesco's communications policies in news reports and editorials while ignoring its useful programs—thus undermining Unesco's reputation and standing. They formed a lobbying group to monitor Unesco and influence its deliberations. They put pressure on Congress to threaten a cut in U.S. funding of Unesco if it persisted in attacks on the free press. And they organized widely publicized international conferences to endorse the free press ideology. When the United States announced its intention to withdraw from the organization altogether, the media organizations refused to take a public stand on the issue. But their coverage favored those who supported the withdrawal and largely ignored its opponents. In short, the media not only reported the media debate but were partisan actors in it.

The media found willing allies in their campaign against Unesco. Political conservatives, spearheaded by the Washington, D.C.–based Heritage Foundation, singled out Unesco as the 'worst case' model of the entire U.N. system and campaigned for withdrawal as a warning shot to other U.N. agencies—and as a first step toward pulling out of the United Nations itself. American Jewish organizations, concerned about challenges to Israel in Unesco, made common cause with the media and the right-wing ideologues. The election of Ronald Reagan in 1980 provided the opportunity to turn this ideology into action. The Reagan administration's charges against Unesco—that it was politicized, anti-Western, anti–free market and anti–free press—echoed the critique of the Heritage Foundation and the media. These charges were then reported by the media as justification for withdrawal. And in December 1983 the administration announced it would withdraw from Unesco after a year's notice if reforms were not made. In retrospect, it seems clear that it planned to withdraw no matter what reforms were undertaken.

In the year that followed, various groups sought to influence public opinion in favor of going ahead with the withdrawal, or of retaining membership in Unesco and seeking reform from within. Arrayed against Unesco were the U.S. government, with its power to manipulate media coverage, and the Heritage Foundation, which ran a sophisticated campaign to have the United States pull out. Heritage Foundation views, expressed in a series of papers and reports from 1982 onward, were adopted by the Reagan administration as the political justification for the withdrawal. The foundation's arguments reached the press through three channels. News reports quoted administration spokespersons, who echoed the Heritage position. Columns and editorials by Heritage Foundation writers appeared under their bylines in the press. And Heritage position papers, mailed to editorial writers and columnists nationwide, became the basis for numerous articles urging the United States to make

good on its threat to withdraw. Opposing the withdrawal were the U.S. National Commission for Unesco, a body set up by the State Department to advise it on Unesco policy, but whose views in this instance were ignored. The commission distributed materials to the press arguing that although the agency had problems, the best course of action would be to retain membership and seek reform from within. Unesco offices in the United States put out press releases, organized talks and sent letters to editors refuting factual inaccuracies in reports. They were assisted by a Washington public relations firm, Wagner & Baroody, that was paid $15,000 a month plus expenses to lobby for continued membership.

Unesco, at the prodding of the United States and other Western nations, undertook a series of reforms to meet the criticisms. At the end of 1984, however, the United States announced that the reforms were too little, too late, and confirmed the pullout. It was joined a year later by the United Kingdom. The departure of these two nations cut Unesco's funding by some 30 percent and undermined the universality of the organization.

OBJECT AND SCOPE

The object of this book is to evaluate American media coverage of the withdrawal. It is not intended to assess the merits of arguments of those who criticized the organization, or those who defended its programs and refuted the charges. There were good arguments to be made on both sides. The critics clearly had a point—and Director General Amadou-Mahtar M'Bow himself acknowledged that Unesco was a "human organization that had its shortcomings." Conversely, Unesco's worldwide activities in the fields of education, science and culture clearly were commendable. Ultimately the debate centered on whether it was in the best interests of the United States to withdraw or to remain a member. The question is whether these conflicting perspectives were presented to the public in a balanced, objective manner.

The primary focus of the book is a systematic analysis of media items relating to the withdrawal. The analysis is both quantitative and qualitative. It seeks to show, through a detailed examination of more than 4,000 television and newspaper reports, editorials and editorial page columns, the extent of the coverage in the nation's media from 1984 through 1987. It examines the thrust of that coverage and attempts to evaluate its quality.

Conspicuously lacking in the bulk of the coverage was any detailed exposition of Unesco's structure, history, mission and programs. Chapter 1 thus provides an overview of the agency's worldwide activities in the

fields of education, the natural and social sciences, culture, and communications. It also examines U.S. participation in each of these areas. The intention is to put the coverage in perspective and to indicate what could have been reported to balance the overwhelmingly negative image that was, in fact, projected. Since Unesco's activities in the communications field were a major factor in the decision to withdraw, Chapter 2 provides perspective on the debate over a New World Information Order. It traces the development of the concept at meetings of the non-aligned nations and at Unesco conferences and examines the reaction of Western media to the proposed new order, documenting steps taken by media organizations to maintain their dominant role in international communications. Among these were efforts to defuse the issue by offering technical assistance and training to developing nations, and moves to have the U.S. Congress exert financial pressure on Unesco to modify its communications policies. Previous studies of media coverage of Unesco activities are summarized at the end of this chapter.

Chapter 3 traces in some detail the events from the announcement by the United States in December 1983 that it planned to withdraw until it did so a year later. Using source documents, news reports, briefings and press releases, it identifies the arguments for and against withdrawal, the individuals and organizations that were involved, and the forums where the debate took place, including Unesco meetings and U.S. congressional hearings. The chronology provides a month-by-month account of efforts by Unesco to adopt reforms that would satisfy its critics, and of Western reaction to those efforts. It documents the highly politicized nature of the debate, with various interest groups striving to maintain U.S. membership or to proceed with the proposed withdrawal. The arguments for and against the pullout are presented in considerable detail to indicate the range of opinion that was available for inclusion in news reports and editorial comment.

Chapter 4 comprises a systematic analysis of the amount and kind of news distributed to American media by the four agencies or syndicates that provided the bulk of the coverage: the Associated Press, United Press International, the New York Times News Service and the Washington Post/Los Angeles Times News Service. It uses content analysis to determine the topics covered in the agency reports and their orientation toward Unesco and the withdrawal. The analysis also compares coverage by the four agencies, their use of sources and the structure of their dispatches. As a whole, the news agency coverage proved to be strongly anti-Unesco and supportive of the withdrawal. About 70 percent of the the themes in the dispatches were hostile to the organization or pro-withdrawal. There was very little difference among the agencies in terms of the topics they emphasized or their orientation toward Unesco.

The agency dispatches are then compared in Chapter 5 with what actually appeared in the nation's media. Based on a file of more than 4,000 items collected nationwide by a commercial clipping service, the analysis examines the extent to which the agency reports were used, the kind of reports that were selected for publication, and how they were edited. The same content analysis scheme as applied to the agency reports is used to examine what appeared in the press. The analysis shows that reports that ran in daily newspapers were even more antagonistic toward Unesco than the agency dispatches on which they were based.

A surprisingly high proportion of all the clippings about Unesco were not news reports but editorials or editorial-page columns. These are also analyzed quantitatively and qualitatively. Chapter 6 gives particular attention to editorials that were syndicated by various services and appeared in identical form in dozens of different newspapers around the country, and to the editorial stance of the influential 'elite' newspapers. The editorials tended to reinforce the anti-Unesco orientation of the news reports, and were in fact even more critical of the organization, reflecting the bias of the editors and publishers. Chapter 7 looks at the editorial columns, including the output of each major syndicated columnist who wrote about the issue, since their columns appeared in hundreds of newspapers with a huge total circulation. Like the editorials, most of the columns were highly critical of Unesco and supportive of the pullout.

Although the Unesco story did not lend itself to television coverage—it had to do with ideas, not action—it did receive some attention on network news programs. Only a handful of events were covered at all, and those that were tended to show Unesco in an unfavorable light. These TV reports, which for many people would have been the sole source of information about the debate, are critiqued in Chapter 8. Once the withdrawal took effect in December 1984, media interest in Unesco faded rapidly. The amount of coverage and the issues raised are discussed in Chapter 9.

Finally, the book focuses on the various parties that tried to influence the course of the debate and, ultimately, the U.S. decision. The antagonists can be divided into two broad camps: those critical of Unesco and in favor of the withdrawal, and those who recognized the value of Unesco's programs and wanted the United States to remain a member, seeking reform from within. The former included the U.S. government, the Heritage Foundation, and certain Jewish organizations, particularly the Anti-Defamation League, B'nai B'rith. Those lobbying for continued membership included Unesco itself, the U.S. National Commission for Unesco, and scientific and cultural organizations that stood to lose as a result of the pullout. Efforts made by these groups to influence media coverage are examined in detail in Chapter 10. A summary and conclusions follow in Chapter 11.

What emerges is a comprehensive assessment of how the media reported and commented on an important news event. The book traces the flow of information from the universe of relevant events that could have been reported, through the prism of the news "wholesalers"—the major agencies and syndicates—to the media gatekeepers who decided what should or should not appear in the nation's newspapers and television programs. It illustrates how the media, the government and certain special interests became involved in a symbiotic relationship that resulted in one-sided, self-serving and uniformly negative coverage of Unesco.

ACKNOWLEDGMENTS

I am grateful to various people and organizations for assistance in preparing this study. The Edward Lamb Foundation, Inc., and Freedom House helped pay for the content analysis. Michael Cochran and Carolyn Byerly, both students at the University of Washington, spent many hours assisting me with the research. Several colleagues at the *Seattle Post-Intelligencer*—notably Alan Boyle, Don Graydon, Paul McElroy, Karin McGinn and Bob Olesen—collected materials and offered useful insights. My son Johan provided the computer expertise to analyze the data and produce the graphics. And Pat Dinning made the manuscript look presentable and carried more than her share of work so that I could get on with writing it.

UNESCO
AND THE
MEDIA

CHAPTER 1

Unesco's Structure and Programs

Press coverage of Unesco focused on a limited range of issues—for the most part criticisms of Unesco's performance. One thesis of this study is that the American public was not given a full range of information about the organization's activities as a basis on which people could form their own conclusions and value judgments. If the performance of the press in providing a full, fair and balanced account of Unesco is to be assessed, one needs to examine not only what was published but what could have been covered. Much of the coverage of Unesco before the U.S. decision to withdraw dealt with its communications policies, specifically with attempts to implement a New World Information Order. Once the withdrawal was announced, the media generally reflected the reasons given by the U.S. government for pulling out—allegations of political bias, an unwieldy bureaucracy and a bloated budget—although communications policies remained a prominent part of the coverage. There were references to the value of Unesco's programs, but they were outweighed by the criticisms. And whole areas of Unesco's activities were ignored altogether. For that reason one needs to examine what the press could have reported—from freely available sources—had it made a real effort to present an objective account of the dispute.

STRUCTURE

Unesco was founded in 1946. Its purpose as set forth in its constitution is "to contribute to peace and security by promoting collaboration among the nations through education, science and culture."[1] Its programs seek

1

the eradication of illiteracy, the promotion of scientific research, preservation of the world's cultural treasures, and the free flow of ideas.

Unesco is the third largest of 15 specialized agencies within the U.N. system. Based in Paris, it is legally autonomous from the United Nations in New York. Unesco has its own constitution, its own budget, and its own staff. However, it reports to the U.N. General Assembly through the Economic and Social Council.

Like other U.N. agencies, Unesco is governed by its member states. Most countries have national commissions that serve as advisory organizations in preparing for and participating in Unesco meetings. They also help implement Unesco programs and evaluate them. The U.S. National Commission for Unesco, for example, is a 100-member body of individuals and non-government organizations created by Congress in 1946 to advise the U.S. government on matters relating to Unesco and to promote understanding of the agency's objectives among people in the United States.

Representatives of the member states meet at a General Conference every two years. Each country has one vote in the General Conference. Most decisions can be taken by a simple majority, but the recent practice has been to iron out differences before a vote is taken and then adopt resolutions by consensus. The General Conference is Unesco's supreme body. It determines the policies and main lines of work of the organization's programs. Detailed implementation of the programs and the budget is left to a 51-member Executive Board, elected to four-year terms by the General Conference. Until the withdrawal, the United States was a permanent member, along with the Soviet Union, the United Kingdom, France and China. The Executive Board meets in regular session twice a year to scrutinize Unesco's programs and spending. It submits the draft program and budget to the General Conference and is responsible for executing the conference's decisions, and for senior staff appointments. A Secretariat headed by the director general, who is the chief administrative officer, services the two legislative bodies. It prepares for meetings and functions as the executive arm in implementing decisions and programs. The director general is nominated by the Executive Board and appointed by the General Conference, usually for a six-year term. In 1980 the Secretariat had a staff of 4,048, consisting of 2,566 headquarters posts and 1,482 posts in the field.

The General Conference adopts a Medium Term Plan that sets out guidelines from a six-year perspective for programs that are implemented over three two-year planning periods. Member states—numbering 160 in 1987—are consulted before the Medium Term Plan and budget are prepared. The Secretariat analyzes their responses and drafts proposals for specific programs. These plans then are discussed by the Executive

Board, which makes recommendations to the General Conference. In practice, nearly all proposals made by the director general and the Secretariat are approved. The current Medium Term Plan was adopted at the fourth extraordinary session of the General Conference held in Paris in the fall of 1982 and covers the years 1984–1989.

Unesco's biennial budget for 1984–85 was $374.4 million, derived from contributions from members. Almost 40 percent of the regular budget is spent on educational projects, 28 percent on science and the rest on social science, culture and communication. Most of the money is spent on projects benefiting developing countries. The budget must be approved by a two-thirds majority of the members. National contributions are assessed on the basis of a formula that takes into account a nation's size and wealth. The United States was the largest contributor, providing 25 percent of the regular budget. There is an upper limit of 25 percent in the U.N. assessment scale; otherwise the U.S. share would have been closer to 35 percent. The Soviet Union was second at 10.98 percent; then Japan at 9.48 percent; West Germany, 8.22 percent; France, 6.19 percent; the United Kingdom, 4.41; Italy, 3.41 and Canada, 3.24. These eight nations together contributed 71 percent of the regular budget. On the other hand, the required two-thirds majority needed to approve the budget could be made up of 108 nations who among them contribute only 2.7 percent of the total.

In addition to its regular budget, Unesco serves as an executing agency for projects funded by other institutions. This involves planning, recruiting consultants, buying equipment, administering fellowships and evaluating programs. Unesco carries out many programs funded by the United Nations Development Program (UNDP), which in the 1981–83 biennium allocated $138.6 million to such projects. Unesco also implements between 10 and 15 percent of the World Bank's educational programs. Funds in trust from bilateral donors form another source of Unesco funding. In 1983 bilateral aid funds from donors like Germany, Norway, the Netherlands and Switzerland amounted to more than $10 million. Total extra-budgetary revenues in 1981–83 amounted to about $294 million. Accounts are audited by an external auditor. In 1983 that was the comptroller and auditor-general of the United Kingdom.

PROGRAMS

Unesco's 14 major programs fall under five substantive sectors: education, natural science, social science, culture and communication. Other programs include human rights, the status of women, and copyright issues. While most of Unesco's efforts are directed at improving these

sectors in developing countries, several programs benefit the industrialized nations, including the United States, either directly or indirectly. Unesco's operations are set out in the many books and documents it publishes. Recent, popularized accounts include Peter I. Hajnal's *Guide to Unesco* and *Unesco on the Eve of its Fortieth Anniversary*, prepared by Unesco staff.[2] The most comprehensive assessment of the usefulness of Unesco programs in relation to American interests is to be found in a document prepared by the U.S. State Department in 1983–84. The *U.S./Unesco Policy Review* was undertaken as part of a systematic study of all multilateral organizations in which the United States participated and to which it contributed.[3] The document describes, from an American perspective, Unesco's strengths and weaknesses. The following summary of the policy review and of official Unesco documents emphasizes positive aspects of the organization's activities that could have been, but usually were not, included in the U.S. press coverage of the withdrawal.

Education

General. Education is the largest of Unesco's program sectors, using 37 percent of its budget. In the 1984–85 biennial budget, this sector amounted to about $86 million. In addition, another $91 million in program funds were administered by Unesco for other organizations including the UNDP, the United Nations Fund for Population Activities (UNFPA), the World Bank and other regional development banks. Many developing countries rely on Unesco for assistance in planning educational programs, for teacher training and for research. It plans and implements programs to combat illiteracy, especially among adults; to promote equal educational opportunity; to improve the quality of education; and to foster international understanding. Unesco also collects and analyzes educational data and publishes the authoritative *Handbook of Educational Statistics*.

Literacy training is part of one major program in the sector, Education for All, which in 1984–85 accounted for $31 million of the regular budget and $24 million in other funds. The focus of the Education for All program is to apply the principles of the Universal Declaration of Human Rights to education. Several subprograms focus on literacy training for girls and women, the handicapped, refugees and migrants. The agency has launched major educational programs in Africa, Latin America and the Caribbean aimed at eliminating illiteracy by the end of the century. Unesco estimates that since 1979 it has taught more than 15 million people to read, and that each year it helps train almost 30,000 teachers. It has led the international campaign that has cut the illiteracy

rate worldwide from 39 percent in 1960 to 32 percent in 1985—although the absolute numbers of illiterates has continued to increase because of population growth. Unesco's 1984 Literacy Prizes give an idea of the range of programs it funds. One prize went to the National Institute for Adult Education of Mexico, which had taught 1 million people to read and write in three years. Another went to the People's Republic of China for its literacy program in Sechuan Province, covering 800 villages and more than a million people. The Literacy Campaign of Turkey was commended for enrolling 3.8 million adults, 70 percent of them women, in a literacy program. And the Cuban National Association of the Blind was cited for training 200 specialists to work with blind illiterates.

Other typical examples of Unesco's educational programs include the distribution of 8 million primary school textbooks and teacher's guides in Jamaica. In Brazil, Unesco is working with UNDP in a project to establish services for the early detection and treatment of deafness, and to set up a Braille printing press. In Thailand, Unesco is providing teacher training among refugees on the Thai-Kampuchea border, and is helping produce visual aids and textbooks there. A Unesco project in Cameroon used radio broadcasts to reach a half-million people with literacy instruction. It has given aid to the Palestine Liberation Organization in the form of higher education fellowships, and has carried out a feasibility study on the creation of a Palestinian Open University. An example of extra-budgetary funding for educational projects is a grant of $1.3 million from the Arab Gulf Program for United Nations Development Organizations (AG Fund) in 1985. The money goes to strengthen teacher training in the Maldives, to increase the output of school textbooks in Chad, and to promote literacy in Peru through the mass media.

A second major program dealing with education goes under the heading the Formulation and Application of Education Policies. This program helps members draw up and implement educational policies. It includes planning and administration of education, teacher training, educational equipment and school buildings. In Sierra Leone, for example, a Unesco project trains primary school teachers to prepare them for rural and community life. Other programs are helping developing countries to design teaching materials in accordance with local needs and to produce them locally, instead of importing them at great expense. Unesco has established regional school-building centers in Africa, Latin America, Asia and the Caribbean to design buildings appropriate for different climates and cultures. They also encourage the design and production of inexpensive, functional school furniture that can be made locally, preferably by hand.

A third major program, entitled Education, Training and Society, deals with issues that arise from the interaction between education, cul-

ture, science and technology. This involves, for instance, developing school syllabuses that will help students understand the impact of human populations on the environment, and how to alleviate the problems they cause.

A Unesco agency, the International Bureau of Education (IBE), based in Geneva, is the world's biggest single source of information on educational organizations, themes, problems and statistics. It is the only source of such data for Africa and Eastern Europe. Its documentation center provides members with a question-and-answer service, and prepares reference books like the *Education Thesaurus*. The IBE, in turn, launched the International Network for Educational Information (INED), which publishes a directory of educational documentation services And is compiling a worldwide data base of education information.

U.S. Participation. Prior to the withdrawal, more than 300 Americans participated in programs relating to scientific, vocational and environmental education, education for international understanding and the teaching of human rights, and for the prevention of drug abuse. Unesco personnel records show, for example, that American academics served as consultants for programs rehabilitating the disabled in Bahrain; in training Portuguese educators and parents in special education; in teaching climatology and astrophysics in Lebanese schools; in developing science and technology infrastructures in the Caribbean; in computer-aided instruction at Beijing Normal University; and in teaching English as a second language in Brazil.[4] Unesco selected these educators on an individual basis, not as representatives of the U.S. government, although the government was represented regularly at Unesco conferences.

The State Department's review notes that Unesco's development activities parallel U.S. foreign policy interests and go beyond the scope of American bilateral assistance efforts. The programs, it said, "contribute to international peace and stability." Also awarded high marks was Unesco's function as a clearinghouse and disseminator of ideas and educational materials—functions "unlikely to be duplicated by any other source." Withdrawal from Unesco, said the review, would be seen as a lessening of American commitment to international cooperation in education. The United States would lose some of its capability to affect Unesco's educational programs, and its absence from Unesco conferences could reduce the influence of Western ideas and values. A withdrawal would also risk "increasing the already sizable influence in Unesco of Soviet bloc and radical Third World countries." And the United States would be in a poor position to encourage Unesco activities that parallel U.S. interests—such as worldwide literacy campaigns and its international clearinghouse function.[5]

Natural Science

General. Unesco's science programs are intended to provide scientists worldwide with research data generated by international projects and to give them access to important research localities. Collaborative projects organized under Unesco's auspices enable countries to share the costs and expensive equipment for large-scale international scientific efforts. Unesco's science sector includes divisions of Science and Techology Policies, Scientific Research and Higher Education, Technological Research and Higher Education, Ecological Sciences, Earth Sciences, Water Sciences, Marine Sciences and the Intergovernmental Oceanographic Commission. Apart from the Paris headquarters, Unesco maintains regional offices for science and techology in Nairobi, Montevideo, New Delhi and Jakarta. In 1984–85, Unesco spent about $70 million from its regular budget for science projects. A similar amount came from other sources, including the UNDP, the U.N. Environment Program, and funds in trust contributed by members. In all, Unesco is involved in about 150 projects in science and technology each year.

The science activities are grouped together into three major programs: the Sciences and Their Application to Development; Science, Technology and Society; and the Human Environment and Terrestrial and Marine Resources. Science projects relating to development include training, with special emphasis on computer science and technology, applied microbiology and biotechnology, and renewable energy. The principal methods used by Unesco in training personnel are workshops, courses and seminars. In 1982 alone, more than 2,500 participants from developing countries took Unesco-sponsored courses in such fields as mathematics, physics, chemistry, biology and microbiology. Unesco also offers consulting services and grants for research and travel, especially for outstanding young scientists from developing countries.

The Science, Technology and Society program is intended to help integrate scientific discoveries and technological innovations into society. It seeks to stimulate public awareness of science and to encourage scientists and the public to participate in formulating scientific policies. Part of the program, therefore, is directed at training science journalists and people in charge of museums or science and technology exhibitions. The journal *Impact of Science on Society* is published under this program.

The Human Environment and Terrestrial and Marine Resources Program is concerned with the effects of human activities on the environment and on supplies of natural resources. One focus is on earth sciences, including, for example, a project to prospect for mineral deposits in Africa using such modern techniques as satellite remote sensing. Studies of the ocean and its resources help scientists understand such phenomena

as weather and climate changes. Regional projects undertaken in cooperation wtih the U.N. Food and Agriculture Organization help coastal states maximize their fisheries management.

Unesco programs complement U.S. efforts to make developing nations aware of global questions like environmental conservation, ocean resource exploitation and management of water resources. For example, in 1985 Unesco organized a week-long conference in Caracas, Venezuela, for university students from 15 Latin American countries. They discussed technologies to protect the environment, agricultural development, industrial expansion and population growth. Unesco supports training of science teachers and has arranged for numbers of its fellows to receive training in the United States.

Unesco's General Information Program serves as an international exchange of scientific information among the developing countries—"probably the only viable program for LDCs on the subject," the State Department review notes.[6] Specific projects range from training in theoretical and experimental physics to use of agricultural byproducts and wastes. Research projects are geared to the needs of developing countries, including arid-zone farming, water conservation and alternative sources of energy.

U.S. Participation. The National Science Foundation, in response to a request for input from the State Department, organized a working group to assess the extent and value of U.S. participation in Unesco's natural science sector. The foundation singled out for special mention one of Unesco's most successful science projects, Man in the Biosphere (MAB). The MAB program involves 105 nations actively participating in research aimed at improved understanding and management of the world's ecosystems. Its projects are aimed at finding practical solutions for problems of managing the world's natural resources. The United States played a central role, holding one of four vice presidencies on the 30-nation International Coordinating Council, and had a National MAB Committee with government and private-sector representatives. Portions of U.S. participation in the MAB program are funded by the Departments of Agriculture, Interior and State, the U.S. Forest and Park Services, and the Agency for International Development. Among MAB research topics are mountains and tundra, tropical forests, marginal lands, urban and island ecosystems, and pollution. The program has set up an international network of 243 biosphere reserves in 65 different countries, including 40 in the United States. The reserves are protected areas for the conservation of ecosystems and the plant and animal resources they contain. They serve as centers for research, training and international scientific cooperation. MAB studies of coastal and esturine resources,

including mangrove ecology, are important research topics for American ecologists.

Other science programs of benefit to the United States include:

- The International Center for Theoretical Physics (ICTP) in Trieste, Italy, which is the world's only effective focus for cooperative research in the discipline by physicists from the United States, Eastern and Western Europe and the Third World. The center receives about 700 researchers from developing countries each year.
- The International Geological Correlation Program (IGCP), which promotes research on the history and geological structures of the Earth. Some 47 projects are being carried out in 100 countries and involve more than 4,000 geologists. The IGCP focuses on basic research aimed at solving such problems as the supply of petroleum and other energy resources. It also studies earthquakes and other natural hazards. The United States was an active participant, and the State Department review notes that the program was "productive and widely respected."
- The General Information Program (PGI), which seeks to improve national ability to gather and use scientific information, and facilitates international information exchange. In 1985, for instance, Unesco organized a seminar in New Delhi for scientific personnel from 13 Asian countries. It showed them how to collect data on scientific projects, how to do surveys, where to get information, and how to analyze the statistics. The PGI is the only viable international program working with the less developed countries (LDCs) on this subject, and the review points out that it benefits the U.S. computer industry by providing information on LDC information needs and capabilities. It provided the United States with its only central source of information about research and development in most countries in the world.
- The International Hydrological Program (IHP) helps nations to manage water resources through research, education and technology transfer. The IHP developed from the International Hydrological Decade, which promoted worldwide research in water sciences from 1965 to 1974. Now more than 130 countries are involved in assessment of surface and groundwater resources, and in water resource planning and management. Three large regional projects on the rational use and conservation of water resources in rural areas were begun in 1981 in Africa, Latin America and the Arab states. One innovative project involves harvesting coastal

fog to provide water for desert regions. Unesco financed an experimental project to build a "fog trap" in the high Andean plateaus of northern Chile. The United States was actively involved in the IHP, with a national committee to formulate policy for U.S. participation that included the private sector, universities and the government.

- The Intergovernmental Oceanographic Commission (IOC) promotes global research on the oceans. Part of this is the Oceanographic Data Exchange which, says the review, provides the United States with access to 60 percent of its marine data from foreign sources. The data exchange includes a system for permanent monitoring of pollutants, and the publication of bathymetric charts and geological atlases. The IOC maintains a tsunami, or tidal wave, warning system to protect the coastlines of 22 countries around the Pacific Ocean, including the western United States and Hawaii.
- The Natural Hazards Program develops research for better assessment and prediction of natural hazards, and designs programs to prevent or reduce loss of life and property from such hazards as earthquakes, tidal waves and floods. American scientists joined in the study of earthquakes and served as consultants to help other countries reduce the risks from volcanic eruptions.
- The Program on Informatics offers training and research in the use of computers in science, technology and economic development.
- The International Brain Research Organization (IBRO) is increasingly active in international neuroscience. Its work, the review notes, "is of considerable interest to the American neuroscience community."[7]

American organizations consulted by the State Department noted that there were both direct and indirect benefits derived from participation in Unesco's natural science programs. It gave American scientists access to important, otherwise unobtainable scientific and technological information, including research data generated abroad by international projects. It gave them opportunities to work with scientists from other countries with whom, for political reasons, they would not otherwise have had contact. These contacts helped promote American models for scientific research and helped establish foreign markets for U.S. technologies. The scientists asserted that if the United States were to withdraw from Unesco without making alternative arrangements, they would lose access to an important international framework for scientific cooperation and data gathering. The U.S. policy objective of helping less developed countries improve their scientific capabilities and infrastructures would be

undermined if it stopped funding Unesco. And it would be more difficult to work with scientists in some countries with which the United States has limited contact.

The National Research Council, a branch of the U.S. National Academy of Sciences, reported in September 1984 that alternative arrangements would have to be found if the United States withdrew. The council identified five Unesco program areas as key activities of major interest to the U.S. scientific community: earth sciences and resources, water resources, the ocean and its resources, the Man in the Biosphere Program, and natural sciences, including the support of the International Council of Scientific Unions (ICSU). The ICSU is an international professional organization, founded in 1931, that brings together different scientific disciplines.

Unesco records show that several hundred American scientists participated in Unesco conferences and acted as consultants in programs and projects between 1979 and 1983. Most were drawn from universities or government agencies like the U.S. Geological Survey, the Bureau of Reclamation, the Department of Agriculture, and the National Oceanic and Atmospheric Administration (NOAA). They worked with developing countries on such topics as remote sensing by satellites, use and conservation of water resources, early warning systems for volcanic eruptions, new and renewable energy sources, the use of computers in microbiology, preparation of geological maps of the ocean floor, and the establishment of biosphere reserves.

Social Sciences

General. The social sciences sector has three basic mandates. One is to build up social science facilities, especially in Asia, Africa and Latin America. The second focuses on strengthening the role of research as a basis for development planning. The third emphasis is the application of social sciences to such world issues as human rights, peace, population growth, development and the environment. Unesco supports scholarly publishing through its *International Social Science Journal* and *Main Trends of Research in the Social and Human Sciences,* and it contributes to research by collecting and disseminating social science information through its computerized data bank.

Unesco social science programs typically fund studies, surveys, international meetings and travel grants. Its social science spending for 1984–85 was about $26 million, or 6 percent of the regular budget. The largest proportion of the money was allocated to programs dealing with general research, training and international cooperation in the social sciences.

Next came programs concerned with peace, human rights and the rights of peoples; then programs relating to the status of women. Smaller amounts were budgeted for studies of world problems, future-oriented studies, and those dealing with the elimination of prejudice, intolerance, racism and apartheid.

Much of Unesco's contribution to the social sciences has involved supporting the establishment of international non-government organizations, often in the form of groups of specialists. It was instrumental, for example, in setting up the World Federation of Mental Health, the International Association of Experts in Comparative Law, the International Sociological Association and the International Economic Association. These groups, formed in the late 1940s and 1950s, expanded in the 1970s with Unesco's encouragement to admit associations of researchers from newly independent countries. Unesco also has sponsored regional institutions in Africa, Asia, Europe and Latin America.

Unesco studies on the role of social science research in development planning have focused on various types and styles of development, seeking to clarify the conditions and factors that permit them. In this regard, Unesco experts have produced studies on the New International Economic Order, and the activities of transnational corporations. Studies at the local level have dealt with various aspects of rural development.

Many of Unesco's social science programs have been devoted to studies on disarmament and peace. It has, for instance, examined the possibility of giving more aid to education as a result of disarmament, and of retraining military research personnel for work in assisting the developing countries in non-military fields. Among Unesco's contributions to the International Year of Peace (1986) are studies of factors conducive to peace and the causes and consequences of conflict. Studies have been carried out on various aspects of the status of women. These include work on the political and economic role of women, their education and their participation in various mass media activities.

U.S. Participation. The United States had sought to achieve a more central role for the social sciences in all Unesco programs. Partly for this reason, the area was elevated in 1972 to a separate sector with its own assistant director general. The U.S. goal has been to help develop strong social science institutions and resources, to provide free and open professional communication, and to facilitate exchange of methods for collecting and analyzing information. In the five years before the withdrawal, more than 100 American social scientists participated in Unesco activities. They were recruited from universities in 17 states, most notably the universities of Massachusetts, New York, Harvard, California and Columbia. And they were active in programs relating to such issues as child

development, human settlements, human rights and peace, socioeconomic indicators, and women. American social scientists, during the period 1979–83, contributed numerous articles to Unesco publications. They participated in seminars on cross-national comparative research and on the role of social science in development. Several were involved in family planning projects in developing countries, and in studies of population trends. Models developed by American social scientists have been revised in the light of data collected at research centers established by Unesco.

The State Department review concluded, however, that although U.S. withdrawal would initially make international contacts more difficult to arrange, American participation in Unesco projects was not vital to the social science community, which had other channels for doing research abroad.

Culture

General. The cultural sector administers programs for the restoration and preservation of the world's cultural monuments. It promotes the cultural identity of individuals and nations by compiling regional histories, protecting ethnic languages, translating literary works, establishing regional cultural documentation centers and researching cultural values. The programs encourage contact among organizations and individuals in the fields of music and the arts. Unesco sponsors traveling art exhibitions, and it supports scholarly publications dealing with culture, history and human development.

Among its best-known projects are the restoration of the Philae monuments and the rescue of the temples of Abu Simbel from the rising waters of the Aswan High Dam in Egypt. In appreciation for the generous contributions from the United States, the Egyptian government made a gift to the American people of Dendur Temple, now on display at New York's Metropolitan Museum of Art. Unesco experts also have worked on preserving and restoring priceless antiquities in Venice, the temple of Borobudur in Indonesia, the Acropolis in Athens, the ancient city of Moenjodaro in Pakistan, and the monuments of Herat in Afghanistan, among others.

The Unesco Collection of Representative Works now comprises nearly 900 translations of important literary works from about 60 languages. Unesco also supports the International Federation of Translators, which helps train literary translators, especially in developing countries. In the field of music, Unesco collaborates with the International Music Council. Together they have produced more than 100 records and cassettes of traditional music from all over the world. Unesco is sponsoring a

world history of music, *Music in the Life of Man*. Fifteen major art exhibitions have been circulated worldwide under Unesco auspices. Among them are reproductions of the art of Africa, China, Islam, Latin America, Persia and Oceania. The agency also sponsored two vast undertakings: the seven-volume *General History of Africa* and the *History of Scientific and Cultural Development of Mankind*. General histories of the Caribbean and of Latin America are in hand, as is a six-volume *History of the Civilizations of Central Asia*.

In addition, Unesco has drawn up alphabets for languages that previously had no written form, and produced grammars, dictionaries, spelling books and readers in those and other languages. One current project encourages the use of African languages as teaching and development media. In Asia, there is a program aimed at compiling words for modern concepts in traditional languages, so that they can be used in education and daily life.

An important part of Unesco's cultural work has to do with setting international standards for cultural activity. Members have adopted conventions for the protection of cultural property in the event of armed conflict; on prohibiting the illegal export or import of cultural property; and on protecting the world's cultural and natural heritage. It has worked to bring about the return of cultural artifacts to their country of origin to fill gaps in museum collections.

U.S. Participation. The Smithsonian Institution was heavily involved in preserving the Nubian temples in Egypt and the Moenjodaro site in Pakistan, It served as the channel for American contributions to Unesco's cultural preservation projects. The Smithsonian also helped formulate Unesco's international regulations to curb illicit dealing in cultural artifacts. Other U.S. institutions involved in Unesco's cultural activities are the U.S. Information Agency, the National Endowment for the Arts, the National Endowment for the Humanities, the Advisory Council on Historic Preservation, and the National Park Service. American historians and anthropologists have worked on Unesco's major historical projects; other experts have helped museum authorities in Third World countries. Between 1979 and 1983, about 100 Americans were recruited to work on preservation and conservation activities, mostly in connection with museums in developing countries or with efforts to preserve ancient monuments. According to Unesco records, Americans organized training courses in dance and choreography in Colombia, and on museum exhibition techniques in Nigeria. They authored chapters of the general histories of Africa, Asia and Latin America. Several served as consultants to museums in countries like Somalia and Zaire. They trained archaeologists in Burma and Peru. And they helped Panama and Guatemala to inventory their cultural property, among other activities.

The State Department review comments that technical books and reports published by Unesco have helped Americans in research and in raising conservation standards. Scholars from many countries have visited the United States under Unesco auspices to share views with their American counterparts. The review pointed out that withdrawal from Unesco would diminish U.S. participation in cultural affairs and limit access to data used by the cultural and academic communities.

Communication

General. There are two main divisions in the communication sector: the Division of the Free Flow of Information, and the Division of Development of Communication Systems. The first seeks to promote freedom of information by removing obstacles that hamper it; the second tries to improve the means and techniques of information distribution. To remove obstacles to free flow, Unesco has, for example, promoted international agreements to remove customs duties on educational, cultural and scientific materials. It has sought to reduce postal charges for publications and to lower the rates for certain kinds of telecommunication services.

Work on improving the means of communication has focused on developing communications infrastructures, networks and resources. Unesco-sponsored training institutes at the University of Strasbourg, the University of Quito, the University of Dakar and the University of the Philippines have trained hundreds of journalists and communication specialists, mostly from developing countries. Unesco also has helped developing nations set up national press or information agencies, some of which have been organized into regional or interregional news pool networks. Typical examples are the Organization of Asian News Agencies, and the Pan-African News Agency, which feeds five regional pools located in Lagos, Kinshasa, Lusaka, Khartoum and Tripoli (Libya). The Caribbean News Agency has led to a quadrupling of the volume of information exchange between news media of English-speaking states in that region. The Latin American Special Information Services Agency supplies articles and programs to the media. The Arab States Broadcasting Union provides broadcasting facilities in support of education at all levels in the region. All are involved in exchanges of news and information. Unesco contracts have helped support Inter Press Service (IPS), an international news agency that specializes in gathering, processing and disseminating news relating to the Third World. Its primary emphasis is on developing horizontal communications links and promoting news and information flow among the developing countries. In addition, IPS distributes news about the Third World to media clients in the industrialized countries.

Part of this developmental function has now been taken over by the International Program for the Development of Communication (IPDC), a semiautonomous body governed by a 35-member intergovermental council elected by the Unesco General Conference. The IPDC was proposed by the United States in 1978 in response to concerns of developing countries about their inadequate communications capabilities. The intention was to redirect Unesco's attention from theory and rhetoric to practical development of communications infrastructures. The IPDC's budget for the 1981–83 triennium was $1,750,000, financed from Unesco's regular budget. In addition, several countries made voluntary contributions. By 1985, the IPDC and approved 110 projects costing some $8 million. Sixty-one of the communications projects were national in scope, 39 were regional, and 10 interregional. Among the allocations were $80,000 to the Pan-African News Agency for a study on computerization of its services; $45,000 to set up a news exchange between members of the Federation of Arab News Agencies and the Latin American News Agencies Pool; and $60,000 each to Sierra Leone to establish a national news agency, to Gambia for a daily newspaper, to Zambia for its school of mass communication, and to Oman to create a Center for the Development of Information and Communication Sciences.

The IPDC also arranged an experimental program of direct exchange of television news via satellite between Africa, Asia, the Arab states and Latin America. An example of bilateral aid channeled through the IPDC is a multimedia training center for journalists from developing countries that was set up in Indonesia in 1985 with Japanese funding. The first IPDC/Unesco Prize for Rural Communication was awarded in 1985 to the Kheda Communication Project in India. It involved setting up a low-power TV transmitter in Gujarat State that can relay programs from India's own communications satellite, INSAT, to community receivers installed in about 400 villages. The villagers not only watched and discussed programs dealing with health, agriculture and economic problems, but also took part in making films.

U.S. Participation. Despite its withdrawal from Unesco, the United States has continued to cooperate in some IPDC programs. It has refused to provide direct contributions to the IPDC special account, but has channeled bilateral assistance to developing countries through the agency.

The United States has derived considerable benefits from Unesco communication programs. Between 1979 and 1983, more than 40 American consultants were paid to work in such projects. In some cases, their participation resulted in the selection of U.S. products and services, especially in building Third World communication networks. They participated in studies of the international flow of television news and pro-

grams, on the New World Information Order and on the Right to Communicate. Several Americans worked on a Global Satellite Project for dissemination and exchange of information. Others worked on the transfer of technology to upgrade Third World communication capabilities.

Under Unesco-sponsored marketing agreements, 70 governments have lifted barriers to the import of various kinds of books, tapes, films and film equipment, scientific instruments and devices used to test industrial materials. In 1983, some $130 million worth of U.S. audiovisual equipment was exported under such agreements.

The State Department review of Unesco's efforts to promote development through improved communications systems generally is positive. However, some of the work of the Division of Free Flow of Information, which has been the forum for debate on a New World Information Order, has proved troublesome to the United States. This will be explored in later chapters.

NOTES

1. The Constitution of the United Nations Educational, Scientific and Cultural Organization, adopted on 16 November 1945 at a United Nations meeting in London. Reprinted in Edmund Jan Osmanczyk, *Encyclopedia of the United Nations and International Agreements* (London: Taylor and Francis, 1985), pp. 827–829.
2. Peter I. Hajnal, *Guide to Unesco* (London: Oceana Publications, 1983); Unesco, *Unesco on the Eve of Its Fortieth Anniversary* (Paris: Unesco, 1986).
3. U.S. Department of State, Bureau of International Organization Affairs, *U.S./Unesco Policy Review* (Washington, D.C., 27 February 1984).
4. Details of participation by U.S. experts in Unesco programs were supplied to U.S. Ambassador Jean Gerard by Director General Amadou-Mahtar M'Bow on 24 October, 1983. The author obtained copies of the report from the U.S. National Commission for Unesco.
5. U.S. Department of State, *U.S./Unesco Policy Review,* p. 8.
6. *Ibid.,* p. 46.
7. Details of Unesco's science and other projects can be found in the "U.S./Unesco Policy Review," and in *Unesco on the Eve of its Fortieth Anniversary.*

CHAPTER 2

The Media Conflict

The U.S. withdrawal from Unesco was the culmination of a long and increasingly bitter debate in that agency over communications issues. Unesco's constitution stipulates that the agency will work toward "advancing the mutual knowledge and understanding of peoples, through all means of mass communication, and to that end recommend such international agreements as may be necessary to promote the free flow of ideas by word and image."[1] This provision was included in the constitution at the instigation of the United States delegation to Unesco's founding conference in 1945. The mandate to promote the "free flow of ideas" reflected the ideology and foreign policy objectives of the Western countries that dominated the agency in its early years. The "free flow" concept was enthusiastically supported by American media organizations, which saw in it an opportunity to further weaken the prewar stranglehold on information held by European news cartels. There were few dissenting voices: the Soviet Union boycotted Unesco until 1954, and most of the world's present nation-states were still colonies, with no voice in international forums. Of the 28 countries represented at Unesco's first General Conference in 1946, only 13 were developing Third World nations. The first big change in Unesco's membership came in the mid-1950s when the Soviet Union joined along with Byelorussia and the Ukraine, which were accorded separate representation. Three Eastern European countries that previously had withdrawn from Unesco rejoined in 1954, and two more signed up in 1956. A second major change began in the late 1950s as the newly independent nations joined the organization. In 1960 alone, 17 new

African members were admitted. Unesco's main function in the communications field during the 1950s and 1960s was to help build up communications infrastructures in the developing world, on the assumption that this would promote modernization and development. Until the mid-1960s, the U.N. itself was the major political forum for debates on problems related to the free flow of information. Unesco played a largely technical role in assisting developing countries to establish and operate news media, and to promote the free exchange of books and periodicals.

A NEW INFORMATION ORDER

The Issue Emerges

The free-flow doctrine came under challenge, however, as more nations achieved independence and a vote in U.N. agencies. By the 1980 General Conference, three-quarters of the 153 member states were from Africa, Asia, the Caribbean, Latin America or the Middle East. Unesco meetings and conferences had become the primary forum for complaints by developing nations about Western domination of international communications channels, and for demands for a more balanced circulation of news. The Soviet Union capitalized on this dissatisfaction, joining the developing nations in accusing the Western-based international news agencies of "media imperialism," and of serving the interests of major corporations in their search for global markets.

Unesco's involvement in the political aspects of information began in 1965 when it issued a report stressing that the media should use space communications systems "for the benefit of all peoples."[2] The 1970 General Conference adopted a resolution inviting member states to "take the necessary steps, including legislative measures, to encourage the use of information media against propaganda on behalf of war, racialism and hatred among nations."[3] The concept of a new information order first surfaced at a Unesco conference in 1970 when developing countries, led by India, called for a more balanced flow of information. The Unesco General Conference in 1972 saw two major challenges to the free-flow doctrine, both in the form of resolutions submitted by the Soviet Union. One insisted that the principle of prior consent be applied to television programs beamed from one country to another by direct broadcast satellites. Only the United States voted against the resolution. The vote appeared to demonstrate growing support in Unesco for statutory control of information flow. The second challenge, which also had wide support from the developing nations, called for the preparation of a declaration on "the fundamental principles governing the use of mass media."[4]

A draft of the declaration was discussed at Unesco's 1974 General Conference. It was sharply opposed by Western delegates, who saw in it a Soviet attempt to gain international sanction for government control of the media. Delegates from developing countries had their own concerns and called for the replacement of the one-way flow of information between the developed countries and themselves with a two-way flow. They also urged that governments should formulate codes of conduct to ensure "unbiased and objective reporting."[5] Western delegates argued, however, that state control of mass media was incompatible with the free flow of information, and the issue was referred to an intergovernmental meeting of experts. The experts met in 1975 and produced a draft declaration that was again considered inimical to Western interests. For one thing, Arab states supported the declaration in return for the inclusion of a reference to a U.N. General Assembly resolution equating Zionism with racism. The United States and 12 other nations then withdrew from the meeting, and the resolution was passed with only 41 states voting. This resolution was introduced at the 19th General Conference in 1976.

The Non-Aligned Movement. The debates in Unesco, meanwhile, were paralleled at meetings of non-aligned countries, where global information flow became a major issue. Heads of state of non-aligned countries, meeting in Algiers in September 1973, adopted an Action Program for Economic Cooperation that urged member states to "reorganize existing communications channels which are the legacy of the colonial past, and which have hampered free, direct and fast communication among them."[6] This debate resulted in the establishment in January 1975 of the Non-Aligned News Agencies Pool, coordinated by the Yugoslav news agency Tanjug, and was intended to provide objective information on economic, social and cultural development in the Third World. Some observers saw the news pool as the first direct challenge to the power of the Western news agencies.[7]

Communications issues figured prominently in three more meetings of non-aligned nations during 1976. A Non-Aligned Symposium on Information in Tunis that March adopted a report titled "The Emancipation of the Mass Media in Non-Aligned Countries."[8] The report focused on ways to improve distribution of news generated in the Third World. In July, information ministers of the non-aligned nations and managers of agencies participating in the news pool met in New Delhi to review the Tunis report and to discuss ways of upgrading communications facilities in the developing countries. A meeting in Colombo of the heads of state of 84 non-aligned nations followed in August. The summit meeting set up a council to coordinate information policies among the non-aligned countries. It adopted a declaration asserting that "a new international order in

the fields of information and mass media is as vital as a new economic order," and that "the emancipation and development of national media is an integral part of the overall struggle for political, economic and social independence for a large majority of the peoples of the world who should not be denied the right to inform and be informed objectively and correctly."[9] The summit meeting gave Tunisia a mandate to raise the international information order issue at the upcoming Unesco General Conference in Nairobi.

Inevitably, the views of what was by now a majority of its membership had influenced Unesco's position on communications issues. The agency's previous unconditional backing for a free flow of information was modified to support instead a free and balanced flow. Unesco sponsored a conference in Costa Rica on Latin American communication policies just before the Colombo summit. Its conclusions were very similar to those adopted at meetings of the non-aligned nations, and the meeting urged Unesco to continue its involvement in communications issues.[10] Unesco Director General M'Bow noted in the fall of 1976 that "one of the greatest forms of inequality in the contemporary world is that involving information" and charged that the international news agencies tended to emphasize negative news about the Third World.[11]

Nairobi, 1976. At Unesco's 18th General Conference in Nairobi in 1976 the communications debate first attracted widespread attention in the world's press. At issue were two resolutions on information policy. One was the Tunisian resolution, calling for a more balanced and diversified exchange of news, and asking Unesco to support the Non-Aligned News Agencies Pool. The other was the Soviet-sponsored mass media declaration that condemned Western news agencies for presenting a distorted view of the developing world and mandated governmental responsibility "for the activities in the international sphere of all news media under their jurisdiction."[12] The United States and other Western governments went along with the Tunisian resolution, partly to circumvent adoption of the draft mass media declaration with its unacceptable endorsement of state regulation of the media. With the support of M'Bow and the African nations, who were concerned that the dispute could tear Unesco apart, the West succeeded in again postponing the issue. The draft declaration was referred instead to a commission that would study the problem and come up with recommendations.

Western concerns about the proposed new information order were summarized by John E. Reinhardt, head of the U.S. delegation to Unesco. At best, he said, "it could mean a greater two-way flow of news, films, television programs, books, scientific and cultural information, and closer relations and a better understanding among individuals and na-

tions." At worst, however, the new information order "could mean legitimizing a limitation on the access to news sources, condoning censorship, placing a restriction on information flow across national borders, and imposing a series of duties, encumbrances, and responsibilities upon the media outside of their reporting functions."[13] In exchange for shelving the declaration, the United States promised to help Third World countries improve their communications capabilities by training journalists and providing equipment and satellite links.

The Nairobi conference also instructed M'Bow to undertake a review of communications issues in contemporary society in the light of developments in international relations and technological progress.[14] This led to the appointment in December 1977 of the International Commission for the Study of Communication Problems, under the chairmanship of Sean MacBride, former minister for foreign affairs for Ireland and the recipient of both the Nobel and the Lenin peace prizes. The 16-member commission reflected the geopolitical makeup of Unesco: four members from Africa, three from Asia, two Latin Americans, three Western Europeans, two North Americans and one each from the Soviet Union and Yugoslavia. The commission was charged to study the current situation in the fields of communication and information and to identify problems that needed action. It was to pay particular attention to problems relating to the free and balanced flow of information, as well as the specific needs of developing countries. The communication problems were to be analyzed "within the perspective of a New International Economic Order and of the measures to be taken to foster the institution of a New World Information Order. By now, as MacBride noted later, the debate on communication issues "had stridently reached points of confrontation in many areas. Third World protests against dominant flow of news from the industrialized countries were often construed as attacks on the free flow of information. Defenders of journalistic freedom were labeled intruders on national sovereignty. Varying concepts of news values and the rights, roles and responsibilities of journalists were widely contended, as was the potential contribution of the mass media to the solution of major world problems."[15]

Paris, 1978. News organizations in the United States and Western Europe, perceiving a threat to their operations in the Third World, began to pay close attention to Unesco's communication policies. This became evident in Western press coverage of the 1978 Unesco General Conference in Paris. Once again the agenda included a revised draft of the Soviet-sponsored mass media declaration, with its call for government control of the media. Herbert Altschull notes that by the time the Paris conference convened, communications had become an important interna-

tional issue, at least as far as the news media were concerned. "Characteristically, the issue was presented in conflictual terms, with the Soviet proposal portrayed in the capitalist media as a threat to democratic freedom and in the Marxist press as a challenge to capitalist exploitation."[16]

An examination of the various drafts of the Mass Media Declaration from 1974 to 1978 shows clearly how the West succeeded in negotiating out most of the offensive language.[17] Gone are any references to state control of the media, to international law, and to words like "responsibility" and "duty" of the media. While the declaration calls for a "free flow and a wider and more balanced flow of information," it leaves it to the media themselves to determine how to improve the balance. The 1978 text includes, for the first time, a statement to the effect that "journalist must have freedom to report and the fullest possible facilities of access to information." And it suggests that access by the public to information "should be guaranteed by the diversity of the sources and means available to it, thus enabling each individual to check the accuracy of facts and to appraise events objectively." Articles in earlier drafts calling for an international right of correction were toned down to an innocuous statement that it was important to disseminate points of view of those who felt that their efforts to strengthen peace and understanding had been prejudiced. Nor did the declaration include earlier calls for an international code of journalistic ethics. Instead, professional organizations and journalism educators were urged to bear the principles of the declaration in mind when drawing up and applying their own codes of ethics.

The "Declaration on Fundamental Principles Concerning the Contribution of the Masss Media to Strengthening Peace and International Understanding, to the Promotion of Human Rights and to Countering Racialism, Apartheid and Incitement to War" was adopted by acclamation, with Director General M'Bow playing a key role in reconciling the differing viewpoints. The U.S. secretary of state reported to the president in January 1979 that:

> the product of the negotiations was a text not only stripped of language implying state control over the mass media, but which also included positive language on freedom of information. Instead of imposing duties and responsibilities on journalists, as various drafts attempted, it proclaimed that they must have freedom to report and the fullest possible facilities of access to information and be assured of protection guaranteeing them the best conditions for the exercise of their profession.[18]

Despite its acceptance by virtually every government, however, there is doubt as to whether nations are bound by international law to respect its provisions. Kaarle Nordenstreng, president of the International

Organization of Journalists, believes they are. He says the declaration not only lays down general and abstract principles for mass media activities, "but it also sets standards for media contents—something which has been almost taboo within the Western libertarian tradition but which is central to the demands of developing and socialist countries." Nordenstreng says that the declaration places the mass media—their contents, rights and responsibilities—within a general framework of interstate relations and international law.[19]

Leonard Sussman argues, however, that the declaration was intended to be a broad statement of purpose. It is clear, he writes, that the declaration "is devoid of any specific rights, duties, obligations or other provisions that would support the thesis that it be accorded the same treatment as a legal instrument." He argues that it is not an international treaty. Nor can it be construed as embodying "international customary law," since it satisfies neither of the requirements for a custom. "It does not embody a uniform inter-state practice, but rather seeks to establish an inter-state practice. Accordingly, because there is no extant uniform practice, there is no legal compulsion by states to adhere to such a practice."[20]

The compromise version of the declaration, however, did not impress some U.S. media. The *New York Times* editorialized that although Western diplomats were congratulating themselves on having turned "a dangerous international declaration on the obligations of the press into an incomprehensible hodgepodge of slogans and prescriptions," the declaration remained an affront to the very idea of communication. "The world deserves to know that the Americans who accepted it as the least offensive document they could write with 145 other nations were not speaking for the free press of the United States."[21]

Belgrade, 1980. The 21st Unesco General Conference, held in Belgrade in 1980, was to be the forum for discussion of the report of the MacBride Commission, a significant attempt to achieve consensus among nations of very different ideological persuasions on ways to achieve a "new more just and more efficient world information and communication order."[22] The report has five parts. The first four, largely prepared by the Unesco secretariat, analyze various aspects of global communication: economic cultural, educational, historical, political and technological. They examine problems of imbalance in communication flow, of disparities in communication development between the most and least advanced countries, and of dominance and control. Among the controversial issues they deal with are protection and licensing of journalists, and codes of professional ethics and press councils. Part V, which was written by the commission members themselves, contains 82 recommendations and the

commission's conclusions. Recommendations called on member states to formulate national communication policies. Others were addressed to journalists; still others to international organizations like Unesco. Seventy-two of the recommendations were unanimous; 10 were subject to disagreements and reservations.

The report contains a strong affirmation of libertarian press values, but also a clear bias against private-sector involvement in communications media. Western delegates objected to the perceived anticommercial bias of the report and to its support for government guidelines. The Soviet bloc, on the other hand, was concerned about recommendations having to do with the abolition of government control of the media. Third World countries were primarily concerned about a more balanced flow of information, which they felt was hampered by the dominance in international news flow of the "Big Four" Western news agencies—Associated Press and United Press International in the United States, Britain's Reuters, and Agence France-Presse.

To avoid confrontation over these issues, the report itself was not voted on at the conference. Instead delegates adopted M'Bow's recommendations that states take action on a national level to implement its proposals. The resolution called for further development of communications capabilities for all countries, and for safeguarding "freedom of opinion, expression and information." Typically, the resolution included passages that reflected the very different concerns of the West, the Soviet Bloc and the Third World. It called for elimination of imbalance and inequalities in world communications, and for "elimination of the negative effects of certain monopolies, public or private, and excessive concentrations." But it also expressed support for a plurality of sources and channels of information, and of freedom of the press. While it recognized the "freedom of journalists and all professionals in the communication media," this freedom was "inseparable from responsibility." The resolution further urged Unesco to continue its work in the "delineation, broadening and application of a new world information order."[23]

The most important new action taken at the 1980 conference was the setting up of the International Program for the Development of Communication (IPDC), a vehicle for technology transfer and training to improve Third World communications capabilities. The IPDC was an outcome of previous offers of aid by the United States to developing countries, and represented a "desire to turn Unesco's attention away from divisive rhetoric towards unifying works of practical construction." The IPDC grew out of an Intergovernmental Conference on Activities, Needs and Programs for Communications Development, which convened in Paris in April 1980. It recommended the establishment of the IPDC, and this proposal was approved by the General Conference later that

year. The objectives of the IPDC are "to increase cooperation and assistance for the development of communication infrastructures and to reduce the gap between various countries in the communication field."[24] It is coordinated by a 35-member board elected to a three-year rotational term by Unesco's General Conference. It is financed partly from Unesco's regular budget and partly by voluntary contributions from member states.

Paris, 1983. Despite Western delegates' success in watering down the more extreme demands for a new information order, press coverage of the conference in the United States was strongly hostile, to the point of urging that the U.S. withdraw from Unesco if it persisted in its attacks on press freedom. Unesco's 22nd General Conference in Paris in 1983 again drew critical attention from Western media. Most of the coverage centered on just one of 13 programs ratified as part of the agency''s five-year plan. The focus was on Major Programme III: Communication in the Service of Man. The program, which reflected the concerns of the Third World, called for countries to develop national communication policies, for training in all aspects of communication, for "free flow and wider and better balanced dissemination of information," and for increased exchanges of news and programs.[25] Third World delegates urged that steps be taken to curb the dominance of the major news agencies; the United States and other Western delegations feared that the plan would lead to curbs on press freedom by giving governments the right to license journalists and establish international codes of journalistic ethics. Two weeks of diplomatic bargaining led to a compromise that established a framework for a new information order, but toned down criticism of Western news agencies, and included a passage supporting the watchdog role of the press in exposing abuses of official power. Clearly, however, the compromise resolutions were merely papering over an ever-widening rift.

THE MEDIA AS PARTICIPANTS

Western media organizations were not detached observers of the debate in Unesco. Alarmed by threats to their interests, they took steps to head off any new information order that would be inimical to their international operations. To achieve this, U.S. media institutions adopted several key strategies. One was to form a new organization, the World Press Freedom Committee (WPFC), which would coordinate and spearhead their campaign. This committee became actively involved in Unesco conferences and meetings, lobbying on behalf of the free flow of information. It organized conferences to articulate traditional Western press

values. And it put pressure on Congress and the State Department to take a stronger line against Unesco's media policies.

Media Pressure Groups

Other media organizations that have played an active role in opposing Unesco's new order include the American Newspaper Publishers Association (ANPA), the International Press Institute (IPI), and the Inter American Press Association (IAPA). The ANPA, a trade organization whose 1,300-odd member newspapers account for more than 90 percent of U.S. daily and Sunday newspaper circulation, and more than 85 percent of Canadian daily circulation, has been particularly active in resisting efforts to impose government control over the news media. According to Harold W. Andersen, former chairman of the ANPA, the group resists "as vigorously as we can any effort, within or outside the United Nations structure, to advance policies which encourage government influence over, or control of, the news media."[26] The ANPA also has input into U.S. policy as a member of the U.S. National Commission for Unesco. Not only print media went on record as opposing Unesco's communication policies. North American broadcast executives, meeting in Ottawa in October 1984, denounced Unesco efforts to curb the free flow of information. They included representatives of the U.S. National Association of Broadcasters, the Canadian Association of Broadcasters and Mexico's La Camera Nacional de la Radio y Televisión.

World Press Freedom Committee

But it is the World Press Freedom Committee that has been at the forefront of the campaign, particularly in the United States. The Soviet-sponsored proposal for state control of media, placed on the Unesco agenda in 1976, "shook the free world press into recognizing that it had serious problems."[27] Convinced, as former Reuters Managing Editor Gerald Long put it, that "the only protection we can get will come in the end from ourselves and our own efforts,"[28] media organizations established the WPFC in May 1976 "to unify the free world media for major threats that develop."[29]

The WPFC brought together under one banner 33 journalistic organizations representing both print and broadcast media, two-thirds of them based in the U.S., but including media organizations in Latin America, Europe and Asia. The U.S. organizations represent virtually every level of the media. Publishers and broadcasters are represented by the ANPA and the National Association of Broadcasters; editors by the American Society of Newspaper Editors and the Associated Press Managing Editors

Association; working journalists by the National Conference of Editorial Writers, the Newspaper Guild, the Overseas Press Club of America, the Radio Television News Directors Association, and the Society of Professional Journalists. The WPFC shared a suite of offices with the ANPA in Reston, VA.

The editors and publishers represented in the WPFC, according to Harold Andersen, who also served as chairman of the committee, are "deeply concerned about the effort by some member states—with the encouragement of the Unesco administration—to create a 'new international information order' under which governments would exert decisive influence—if not outright control—over news media within their borders." The press of the free world, says Andersen, "simply will never accept this kind of international policy."[30]

One way the WPFC has been working to head off a new information order is to gain the support of Third World countries by offering them equipment and training to meet their media needs. Funds collected from non-government media are used to mount seminars and provide textbooks for journalists in Africa, Asia, the Caribbean and Latin America. It also acts as a clearinghouse for print and broadcast equipment donated by American and Canadian media.

The primary objective of the WPFC, however, has been to act as a watchdog for Western media interests. It has "vigilantly monitored international conferences where the free world media have been under scrutiny, and has tried to offer reason and moderation to the discussion."[31] The WPFC's first major lobbying effort at Unesco was aimed at derailing the Soviet draft declaration on uses of the mass media that was presented at the General Conference in Nairobi in the fall of 1976. The WPFC, together with other international media organizations and Western government representatives, argued strongly against the draft resolution and won a two-year delay during which the resolution was to be rewritten.[32]

When the declaration came up for discussion again at the 1978 conference in Paris, the Western governments and media organizations negotiated intensively with Third World delegates and succeeded in eliminating from the final document all references to press controls. In addition to the Unesco general conferences, the WPFC has sent delegates to several other meetings on media issues organized by Unesco or the non-aligned countries. Representatives of the WPFC have also met with Director General M'Bow to discuss Unesco's media policies.[33] In May 1984, Andersen told a WPFC meeting that if it had not been for the vigilance of the WPFC and other watchdog groups, "the licensing of journalists would be much further down the road." And he added that the WPFC's close relationship with the State Department was a "primary factor" in the U.S. decision to withdraw from Unesco.[34]

Another strategy adopted by Western media has been to assert their own values vigorously as a counter to the arguments for a new information order. The best example is the Declaration of Talloires, adopted in May 1981. The Talloires meeting appears to have been convened partly as a reaction to a Unesco meeting earlier that year. Unesco's 21st General Conference in Paris in the fall of 1980 was generally considered a victory by Western delegates because they succeeded in blocking the adoption of an international code of ethics and licensing of journalists. In February 1981, however, the Unesco Secretariat convened a conference in Paris on codes of ethics and protection of journalists. On the agenda was a proposal by Pierre Gaborit, a French political scientist, that there be an international commission for the protection of journalists. This commission would, among other activities, study journalistic professional ethics with a view to promoting common attitudes. It would also issue international identification cards to journalists. To the West, this implied licensing of journalists to ensure that they complied with the "generally accepted" ethics of their profession.[35] Such proposals were anathema to Western media who apparently assumed, despite denials by M'Bow, that Gaborit's proposal reflected official Unesco policy. They were incensed also by reports that the meeting was to be held in secret and that Western journalists had not been invited to participate. The *Chicago Tribune*, for example, referred to the meeting as a "sneak play . . . for which notices went to communist and Third World delegates but not to American delegates."[36] This editorial was read into the *Congressional Record* on June 9, 1981. The U.S. State Department complained to the Unesco Secretariat, who then invited four additional organizations: the International Federation of Newspaper Publishers, the International Press Institute, the Miami-based Inter American Press Association and the World Press Freedom Committee.[37] Leonard H. Marks, secretary-treasurer of the WPFC and a former director of the U.S. Information Agency, declared that he opposed any new order that meant "government or Unesco control over the media, reporters' access, their freedom to cover what they want to cover, and censorship of their stories."[38] Although no decision was taken, the meeting resulted in a new outcry against Unesco in the Western press.

"Voices of Freedom"

Following this meeting, the WPFC, in conjunction with Tufts University's Fletcher School of Law and Diplomacy, sponsored a "Voices of Freedom" conference in Talloires, France, in May 1981. The 63 delegates represented 60 print and broadcast organizations in 21 countries, and included the Big Four wire services. Led by U.S. delegates, they adopted

what came to be known as the Talloires Declaration on Press Freedom, an unprecedented "Bill of Rights" for the free press. It pledged "cooperation in all genuine efforts to expand the free flow of information," and promised "concerted action" to uphold the "basic human right" of press freedom.[39] But the declaration called on Unesco to "abandon its attempts to regulate news content and formulate rules for the press." The *New York Times* welcomed the declaration, which was widely publicized in the United States and entered into the *Congressional Record* on June 17, as "the first time Western and other free newspapers and broadcasting networks took a united stand against the campaign by Soviet bloc and Third World countries to give Unesco the authority to regulate the flow of news and information."

For the Western media to bring about change in Unesco policies, however, they had to exert more direct pressure. And that meant enlisting the aid of Western governments, who provide about 75 percent of Unesco's budget. The United States alone accounted for 25 percent of the agency's income, and threats of withholding that contribution could be a powerful lever in effecting desired reforms. In the United States, this involved working through Congress, which appropriates funds for international organizations.

THE ROLE OF CONGRESS

Western media were alert to the Unesco challenge well before it gained the attention of Congress. As *Editor & Publisher* put it, commenting on proposals to license journalists, "the free press of this hemisphere led the fight against many of these proposals long before the U.S. Government woke up to the dangers and started to participate officially in Unesco sessions."[40] Getting the support of Congress was not difficult. Officials are generally aware of the power of the media in election campaigns, and most needed little convincing, having been reared on the free press ideology. Altschull notes that the "power of the folklore of the press" was evident in congressional debates on Unesco's communication policies where members gave "a series of ringing speeches endorsing the American concept of a free press, the First Amendment, and even speeches by Thomas Jefferson."[41]

The media exerted influence on Congress in several ways. News reports, articles and editorials set the agenda for the Unesco discussion. Many of these items were quoted in House and Senate debates, and read into the *Congressional Record*. Media representatives gave evidence at congressional hearings and argued in print and in private for a stronger line against Unesco.

Congressional Hearings

The media were prominently represented at hearings before two subcommittees of the House Foreign Affairs Committee to review U.S. participation in Unesco. These hearings began in March 1981 and continued in July. The hearings were held to review the Belgrade conference, prospects for the future, and ways in which the U.S. could improve its participation in Unesco. At issue was a resolution sponsored by Rep. Millicent Fenwick, R-N.J., and Rep. Bob Shamansky, D-Ohio, expressing the House's opposition to Unesco's attempts to regulate news.

Most of the dozen people invited to give testimony were members of the U.S. delegation to the Belgrade conference and representatives of media organizations. Robin Chandler Duke, chairwoman of the U.S. delegation, observed that the U.S. had "not lost the ball game in Belgrade on communications," although the U.S. no longer had the support of the majority of members. Duke recommended, however, "I think it is more productive to stay with it, to fight it through and be constructive, as I think we were in Belgrade." This recommendation was supported by John E. Fobes, chairman of the U.S. National Committee for Unesco, who argued that the U.S. could shape the debate in Unesco "only if we participate."[42]

Media representatives, while critical of Unesco, generally argued also that the U.S. should remain a member and work for reform from within. For example, Philip Power, chairman of Suburban Communications Corp., stated that "pulling out of Unesco would be a very serious mistake." And Leonard Marks of the WPFC observed that the committee had asked each witness whether the U.S. should withdraw from Unesco: "The general consensus has been that we should stay in there and fight . . . we would lose by withdrawing at this time because of the media situation." However, Murray J. Gant, editor of the *Washington Star*, calling for vigorous opposition to "all initiatives within Unesco that threaten a free press," recommended that "we should keep open as an active option the withdrawing of support and representation in Unesco itself."

Hamid Mowlana, director of the Program in International Communication Studies at the American University in Washington, D.C., was the only academician invited to give testimony. He declared that "the debate over the New World Information Order is, in a significant way, discussion of inequalities born of the economics of modern mass communications," and that "the American media often see a coincidence between American ideals, their own commercial self-interest, and the appropriate direction for world communities." Mowlana noted later that he was allowed to give his testimony, which contrasted sharply with that

of the other witnesses, "only after all other witnesses had been heard and the resolution already endorsed. Most interesting was the fact that the major U.S. media covering the hearings, including the *Washington Post*, the *Washington Star*, and the *New York Times*, ignored my testimony. Ironically I had to read the coverage of my own statement not in the local newspapers but in *The Times* of London."[43]

The International Program for the Development of Communication

The first meeting of the International Program for the Development of Communication (IPDC), scheduled for Paris in June 1981, set off a flurry of news reports, editorials and articles about Unesco. In May 1981, for example, the *Wall Street Journal* carried an article by Leonard Sussman, executive director of Freedom House, lauding the Talloires Declaration as a "free press counterattack" to actions taken at Unesco meetings. The article pointed out that countries with controlled presses held a majority of votes in Unesco. If those countries persisted in their campaign to "harass the free press," Sussman wrote, then the U.S. should consider withdrawing financial support from Unesco.[44]

In June the *Washington Star* published two pieces attacking Unesco's communication policies, one by its own editors and the other by Rosemary Righter, who covers Unesco for the London *Sunday Times* and is a strong critic of the agency. The *Star* article commented that "the information issue is important enough to merit drastic action if basic Unesco principles are compromised by the IPDC."[45] Both articles were read into the *Congressional Record*. Also in June, Elliott Abrams, assistant secretary of state for international organizations affairs, warned Unesco that the U.S. might quit the agency if it persisted in plans to regulate journalists in the performance of their professional duties.[46]

The debate extended to Congress that month, where Sen. Dan Quayle, R-Ind, a lawyer and newspaper publisher, introduced a resolution in the Senate to express opposition to Unesco's "attempt to regulate news content and to formulate rules and regulations for the operation of the world press." The resolution further expressed the Senate's opposition to "efforts by some countries to further control access to and dissemination of news." Quayle's resolution then was offered as an amendment to the Department of State authorization bill.[47] A further amendment by Sen. Patrick Moynihan, D-N.Y., was intended to put "teeth" into the motion. It specified that the U.S. would withhold from Unesco "our share of the money Unesco chooses to spend implementing its misguided New World Information Order."[48] The amendment was approved by a vote of 99 for, 0 against.

The Beard Amendment

In the House, Rep. Robin Beard, R-Tenn., announced his intention of further strengthening the language of the amendment. Beard proposed to "prohibit funding to Unesco if that organization implements any policies or procedures designed to regulate news content and formulate rules and regulations for the operation of the world press."[49] Beard backed up his proposal by reading into the *Congressional Record* the "excellent editorial" that had appeared in the *Washington Star* on June 12 about Unesco's "new order," and a letter from President Reagan endorsing the Declaration of Talloires and supporting his proposed amendment.

The House passed the Department of State authorization bill incorporating the Beard Amendment in September. It required the president to report to Congress within six months of the act taking effect his assessment of the extent to which U.S. contributions to Unesco programs, "especially its programs and activities in the communications sector," serve the national interests of the United States. It specified that no more U.S. funds could be paid to Unesco "if that organization implements any policy or procedure the effect of which is to license journalists or their publications, to censor or otherwise restrict the free flow of information within or among countries, or to impose mandatory codes of journalistic practice or ethics." And it required the Secretary of State to report to Congress each year on compliance with this section. The Beard Amendment was approved in the House by a vote of 372 to 19. Differences between the House and Senate versions of the bill (the language of the Unesco provision was not in dispute) were not resolved until August 1982, when President Reagan signed the measure into law.

TECHNOLOGY AND POLITICS

In its attempts to influence Unesco communications policies, the United States has used both the carrot and the stick approaches. The stick was the threat to withhold funds, as exemplified in the Beard Amendment. The carrot was to offer Third World nations assistance in building up their communications infrastructures. At the 1974 General Conference, the U.S. delegation, in opposing the draft declaration on mass media, asserted that the way to redress the imbalance was not to impose restrictive measures on countries with advanced systems, but to help developing nations strengthen their own capabilities. The United States took a similar line at the 1976 General Conference, and again in 1978, when John Reinhardt, head of the U.S. delegation, offered to explore the possibility of a mechanism for promoting both bilateral and multilateral assistance

programs in communications development. This was to lead eventually to the establishment of the International Program for the Development of Communication. Other offers of U.S. assistance included use of the INTELSAT system for projects serving rural development in various regions, and an offer to send senior U.S. scholars and media practitioners to regional training centers to upgrade their professional programs.

The underlying premise was that technology would make it possible to meet the core demands of proponents of the new information order: that all population groups would be able to make their voices heard, and that one-way communication would give way to two-way exchange. The IPDC also has put its trust in technologies. Among the projects it has funded are facilities for international exchange of information through satellite systems and the application of communications technology to rural areas.

The technical progress that has taken place in international communications is impressive. The passive reflecting satellite Echo I demonstrated in 1960 that a radio signal could be bounced off a satellite and picked up by another earth station thousands of miles from the first. Two years later Telstar carried into space transponders that amplified signals received from earth, and relayed them back to their destination. By 1965 the first geostationary communications satellite was in place. Early Bird, parked over the Atlantic, could carry 240 simultaneous telephone calls between North America and Europe. The fifth generation of Intelsat satellites, now being deployed, carry 12,000 voice circuits, plus two color TV channels, with worldwide coverage.[50]

As capacity has increased, costs have dropped. The cost per circuit per year in 1965 was $22,000. But the next generation of satellites will handle 100,000 circuits at $30 a year each.[51] The costs of associated computer equipment have fallen equally rapidly. In the five-year period between 1974 and 1979, while the costs of most goods and services was doubling, computer costs dropped by 95 percent—a trend that has continued since.[52]

Implications for Information Exchange

The implications of this for information exchange between the developing world and the industrialized countries are obvious. The United States and the Soviet Union are vying with each other to link up Third World countries to their respective satellite systems, Intelsat and Intersputnik. Both offer earth stations as part of their aid packages.[53] Since the satellites are virtually cost-insensitive to distance, people in remote and rural areas theoretically have access to transmitted materials as cheaply as

the city dweller in a developed country.[54] Today the Intelsat system has more than 100 member nations, who between them generate more than 95 percent of all international communications traffic.

Most of the members of Intelsat are developing countries, and between them they control a third of the corporation's investment shares, which are based on use of the system. To encourage smaller users, Intelsat charges equal prices regardless of volume. It also leases spare capacity for domestic use at half the usual rate, on a pre-emptable basis.[55] Several developing countries now have domestic satellite systems based on spare capacity on Intelsat. Regional systems have linked developing countries directly together for the first time. Systems either in operation now, or in the planning stage, include the ASEAN network using Indonesia's PALAPA satellite; an Arab regional system, Arabsat; an African system for the 38-member Panaftel group, Afrosat; and an Andean system to serve Latin American nations.[56] The Pacific Regional Satellite Communications system, proposed by Japan's Research Institute of Telecommunications and Economics (RITE), would use a single powerful satellite to link both developed and developing nations around the Pacific Rim into a vast network encompassing nearly half the world's population.[57]

The availability of low-cost transmission facilities, together with the establishment of national news agencies in more than 120 countries, has greatly increased the flow of news across frontiers. Narinder Aggarwala of the United Nations Development Program estimates there are now no fewer than 16 regional news pools operating among developing countries that could not have existed before. A typical example is Acción de Sistemas Informativos Nacionales (ASIN), a regional pool of 16 national news agencies of Latin American and Caribbean countries. ASIN uses satellite links to exchange news daily. In some cases there is also an exchange of news between regional systems. ASIN, for instance, now has a reciprocal news exchange with the Middle Eastern news pool, FANA. Another example of an interregional system is the News Agencies Pool of Non-aligned Countries.[58] The new technologies have also made possible the growth of a new international news agency, Inter Press Service, which focuses on Third World countries.[59]

The Growing Gap

These encouraging developments do not mean, however, that the developing countries are closing the gap between themselves and the advanced information societies. If anything, the new technologies are widening the communications gap between the rich and poor nations.[60] While the most advanced countries are awash in new information sys-

tems, the poorest nations have barely wet their feet. One communications finance expert has estimated that other countries will have to invest $50 billion a year over the next 30 years just to bring their communications systems up to *present* standards in the United States.[61] By then the U.S. itself will have vastly increased the range and size of its own system, continuing to outstrip its competitors.

One reason for the growing gap is that the information societies are spending vast sums on research into new technologies. By one estimate, even developing countries that are advanced in electronics, such as South Korea, had only 0.4 researchers per 1,000 of their population in 1978, compared to 2.6 in the United States and 2.4 in Japan for the year 1977.[62] Furthermore, expenditure per researcher was about $21,500 in Korea, compared to $47,560 in Japan and $80,680 in the United States.

While news agencies in the developing nations have upgraded their communications capabilities through the use of satellites, these often are low-capacity telex channels. By contrast, the U.S. agencies Associated Press and United Press International are in the forefront of technological innovation. The AP, for example, now distributes its news directly into the computers of 1,700 subscribers in the United States via WESTAR satellite, effectively eliminating the use of surface channels and telex printers. The AP channel also carries dozens of supplementary news services and syndicated materials. UPI has linked its journalists world-wide into a single high-speed network. Most newspapers in the United States now get their news agency copy directly from satellite receivers and do their editing electronically. Because of the extra costs involved in keyboarding hard copy into their systems, many editors now are reluctant to accept news delivered by traditional means, such as telex. As a result, unless Third World news services can get their materials carried on the U.S. domestic distribution systems, they are unlikely to break into the world's largest media market.

The impact of the new technology on news, therefore, has been to increase the amount flowing within countries, between Third World countries through regional pools, and from the North to the South through improved communications links. It has also made possible a larger flow of news from South to North. But little has in fact been achieved in this dimension.

Political and Economic Constraints

The reason is that what is technically possible is a very different matter from what is politically and economically feasible. As Wilson Dizard points out, communications and information affairs have economic, political and technological aspects:

Microelectronic technology is, for the present, the driving force among these factors, with its active promise of a new era of abundant resources. Economics is next, as industry demonstrates its ability to transform technological capabilities into marketplace realities. The most critical side of the triangle is the political one. Here is where understanding and actions are weakest, threatening the chances that viable strategies for dealing with the new environment will emerge. The choice, in simplest terms, is whether resources adequate to meet our needs can be assured through a linear extension of past political and social practices or whether a new set of strategies is called for.[63]

That is precisely the dilemma facing those who seek a free, *balanced* flow of news between nations on a North-South axis. The difficulty lies in the very different attitudes in the developed and developing worlds toward the role of news media, their function in society, and the very definition of what is news. The debates in Unesco concerning a New International Information Order illustrate very clearly these differences. To Western journalists, news is simply an objective, impartial report of an event. To some Third World leaders, news is any statement that can advance the objectives of the government. Much of the news in Western media, it is alleged, focuses on the odd, the aberational, the negative. Many Third World journalists see the real news as their slow, painful process of development, with its victories and setbacks, rather than the coups and earthquakes that beset them. Shrill voices have been raised on both sides. To Mustapha Masmoudi, a leading spokesman for the Third World point of view, "the flagrant quantitative and qualitative imbalance in communications flow between the North and South, amounts to a violation of national territories and private homes, and a veritable form of mental rape."[64] One American newsman responds that the New International Information Order is "part of a campaign by the Third World, with its Marxist and Soviet allies, to erect a global dictatorship of thought."[65] Given these very different ideological perspectives, it is not surprising that the new technology cannot by itself guarantee a free and balanced flow of information.

Inter Press Service

The political and economic factors involved in attempts to change existing international news flow patterns are perhaps best illustrated by the experience of two recent attempts to achieve it. The first is the case of Inter Press Service (IPS), an international news agency that specializes in news relating to the Third World. Its primary emphasis is on developing horizontal communications links and promoting news and information flow between the developing countries. In addition, the agency distributes

news about the Third World to clients in the industrialized countries of the North, thus enhancing the South-North flow.

IPS is the most recent of the international agencies. Founded in 1964 with the aim of providing an "information bridge" between Latin America and Europe, it has since expanded its operations to include parts of Africa, Asia, the Middle East and North America. As of 1986, IPS had bureaus or correspondents in more than 60 countries, and had distribution or news exchange agreements with some 30 Third World news agencies. Bureaus in such developed countries as Austria, France, Germany, the Netherlands, Sweden and the United States are translating and adapting IPS material for use in local media. The agency is continuing to expand its coverage of the Third World.

IPS is registered in Italy as a non-profit cooperative organization. Its international operations are conducted through a wholly owned subsidiary, IPS Third World, which is headquartered in Panama. Separate affiliates have been established in several Western countries to distribute IPS materials. Third World nationals, and particularly South Americans, form the majority of IPS's staff and correspondents, even in some European bureaus.

Although IPS is primarily a Third World news agency, its telecommunications network is centered in Rome, largely because despite the advances that have been made, it is still cheaper and more convenient to operate from a northern capital than from a developing country. From Rome, satellite teleprinter channels fork out to regional centers, and branch into local bureaus. Surplus capacity in the network is used by national news agencies to exchange information, thus providing direct links and building information flows between developing nations.

IPS has two basic services: Spanish, which has a volume of about 30,000 words a day, and English, with about 20,000 words a day. Selections from these core services are translated by regional bureaus into Arabic, Dutch, French, German, Norwegian, Portuguese and Swedish.

About 80 percent of the news distributed by IPS is produced by its own correspondents. IPS also has contracts with several national news agencies in the Third World to distribute their materials, unaltered, to IPS clients. Such items carry the credit line of the contributing agency. The agency carries several special feature services, including two that focus on the role of women in the developing world.

The IPS services are characterized by an emphasis on news about the Third World, and the Third World in relation to the industrialized West. Little attempt is made to compete with the major transnational agencies in coverage of spot news. Instead IPS provides a kind of daily news feature service, focusing on developmental themes.

By the budgetary standards of the Big Four agencies, IPS is a

shoestring operation. It has no wealthy national base to finance its foreign operations. The countries it has traditionally served have few privately owned media that can afford substantial subscriptions. Were it not for inexpensive satellite links, it probably could not exist. The agency's total budget for 1982 amounted to about $4 million (in the same year UPI's budget was $110 million; that of the AP was $190 million). About a third of the IPS budget derived from the sale of news and other services to national news agencies or direct to media subscribers. Another third came from contracts with national agencies for carrier and distribution services. Contracts with several United Nations agencies to provide coverage of their activities, with various organizations for special projects, and with non-media clients for subscriptions and services, accounted for about 10 percent each. Some of these contracts are subject to abrupt cancellation as political circumstances in the contracting countries change, and the agency is frequently strapped for cash. It finds itself squeezed between the powerful commercial agencies on the one hand, and Third World government and inter governmental initiatives to promote news flow on the other.

One reason for the agency's precarious financial position is that IPS has a definite philosophical perspective. It is associated with Unesco's efforts in the information field. To the developing countries, IPS represents a strong protagonist of the New International Economic Order, and its linkage with the New International Information Order. It is perceived as supporting the more "progressive" movements in Africa, Latin America and the Middle East, while opposing right-wing governments. To Westerners, IPS argues that its focus on the Third World does not mean that it is biased against the West, and that its news services are every bit as objective as those of the major agencies, differing only in the topics and themes they emphasize. Nevertheless, criticisms in some quarters of the agency's perceived ideological orientation meant that when IPS tried to break into Western markets, particularly the United States, it ran into a political storm.

Interlink Press Service

The impact of political, ideological and economic criticisms of initiatives by Third World agencies to enter the global communications market can be seen in the outcome of an attempt to sell IPS materials in the United States. Distribution of the agency's services in the U.S. was handled by Interlink Press Service, a non-profit organization set up in New York in 1980. It translated and adapted IPS material, as well as news from a variety of other alternative sources, for the U.S. media market. Breaking into that market was not an easy task, for technological, political and

economic reasons. Technologically, Interlink was innovative. It received feeds from IPS via INTELSAT channels, and in turn fed American news into the IPS international network. Early attempts to distribute the service domestically to U.S. subscribers by mail were unsuccessful, partly because the time involved meant it was not competitive; partly because of the reluctance of editors to accept copy that had to be keyboarded into their computers. But Interlink's attempts to distribute its copy over the AP satellite channel were not successful either. The AP would not carry the service unless it had a certain number of guaranteed subscribers to begin with. The editors would not buy the service until they could try it out first—and they couldn't because it wasn't available on the AP satellite. Interlink resorted to yet another new technology—distributing its copy on a nationwide time-sharing computer network. Any subscriber could dial up the network, making only a local phone call, and access the Interlink files. That worked well for some institutional users, like church groups and universities, but was not acceptable to news media, accustomed to getting news fed directly into their computers off satellites. As a result of lack of support, and little prospect of gaining much, Interlink shut down in 1986. North American subscribers can still get the Inter Press Service, but no longer tailored to their specific audiences. Politically, IPS still has to fight the perception that Third World journalists, whatever their qualifications, are under open or hidden pressure to write in a way pleasing to their governments. As one editor is quoted as saying, "In the Third World, the good journalists are in jail and those who aren't in jail aren't good."[66]

The point to be made here is that IPS/Interlink potentially could play an important role in improving the balance of international news flow. It offers an alternative source of news from a Third World perspective. It has access to technology that makes it possible to distribute that news. But so far political and economic restraints have stymied its growth.

In part, the opposition to IPS is one reaction of the Western media to pressure from the Third World to implement a New Information Order. Caught off guard when the issue was first raised in the 1970s, Western governments and media, led by the United States, have become more aggressive in defending their interests. As the most visible attempt to implement the principles of the New International Information Order, IPS seems to have been accorded special attention. The Western attack on IPS was based on two grounds: ideological and commercial. The ideological criticisms relate to IPS's association with Unesco, with the new information order, with national news agencies of some authoritarian countries, and with liberation movements. On the other hand IPS is seen by Western news agencies as a potential competitor whose activities conceivably could lead to cancellation of their contracts with Third

World countries, and to denial of access to those countries by their correspondents.

The Development Information Network

These issues emerge clearly also in the controversy over the Development Information Network. DevNet (or DIN) is an ambitious proposal to improve horizontal flow of communication between developing countries. It is intended to improve information flow South–South, not South–North. The concept arose from the realization that information has a vital role to play in the development process. In 1979 the UN Development Program commissioned IPS, with its experience in Third World information links, to undertake a multiregional feasibility study of a South–South development information network.[67] In its report to UNDP, IPS concluded that "a new flow of information, with distinct characteristics, can be created through a computer-operated South–South network, providing a full horizontal exchange of mutually supportive development information between developing countries."[68] The plan is to establish a network, using surplus capacity on existing satellite channels leased by developing countries for their telecommunications. The network would link 60 national centers in the first three years. Later it would be extended to all developing countries. DevNet would use Third World personnel, hardware and software as far as was practical. DevNet was estimated to cost about $40 million in the first six years. The UNDP would provide start-up funds of up to $2 million, with the rest coming from voluntary contributions from nations around the world, and from subscriber fees. DevNet was to be operated by a Malta-based group called Communication for Development (CODEV). CODEV is closely associated with IPS: it has several directors in common, including IPS Director General Roberto Savio; it has an office at the same address as the IPS headquarters in Rome.

But on the eve of the signing of a contract between UNDP and CODEV to begin a pilot project for DevNet, the United States government, acting on behalf of U.S. media interests, stopped it short, with a clearly implied threat of economic retribution if the agency went ahead (in 1982 the U.S. contribution to UNDP was $126 million). The ostensible reason for the DevNet, contract being blocked was technical and procedural: UNDP could not award so large a contract to a single bidder —CODEV. The real reasons were political and economic.

Just before the contract was to be signed, the U.S. State Department sent a cable to the U.S. Mission to the United Nations instructing it to discuss the contract with UNDP Administrator Bradford Morse.[69] "We perceive serious problems with the contract," said the State Department,

"as well as with the possible political ramifications of the DIN. Mission should make it clear to Morse that the UNDP faces a political backlash in the U.S. if our understanding of the contract is correct. He should be asked specifically to postpone award of the contract or its further implementation until a thorough review is made."

Both the ideological and commercial objections to IPS emerge in a series of "talking points" the U.S. ambassador was instructed to raise with Morse. The United States, it said, did not believe the UNDP considered the range of potential contractors or gave consideration to the political sensibilities of such member states as the United States in its choice of CODEV. "The latter is largely an initiative of Inter Press Service Third World News Agency (IPS), an organization which has consistently opposed U.S. interests in economic, political and information matters. For example, on Middle East issues the IPS steadily supports PLO themes."

The cable states further that IPS "publicizes a standard 'anti-imperialist' line and unabashedly promotes the most radical version of a New International Economic Order and a New World Information Order. It is regarded as a stalking horse for Third World press interests and is an object of deep suspicion both to U.S. private media and the U.S.G[overnment]."

The ecomonic argument is stated with equal candor. The IPS, says the cable, "officially describes itself as a non-profit clearing house of development information and as a supplement to general news dissemination through the commercial news agencies. In fact it is much more than that. IPS management has ambitiously presented itself in recent years to governments in developing countries as an alternative to the commercial news agencies. One of its tactics is to offer to carry host government materials over the IPS network in return for contracts to supply IPS materials to the local media."

The State Department cable argues that "in awarding the DIN contract to CODEV (read IPS), the UNDP will be providing UN money to build the IPS into a world class competitor of the commercial news agencies. Through the DIN, the IPS stands to gain access to a vastly increased distribution network for its own materials, and to dispose of facilities and resources rivaling those of the commercial agencies. The scale of the new project—some $40 million over 5 years—makes this one of the most important developments on the world information scene."

Presstime, the organ of the American Newspaper Publishers Association, stressed the link between IPS and NIIO issues when reporting on the stalled CODEV contract.[70] *Presstime* quotes John Koehler, then assistant general manager of the World Services Division of the Associated Press, as saying: "We welcome competition wherever it is. What

concerns us is what happens if UN money is used to build up an agency that would keep us out of areas where we need to go to do our job."

The DevNet contract was never signed, and although opposition to the project in the United States appears to have diminished, several Third World countries that were to have supported the system found themselves unable to do so as their economies weakened. A revised version of the project, with a different funding base, is now being developed in Rome.

The criticisms of IPS affected not only the CODEV contract but a number of other contracts with specialized U.N. agencies, which were cut or canceled. The opposition to IPS came from the same sources as those active in the campaign against Unesco. They included the U.S. government, particularly the State Department Bureau for International Organization Affairs. The bureau acted in concert with the World Press Freedom Committee, led by Leonard Marks, a former head of the U.S. Information Service. Also active in the campaign to block IPS was Stan Swinton, then head of international operations for the Associated Press.

IPS Responds

Officials of IPS, faced with Western criticisms, have taken steps to counter what they believe to be misunderstandings about their operation. Roberto Savio, director general of IPS, addressed the issue of the agency's links with national news agencies in testimony submitted to a U.S. congressional committee.[71] Savio pointed out that a recurring theme in the West is that one cannot have a free and professional press when the structures are owned by the state; only private enterprise can guarantee free information flow. This concept, he says, is based on the specific experience of industrialization in the Western world. There, the creation of an industrial society built a mass market for information, which allowed newspapers to sustain themselves. News agencies in turn were sustained by the press. The situation in the Third World is totally different, says Savio. Few countries are industrialized; they are poor; they lack a mass market, and so cannot sustain commercial media. For the Third World, he says, the problem is simple: communication is essential for national development. But either the state intervenes to support the media, or the media do not exist.

There is no disagreement that IPS favors many of the objectives of a New Economic Order and a New Information Order. Whether it promotes "the most radical version" of the two is open to question. There has been some inflated rhetoric. But the current position IPS takes on the New Information Order eschews the more extreme demands. IPS convened a conference in Rome in September 1982 with the theme "A

Challenge for the 80's: Implementing Communication for Development." A draft declaration by the participants defines the New Information Order as a process for building new communications and information infrastructures in the world. The approach is pluralistic: "The NWICO is a long-term undertaking in which different countries are at different stages in this process and will, as independent and sovereign nations, continue to adopt different policies and approaches in accordance with their needs and resources."[72]

One key clause of the declaration deals with the relationship between the state and the media: While the New World Information and Communication Order "requires the state to guarantee access to information for all social sectors, foster new channels of communication and guarantee the right to communicate in its widest sense, this should not be seen as an excuse for government control or subjugation of the media, should not limit freedom of expression nor be construed as authorizing censorship and media control by any public or private institutions."

The concern among Western agencies that IPS could become a significant competitor, perhaps replacing them eventually in some Third World markets, appears to be based in part on statements by IPS officers that it seeks to be an "alternative" agency. Savio says there appears to be a fear on the part of AP and UPI that IPS could become so efficient that Third World countries would take only IPS, and deny access to the others. "We are not competing directly," says Savio. "There is no instance in which AP, UPI, Reuters, or any other agency has been kept out of a country because of IPS." What IPS offers, says Savio, is an alternative kind of information, not an alternative to the services of the major agencies.

The attack on IPS has been particularly vehement in the United States. In Europe, where the political center of gravity is closer to that represented by IPS and there is a long tradition of government subvention of the media, there is much greater tolerance of and support for what IPS is trying to achieve. Governments in countries like West Germany, Sweden, the Netherlands, Austria and France have channeled funds to IPS, often through their development aid agencies or through non-government organizations set up for such purposes. Typically the funding is temporary, helping support a bureau that translates and adapts IPS news for the local market. The intention is that the bureaus should become self-supporting from subscriptions once they are established. Some of these operations, particularly those in West Germany and Sweden, have been remarkably successful in attracting media clients.

It has, however, taken a deliberate political decision by the governments involved to fund the service. This in turn is based on a perception that the world is becoming increasing interdependent, both politically and

economically, and that it is in their own self-interest to promote an understanding among their citizens of Third World issues. The new technologies have made it possible for the new initiatives to germinate. But without the right political and economic climate, there is little chance of their taking root and flourishing.

PREVIOUS STUDIES

There have been several previous studies of media coverage of Unesco activities during the period outlined above. These include a report on news coverage of the 1980 Unesco General Conference in Belgrade, prepared by the U.S. National News Council, and a report on the coverage of the Paris conference in 1982, prepared by George Gerbner, dean of the Annenberg School of Communication at the University of Pennsylvania.

National News Council

The National News Council study by A.H. Raskin, associate director of the council, examined 448 news clippings and 206 editorials from newspapers throughout the United States.[73] About 80 percent of the news stories printed came from the AP or UPI, so there was a high degree of duplication. The six-week conference in the fall of 1980 dealt with scores of Unesco activities, including its work in combating illiteracy, developing alternate energy sources, protecting historic monuments, and broadening educational and research programs for scientists and engineers. But, says Raskin, not one story emanating from the conference dealt with these topics. Instead, the focus was on political confrontation at the meeting, and particularly the debate over Unesco's communications policies. News analysis and factual stories, said the report, "concentrated almost exclusively on Western worries about the Unesco initiative, with little presentation of opposing viewpoints." The editorials "without exception . . . expressed apprehension about Unesco's involvement in attempts to establish policy on matters affecting the worldwide flow of information."

Roger Revelle, professor of science and public policy at the University of California, San Diego, who was a U.S. delegate at Belgrade, is quoted in the study as saying, "When one reads the press reports of the 21st General Conference, it seems that Unesco is concerned only with the 'media,' that is newspapers, radio and television, and their relations to governments. The major activities of Unesco in science, education and culture are rarely, if ever, mentioned."

Raskin also quotes Western media representatives who rejected the charge that international news organizations are biased against Unesco. Stan Swinton, former head of the Associated Press's World Service, insisted that AP correspondents apply total fairness in reporting Unesco communication policy. While conceding that not all of Unesco's activities at Belgrade were covered, Swinton felt that "if it were not for the controversy over the 'new communications order,' nobody from the press would have been there at all. It's like soft landings at an airport, a non-story." The study quotes H. L. Stevenson, vice president of UPI, as ascribing many of the complaints of one-sidedness in Western news reporting of the Unesco debate to the gatekeeping system. "We can crank out stories of all sorts," Stevenson told the News Council researchers, "and much to our amazement see them never get printed. We get frustrated about that."

Nevertheless, the report maintained that news reports from the Belgrade conference were distorted—not by editorialization in the writing, but by the selective process.

> The first sifting out of material that did not fit Western journalism's mind-set was by reporters in their assessment of which developments were worthy of note. The process of excluding contrary material was then reinforced by the tendency of gatekeepers at the foreign desks in newspapers at home to discard stories that did not highlight the conflict angle. Maximum attention was given to stories indicating that the West was being outmaneuvered on the freedom front and little space was given in most of those stories or in others reviewed in the survey to expositions of opposing viewpoints.

Raskin concludes that "the imbalance that characterized most of the Belgrade coverage in this country provided an inadequate foundation for independent judgment by Americans of the correctness of the editorial positions their newspapers were taking on the Unesco communications issue. Equally troublesome, the imbalance set a poor example of Third World journalists and other skeptics on what they should find admirable as a model of press freedom and immunity from governmental control in Western journalistic practice."

Freedom House

Two other studies of coverage of the Belgrade conference are cited in the National News Council report. One is an independent study by Leonard Sussman of Freedom House of 63 news accounts and 37 editorials.[74]

Sussman classified 60 percent of the news reports as "unfavorable," 32 percent as "balanced," and 8 percent as "favorable." Of the editorials, 92 percent "strongly attacked" the work of the conference. Sussman, a leading critic of Unesco's media programs, was concerned, however, that

> the coverage was unbalanced because many reports of the events at Belgrade emphasized the dire potentialities of press control as though they had already materialized. Votes taken or a consensus reached were faithfully reported. But *all* of these actions were directed toward further studies and meetings over the next three years. These actions unquestionably target the free press for future governmental restrictions or, at least, repressive standards however enforced. This is undeniably a threat—but too often the reports and certainly the headlines gave the impression doomsday had already arrived. Neither public understanding nor an effective defense of press freedom is helped by exaggerating the present state of the challenge.

Joseph A. Mehan, chief of public information for Unesco in New York, prepared a report on the Belgrade conference for the News Council. He noted that although the six-week conference covered 53 activities from integrated rural development to copyright systems to the status of women in society, Paul Lewis in the *New York Times* described the conference as "a United Nations conference on communications and news organizations."[75] This, said Mehan, "symptomizes the disgraceful American coverage of the Unesco general conference."[76] A Unesco review of 302 press clippings from U.S. publications while the Belgrade conference was under way found not one on any topic other than the communication issue or four other controversial subjects: a speech by Yassir Arafat of the Palestine Liberation Organization, a denunciation of the Soviet Union by a defecting Afghan delegate, and the re-election of Director General M'Bow. The Unesco survey found 229 editorials in the U.S. press denouncing Unesco on communications issues. According to Mehan, not one editor offered comment on any other aspect of the conference, and "none suggested an alternative or viable perspective from another perspective, i.e. the Third World." Mehan concluded that

> it would be utterly impossible for an alert American citizen, desirous of informing himself on either the programmatic role Unesco plays in the international scene or the immensely complicated communications issue, to make an intelligent judgment based on the abysmal quality of the America reporting. It is incredibly ironic that the America press which stridently claims it is protecting the rights of a free press and the free flow of information, restricts and distorts that flow on the communications issue to the America public.

Annenberg School of Communications

The next Unesco general conference took place in Paris in the fall of 1982. Coverage of that event was studied by George Gerbner, dean of the Annenberg School of Communications, under contract to Unesco.[77] Gerbner analyzed reports that appeared in U.S. newspapers, in wire stories from the AP and UPI, Unesco press releases, and responses to a letter of inquiry sent to journalists who covered the conference. The aim of the study was to analyze the extent and nature of the coverage, and to show the operation of news values and other factors at work by comparing the actual conference with its news coverage.

Gerbner found that coverage of the conference in the nation's press was sparse. Only about one in 15 daily papers printed anything, and most of the 116 papers that printed anything carried only one small item. What coverage there was controlled by a few central organizations and sources, with two-thirds of the reports coming from AP or UPI, and lesser numbers coming from the New York Times News Service and Reuters.

Although the conference covered a wide range of topics, the news coverage focused almost exclusively on communications issues: Unesco's promotion of a New World Information Order and related themes. Responses to letters of inquiry from Gerbner to U.S. journalists who covered or edited stories about the conference indicated that Unesco's Office of Public Information had served correspondents well in providing drafts of speeches and other information. This, however, had no effect on shaping the basic terms of U.S. press coverage. Gerbner quotes one correspondent who was well aware of the priorities of his home office:

> I was trying to give an overview of the conference and show that there were other issues besides communications that Unesco deals with in its medium-term plan . . . . However, the desk felt that there had to be greater emphasis on communications, specifically what happened to the New World Information and Communication Order, because that was the only reason editors would pay attention to a story about Unesco.

In addition to the 177 news reports analyzed, Gerbner studied editorials relating to the conference. "All but one were negative," he wrote, "ranging from the skeptical to the strident." In some cases identical editorials appeared in several different newspapers. For example, 15 papers printed an editorial "How the West Won One" that was distributed by the Copley News Service. Another five papers carried an editorial from the Hearst News and Feature Service. Gerbner noted that "a defensive, belligerent and often paranoid tone pervaded most editorials

published about the conference. There was little recognition of American points of view other than that of the press and its trade associations and public relations spokespersons."

Gerbner concluded that the American press had viewed the session mostly from its own institutional vantage point: "The press constructed a picture of the meetings more from selected speeches and prior information than from the actual resolutions and official actions of the conference. That construction showed a preoccupation with real and imagined threats to private control of the press to the virtual exclusion of other issues."

NOTES

1. The Constitution of the United Nations Educational, Scientific and Cultural Organization, adopted on 16 November 1945 at a United Nations meeting in London. Reprinted in Edmund Jan Osmanczyk, *Encyclopedia of the United Nations and International Agreements* (London: Taylor and Francis, 1985), pp. 827–829.
2. Peter I. Hajnal, *Guide to Unesco* (London: Oceana, 1983), p. 243
3. Ibid., p. 244
4. "Draft Declaration of Fundamental Principles Governing the Use of Mass Media" (Unesco document COM-74/CONF. 6l6/3, 23 January 1974).
5. See Kaarle Nordenstreng, *The Mass Media Declaration of Unesco* (Norwood, N.J.: Ablex, 1984), p. 79 ff.
6. "Action Program for Economic Cooperation," reprinted in Odette Tankowitsch and Karl Sauvant, *The Third World without Super Powers: The Collected Documents of the non-Aligned Countries* (Dobbs Ferry, N.Y.: Oceana, 1978), pp. 225–226.
7. Leonard H. Marks,"New World Information Order: A Bad Idea that Refuses to Die," in Leonard H. Marks, ed., *The Media Crisis* (Miami: World Press Freedom Committee, 1981), p. 29.
8. Jonathan F. Gunter, "The United States and the Debate on the World Information Order"(Washington: USICA, 1979), p. 48.
9. Ibid., p. 50.
10. A. W. Singham and Tran Van Dinh, eds., *From Bandung to Colombo* (New York: Third Press Review Book, 1976), pp. 163–164.
11. *Final Report: Intergovernmental Conference on Communication Policies in Latin America and the Caribbean* (Paris: Unesco, 1976), pp. 23–24.
12. "Draft Declaration on Fundamental Principles Governing the Use of the Mass Media in Strengthening Peace and International Understanding and in Combating War Propaganda, Racism and Apartheid" (Unesco document 19C/91, 1 July 1976).
13. Leonard R. Sussman, "The Controversy . . . And How It Began," in Marks, *The Media Crisis,* p. 3.

14. Amadou-Mahtar M'Bow, "New World Information Order: An Idea Whose Time is Near," in Marks, *The Media Crisis*, p. 17.
15. Sean MacBride, Preface to Unesco, *Many Voices, One World* (Paris: Unesco, 1980), p. xvii.
16. J. Herbert Altschull, *Agents of Power: The Role of the News Media in Human Affairs* (White Plains, N.Y.: Longman, 1984), p. 217.
17. The various versions of the text are reprinted in Nordenstreng, *The Mass Media Declaration of Unesco*, pp. 271–381.
18. The unpublished report is reprinted in Nordenstreng, *The Mass Media Declaration of Unesco*, p. 129.
19. Kaarle Nordenstreng, "Struggle around New International Information Order: Paris Compromise May Not Be the Last Word," *Communicator*, October 1979.
20. Leonard R. Sussman and David W. Sussman, "Mass News Media and International Law," *International Political Science Review*, 7 (July 1986), pp. 344–360.
21. *New York Times*, 27 November 1978.
22. Unesco, *Many Voices, One World*, frontispiece.
23. Sarah Goddard Power, "Assessment of Information and Communication Issues," 21st General Conference of Unesco, Belgrade, September–October 1980 (Washington, D.C.: U.S. State Department, 1980).
24. Ibid.
25. *Unesco's Second Medium-Term Plan* (Paris: Unesco, 1982).
26. Harold W. Andersen, "Cooperate—But Not at the Expense of Our Principles," in Marks, *The Media Crisis*, p. 26.
27. Tina S. Hills, "MacBride Report Prescribes Peril Instead of Protection," in Marks, *The Media Crisis*, p. 40.
28. Gerald R. Long, "A Search for Truth . . . Or a Denial of Truth," in Marks, *The Media Crisis*, p. 56.
29. "The World Press Freedom Committee Story," in Marks, *The Media Crisis*, p. 107.
30. Andersen, "Cooperate," p. 25.
31. Introduction to Marks, *The Media Crisis*, p. ix.
32. Sussman, "The Controversy,"p. 1.
33. Andersen, "Cooperate," p. 26.
34. Quoted in "Unesco Watchdog Seeks Funds," *Editor & Publisher*, 5 May 1984, p. 14.
35. Altschull, *Agents of Power*, pp. 240ff.
36. "A Journalistic Anniversary . . . with a Timely Message," *Chicago Tribune*, 1 June 1981, p. 17.
37. Gunnar Garbo, *A World of Difference* (Paris: Unesco, 1985), p. 62.
38. Quoted in Altschull, *Agents of Power*, p. 242.
39. World Press Freedom Committee, "The Declaration of Talloires," reprinted in *Freedom at Issue* (New York: Freedom House) September–October 1981.
40. *Editor & Publisher*, 29 September 1984, p. 6.
41. Altschull, Agents of Power, p. 246.

42. U.S. House of Representatives, Committee on Foreign Affairs, Hearings and Markup, "Review of U.S. Participation in UNESCO," 10 March, 9 and 16 July, 1981, p. 3.
43. Hamid Mowlana, *Journal of Communication*, 34 (Autumn, 1984), p. 139.
44. *Wall Street Journal*, 16 June 1981, p. 30.
45. *Washington Star*, 12 June 1981.
46. *Congressional Record*, 97th Congress, 1st session, 9 June 1981, p. E2180.
47. *Congressional Record*, 97th Congress, 1st session, 17 June 1981, p. S6365.
48. Ibid.
49. *Congressional Record*, 97th Congress, 1st session, 25 June 1981, p. E3215.
50. Thomas Y. Canby, "Satellites That Serve Us," *National Geographic*, 164 (September 1983).
51. Thomas R. Ide, "The Technology," in Gunter Friedrichs and Adam Schaff, eds., *Microelectronics and Society* (Oxford, England: Pergamon Press, 1982), p. 60.
52. Oswald H. Ganley, *International Implications of United States Communications and Information Resources* (Cambridge, Mass: Harvard University, 1981), p. 79.
53. Ibid., p. 18.
54. Ide, "The Technology," p. 60.
55. Ganley, *International Implications*, p. 207.
56. "Satellites: An InterMedia Survey," *InterMedia*, 14 (July/September 1986), pp. 26–81.
57. Research Institute of Telecommunications and Economics, "A Study on the Pacific Regional Communications System" (Tokyo: RITE, 1983).
58. D. R. Mankekar, "The Non-Aligned News Pool," in Jim Richstad and Michael H. Anderson, eds., *Crisis in International News* (New York: Columbia University Press, 1981), pp. 369–379.
59. C. Anthony Giffard, "Inter Press Service: News from the Third World," Journal of Communication, 34 (Autumn 1984), pp. 41–59; C. Anthony Giffard, "Inter Press Service: New Information for a New Order," *Journalism Quarterly* (Spring 1985), pp. 17–23.
60. William A. Hachten, *The World News Prism: Changing Media, Clashing Ideologies*, (Ames: Iowa State University Press, 1981), p. 116.
61. Robert LeBlanc, "Changes and Opportunities in Telecommunications," *Telecommunications Industry Monthly* (New York: Salomon Brothers, 1 February 1981).
62. Juan F. Rada, "A Third World Perspective," in Friedrichs and Schaff, *Microelectronics and Society*, p. 225.
63. Wilson P. Dizard, *The Coming Information Age* (White Plains, N.Y.: Longman, 1982), p. 27.
64. Mustapha Masmoudi, "The New World Information Order," in Richstad and Anderson, *Crisis in International News*, pp. 77–96.
65. Jeffrey St. John, "Restraints on International News Flow," paper delivered at the Edward R. Murrow Symposium, Washington State University, 1979.
66. Quoted in Donald L. Shanor, "Voices from the Third World: A Report to the Ford Foundation," (unpublished monograph, 1984).

67. Roberto Savio and Phil Harris, "IPS: The NIIO in Practice," *Media Development*, 27 (April 1980), pp. 38–42.
68. Ibid.
69. Peter Hall, "What's All the Fuss about Interpress?" *Columbia Journalism Review* (January/February 1982), pp. 53–57.
70. "UN Agency Postpones Action on New Information Network," *Presstime*, February 1982.
71. Roberto Savio, Statement to the Subcommittee on Human Rights and International Organizations, Committee of Foreign Affairs, U.S. House of Representatives, 97th Congress, 1st session (Washington, D.C., 16 July 1981).
72. "A Challenge for the 1980s: Implementing Communication for Democracy and Development" (Rome: Inter Press Service, 1982).
73. A. H. Raskin, "U.S. News Coverage of the Belgrade Unesco Conference," *Journal of Communication*, 31 (Autumn 1981), pp. 164–174.
74. Sussman's study is quoted in Raskin, "U.S. News Coverage."
75. The *New York Times* report is quoted in Joseph A. Mehan, "U.S. Media Coverage of the Unesco General Conference, Belgrade," (Unesco memorandum, 16 December 1980 New York,).
76. Ibid.
77. George Gerbner, "The American Press Coverage of the Fourth Extraordinary session of the UNESCO General Conference, Paris 1982" (Philadelphia: Annenberg School of Communications, 1983).

CHAPTER 3

The Year of Crisis

The period covered by this study begins with the announcement in December 1983 that the United States had given Unesco the formal one-year notice of withdrawal that Unesco's charter requires before a member can leave the organization. Much of the subsequent action obviously took place behind the scenes, but a chronology of recorded public events and documents helps to illuminate the issues and evaluate the press coverage that ensued. The chronology is not intended to be exhaustive. Based on source documents, press releases, briefings and news reports, it is meant to identify the forums where the discussion took place, the main actors involved, and the arguments for and against withdrawal. Although foreign policy is primarily the responsibility of the executive branch of government, and the decision to withdraw was made by the administration, much of the public debate took place at hearings before various congressional committees. These arguments are presented in some detail because they indicate the parameters of the debate and the range of opinion that was available for news reports and opinion pieces in the press.

DECEMBER 1983

Recommendation to Withdraw

The recommendation that the United States should withdraw first appears in a classified document dated December 16 from Gregory J. Newell, assistant secretary of state for international organization affairs, to Secret-

ary of State George Shultz. Newell recommended that the United States withdraw, since continued participation in Unesco "did not serve the interests of the United States" and referred to the in-depth policy review of Unesco he had commissioned in mid-1983, which he said "confirmed prior impressions that the organization does have deep-seated problems." There appeared to be a persistent pattern of:

1. extraneous politicization of virtually every subject dealt with: Israel, South Africa, human rights, disarmament, communications, etc.;
2. an endemic hostility toward basic institutions of a free society, especially a free market and a free press; and
3. the most irresponsible and unrestrained budgetary expansion in the U.N. system.

Noting the there would be opposition to the decision from other nations—including France and Israel—as well as from U.S. interest groups in the educational, scientific, cultural and media establishments, Newell's "action memorandum" included a proposed strategy for disengagement from Unesco. In addition to the standard diplomatic consultations and notifications, the document called for a campaign to manipulate the press to generate public support for the withdrawal. It suggested sending articles backing the administration's view to the *Washington Post* and the *New York Times* and called for "articles of support" to be submitted to the press by "private sector individuals" and for a letters-to-the-editor campaign.[1]

U.S. National Commission for Unesco

Domestic opposition to the withdrawal surfaced on December 16 when members attending the U.S. National Commission for Unesco annual meeting voted in support of a resolution that called for efforts to reform Unesco, but also urged the United States not to withdraw. Most of the commissioners argued that the United States would be in a better position to effect reforms if it remained a member. James B. Holderman, chairman of the commission, argued that "the best means of serving U.S. interests in Unesco is to press for reform within."[2] Others held that only a strong gesture, like a temporary withdrawal, would have any influence on the organization.

The commission adopted, by a vote of 41 to 8, a resolution noting that strong American leadership and "a certain spirit of accommodation" shown by the 22nd General Conference of Unesco had made possible the

development of a consensus more consistent with U.S. views on important aspects of several contentious issues, especially in the field of communications. The commission concluded that continued U.S. membership in Unesco was in the national interest. It called for the "exercise of positive American leadership in Unesco affairs in place of the restrictive, damage-limiting stance we have so often adopted," and it urged the State Department to develop channels of consultation with the director general of Unesco to make continued U.S. participation mutually valuable and productive.[3] According to a report in London's *The Guardian*, Newell, addressing the commission meeting, said that the State Department review of Unesco was still going on. "There has not been a decision made. There has not been a recommendation to the Secretary of State."[4] This appeared on the same date as Newell's secret memorandum to Shultz recommending withdrawal.

Presidential Approval

The White House approved the State Department's decision to withdraw on December 23. A letter from National Security Adviser Robert C. McFarlane to Secretary of State Shultz said that President Reagan had approved the recommendation with reluctance, but "given our inability to reform Unesco in any substantive way over the past three years, its continued politicization of almost every issue, its attack upon a free flow of communications and unrestrained budgetary expansion, we see little hope for productive membership."[5] The letter said, however, that

> the President wishes us to continue to expend every effort to effect meaningful changes over the next year to eliminate the suppression of minority views and political diversions and restore fiscal integrity. In pursuing the effort he wishes you to consider significant upgrading of our representation in Unesco and appointment of a panel consisting of senior representatives of the academic community, the media and the corporate world to advise us over the next year. He is prepared to review the decision to withdraw should concrete changes materialize.

Over the next two weeks there were almost daily reports on one news service or another, quoting administration officials as saying that withdrawal was imminent. Both the *New York Times* and the *Washington Post* reported on December 24 that Secretary of State George Shultz would recommend to President Reagan that the United States pull out, and similar reports were carried by the AP and UPI.

Formal Notice

The United States ambassador to Unesco, Jean Broward Shevlin Gerard, handed M'Bow a letter from Shultz giving formal notice of the intention to withdraw on December 28. The letter expressed the administration's central complaints. Shultz stated that the United States was concerned "that trends in the policy, ideological emphasis, budget and management were detracting from the organization's effectiveness" and that these trends had "led Unesco away from the original principles of its constitution. We feel that they have served the political purposes of member states, rather than the international vocation of Unesco."[6]

These concerns were amplified by administration officials. Announcing the formal withdrawal, the State Department's deputy spokesman, Alan Romberg, said that Unesco had "extraneously politicized virtually every subject it deals with," that it had "exhibited hostility toward the basic institutions of a free society, especially a free market and a free press," and that it had demonstrated "unrestrained budgetary expansion."[7]

Gregory Newell gave an on-the-record briefing at the State Department the afternoon of December 29. He began with an opening statement, then answered reporters' questions.[8] The statement, copies of which were made available to the press, read:

> Unesco policies for several years have served anti-U.S. political ends. The Reagan Administration has frequently advised Unesco of the limits of U.S. toleration: for its misguided policies, its tendentious programs, and its extravagant budgetary mismanagement. For nearly three years now, the Administration has applied to Unesco the same goals and priorities that guide our relations with all multilateral institutions. But Unesco alone, among the major U.N. organizations, has not responded.
>
> Now, at the conclusion of a long effort to reason with Unesco, and a careful reassessment of our relationship to it, the President has concluded that U.S. participation in Unesco, as it is currently organized, directed and focused, does not serve the interests of the United States. Our conclusion is firm. The United States has accordingly given notice that it will withdraw from Unesco effective December 31, 1984.

Asked by a reporter for concrete examples of what the United States was objecting to by way of politicization, Newell said that in the first instance, a great deal of time was spent discussing Soviet-inspired peace initiatives. In the last Unesco budget, more than three-quarters of a million dollars had been approved for peace and disarmament initiatives, "again inspired from the Eastern bloc," while only $32,000 had been

approved for the education of refugees, of whom there were 10 million worldwide. This, said Newell, seemed to be a misuse of funds and politicization of the educational sector of Unesco. A second item was human rights. In terms of Unesco's mandate it subscribed to the Universal Declaration of Human Rights, "yet they continually push for collective rights, people rights, cultural rights, etc., which are of the state and not of the individual." A third area would be in academic freedom, "again under the same statist concept."

Asked about criticisms of Unesco's budget, Newell said the administration had adopted a policy of zero net program growth throughout the United Nations system. Most agencies had responded by coming in at or near zero. But Unesco had recommended to its last General Conference a 9.7 percent increase, then worked on a Nordic proposal of a 2.5 percent increase as a compromise. In real terms this worked out to a 3.8 to 5.5 percent increase. Asked to comment on U.S. objections to Unesco's "proposed restrictions on the press," Newell said that the concern was with licensing of journalists. "That means some journalists might not be licensed; with codes of conduct, we find that unacceptable." He noted that the recent General Conference "provided a much different tone" on communications issues than had been the case in the past. However, "our feeling is that the General Conference was merely a transitory change of behavior. Programmatically, nothing in communications that I have seen—and I went to Paris during the communications presentation—has changed."

Newell said that the six-month policy review of Unesco by the State Department had led to the conclusion that "there is no conceivable way that Unesco could change its policies, its direction, its practices, such that we would be enticed to remain as part of the organization." Having said that, however, Newell remarked that elements of Unesco were important to the United States in the development area. And he held out the possibility that the United States might reconsider its decision before the withdrawal took effect. "Should there be significant progress moving away from politicization, number one, statist approaches, number two, and reordering its house managerially and fiscally, then we would be open perhaps at the end of the year to look again to make sure that the decision which the President has made remains. But for the time being it is our conclusion that those changes are just not in the offing."

Asked how Unesco could demonstrate significant change, Newell said that in the first place it should abandon discussions on disarmament and peace. The appropriate place for those was the Committee on Disarmament in Geneva, not in Unesco. On human rights, Unesco should live up to its mandate as enunciated in the Declaration of Human Rights

"rather than getting off on collective rights which are not part of that Declaration." In terms of communications, it should back away from and cease support for mechanisms that would lead to a New World Information and Communications Order. It would likewise have to move away from the New International Economic Order, "which they inject into virtually every resolution that comes forward," and Unesco would have to impose a ceiling on its budget.

The flurry of reports of the announcement was followed by several reactions to the move. The 50-nation African bloc at Unesco appealed to the United States to reconsider. The Soviet Union and Spain, among others, denounced the decision, while several Western nations were reported as saying that they also would review their membership. Unesco's first official comment, from Assistant Director General Henri Lopes, dismissed the charges of politicization and mismanagement, calling the criticisms "a tissue of lies."

JANUARY 1984

M'Bow Replies

M'Bow, in a letter to Shultz dated January 18, expressed his concern over the impact the pullout would have on the universality of Unesco. In response to Shultz's criticisms about the new trends in Unesco, M'Bow noted that the majority of decisions taken since 1976 had been reached by consensus of all states represented. The growing diversity of the membership over the years had brought about changes in the subjects dealt with by Unesco. Most deprived countries had realized the importance of asserting their cultural identity, and that their problems could not be solved without development of education, without a surer grasp of science and technology, and without "an increase in their potential in the various fields of information and communication." M'Bow suggested that the United States should distinguish between the viewpoints of individual member nations, or groups of states, and the activities of the organization itself. He expressed the hope that the United States would decide to remain in Unesco.[9]

Soviet Premier Yuri Andropov wrote to M'Bow expressing support for Unesco and criticism of the U.S. pullout.[10] Support for Unesco also came from several Third World countries and institutions.[11] The Islamic Conference Organization, meeting in Casablanca in January, appealed to the United States to reconsider its decision "in view of the important role played by the United States in the constitution and development of Unesco and the fact that the withdrawal of any member state comprom-

ises the organization's utility." The Conference of Information Ministers of Non-Aligned Countries, meeting in Jakarta that month, likewise reaffirmed "the need to preserve the organization's universal character and expresses its total support for and confidence in the director general. Dr. Peter Onu, acting secretary general of the Organization of African Unity (OAU), wrote expressing the "stupefaction" of OAU members at the American decision, which would have "serious consequences on the program, mission and the very originality of Unesco, which will thus be deprived of one of its most important members."

FEBRUARY 1984

State Department View

William G. Harley, a communications consultant to the State Department, issued a memorandum to the news media on February 9 containing questions and answers about the decision to withdraw. The chief reasons it gave for the action were Unesco's anti-Western tone, statist tendencies, lack of responsiveness to United States demands that it change its ideological orientation, its rejection of sound management principles, and its efforts to establish a New World Information Order "which embodies elements threatening to a free press and a free market."[12]

National Security Adviser McFarlane sent a memorandum to Secretary of State Shultz on February 11, following up on his suggestion that an advisory group drawn from press, academic and business communities be appointed to advise government on Unesco policy.[13] The president, said McFarlane, had "expressed a desire for us to expend every effort over the next year to eliminate suppression of minority views and political diversions and to restore fiscal integrity to Unesco." To accomplish this, he wrote, "we will need to launch a major campaign to turn Unesco around during 1984. If we fail, we leave." McFarlane suggested the campaign might include the following elements:

- A clear action plan. What we need to accomplish and how we can do it. This will need precise milestones to measure our accomplishments.
- We will need to mobilize our international supporters to assist in this effort. For example, a number of West European delegations have expressed concern over the trends and developments in Unesco and several have explicitly or implicitly sympathized and supported our December decision.
- Our strengthened Unesco "team" should re-examine and challenge

existing contracts. The team should also be involved more directly in personnel assignments where the Soviets have had a free ride too long.

A few days later, in mid-February, the administration announced that it would name a panel of American educators, scientists, cultural and media figures to monitor Unesco "to see if there are any concrete program changes." If the panel decided there were improvements, said Newell, the administration would reconsider its decision.[14]

U.S./Unesco Policy Review

The State Department released its U.S./Unesco Policy Review on February 27, sending copies to Charles H. Percy, chairman of the Senate Committee on Foreign Relations, and to Dante Fascell, chairman of the House Foreign Affairs Committee.[15]

Newell's six-page covering letter summarized the policy review and concluded that "the Administration has judged that it is no longer worthwhile for the United States to remain a member of an international organization in which negative considerations so far outweigh the technical benefits provided, whether to ourselves or to the developing world." Ten months remained, however, during which the United States would work with all interested groups to effect meaningful change in Unesco. And a small group of select non-government figures who represented the public interest would help monitor Unesco during the coming year and advise the State Department whether significant change had in fact occurred. "We are not optimistic on this score," Newell wrote. "Our decision to withdraw from Unesco involved a judgment that significant structural and programmatic change in the organization was not realistically attainable in any reasonable time frame under existing circumstances."

The review is the key document in the Reagan administrations justification for withdrawing from Unesco. The Unesco evaluation was part of an 18-month review of about 90 multilateral organizations. Its avowed purpose was to reassert American leadership in multilateral affairs; to curb budget growth; to ensure that the United States was adequately represented on the secretariats of international agencies, and to promote a role for the private sector in international organizations. The State Department began its review of Unesco in June 1983. It solicited views from public and private institutions that participated in or benefited from Unesco's programs. Among those contributing to the review were the U.S. National Commission for Unesco and 13 U.S. government agencies, including the Agency for International Development, the Commission for Libraries and Information Sciences, the departments of Education, of

State, and of the Interior; the U.S. Information Agency, the Library of Congress, the National Academy of Sciences, the National Endowments for the Arts and for the Humanities, the National Science Foundation, the Smithsonian Institution and the U.S. Geological Survey. Also included were assessments from 78 U.S. diplomatic and Agency for International Development missions abroad.

The review appears to have existed in various versions. The original report of more than 700 pages comprised a collection of raw data and internal working documents. Only parts of this, such as the submissions of the National Science Foundation and of the U.S. National Commission for Unesco, were ever released, although some of the material was repeated in testimony at congressional hearings. These reports were boiled down into the 64-page U.S./Unesco Policy Review. That in turn was further abbreviated into a 13-page executive summary, which was widely circulated. Newell's covering letter to Percy and Fascell is a further condensation. At each stage of summarization, the proportion of negative commentary on Unesco increases, which gave rise to suspicions that the summary report was tailored to the requirements of the decision to withdraw.[16]

The 64-page version of the review examines each sector of Unesco's activities in terms of the organization's mandate, the extent and nature of U.S. participation, and the benefits of membership, both direct and indirect. It also examines "problem areas" in each sector and weighs the consequences of withdrawal and alternatives the United States might pursue in case of a pullout. The review concludes with an assessment of Unesco's institutional and political functioning, its management, and its budget.

As indicated in Chapter 1, the review found much to commend in the programs. "On the whole," it concluded, "comments from the field are more positive about Unesco's performance, in terms of program quality and effectiveness, than critical. Unesco is covering a wide range of sensitive activities having long-term political and developmental importance, and is discharging its development mandate fairly well." But it also identified several problems. In the Education Sector, the review complained of the "continued emergence in Unesco debates of statist, collectivist concepts and thinly-disguised anti-Western ideological initiatives" that posed serious long-range problems for the United States. It singled out programs carried out in cooperation with the Palestine Liberation Organization and those stressing peace and disarmament with an anti-Western slant.

In the Natural Science Sector, U.S. dissatisfaction was directed mainly at Unesco's organizational shortcomings, which included high administrative costs, poor staff quality and inadequate evaluation of projects.

Problem areas in the Social Science Sector had to do with the fragmented and small-scale nature of Unesco's social science activities brought about by the disparate and often conflicting demands of member states. This made it difficult for the American social science community to develop institutional links with them. The social science programs, said the review, tended to be highly theoretical and of limited practical significance.

The Cultural Sector, it noted, had been relatively free of the political problems that had plagued some other programs. One highly visible exception had been efforts to penalize Israel. In the Communication Sector, the major sticking point was the Division of Free Flow of Information, which was "predicated on assumptions inimical to traditional Western notions of a free press." Communication issues had become increasingly politicized during a decade-long debate on the concept of a New World Information Order. While recognizing an imbalance in access to and dissemination of information, the United States rejected solutions to the problem that could lead to state control of the private media, licensing of journalists, censorship of the press, and dilution of the concept of free flow of information.

The review also identified U.S. concerns about Unesco's institutional functioning, its management and its budget. The basic institutions, it said, did not function well and bore little relationship to the smooth, cooperative and open system that the founders of the organization had envisaged. The General Conference, for example, was intended to be a creative and policy-determining body. In practice it was "numbed by the staggering agenda its own procedures and momentum impose on it." It was passive before a Secretariat that "frames its work, sets its pace, drafts its resolutions, and in other ways arrogates to itself the General Conference's responsibilities." The organization had little chance of returning to its founding principles until the General Conference assumed the broad role which the founders envisaged for it.

The Executive Board, being smaller than the General Conference, was a more workable instrument. Yet it shared many of the same institutional weaknesses of the General Conference, "most notably the abdication of its independent responsibility to a Secretariat ready and willing to fill in the gaps." Rarely did the board question program and budget material submitted by the Secretariat; there was no practice of informal give-and-take over financial and program matters which was customary in parliamentary systems. Technical and scheduling problems were adduced to prevent free discussion, requests for information were ignored unless endorsed by many members, and replies were given in prepared statements not subject to further inquiry.

The review complained that in Unesco, management information was "more often used to obscure and mask reality than to express it."

Thousands of pages of material were submitted to the Executive Board and General Conference each two-year cycle. "Almost without exeption, the effect and purpose of this staggering outpouring of paper is to justify and applaud whatever it is the organization is doing. Rarely does a document surface which provides information and data on programs or activities which are not accomplishing their purpose, which are not worth the cost, or which are not fulfilling whatever goals were established for them." The review commented that an organization of 161 member states, with a staff of some 2,300 persons and a budget of about $200 million a year, could not operate over a period of years without making mistakes. "Yet that is precisely the conclusion one would reach if one read only the organization's own descriptions of its activities."

The review was highly critical of Unesco's management, which it said was characterized by a tendency to overcentralize decision making and a reluctance to delegate authority. It lacked rigorous criteria for program formulation and evaluation. Commenting on personnel matters, the review said there was a poor selection of staff. Although highly qualified professionals from all over the world continued to apply for positions, "more and more frequently, persons of third and fourth rank are selected." Morale was low, and promotions were made on bases other than professional competence. While the Secretariat included a number of conscientious, hard-working people, "others either have little to do or are incapable of doing the work assigned." This had led to an excessive use of outside consultants.

The review complained of Unesco's "politicization" as manifested in activities that were basically political in purpose. These included aid to "liberation" organizations; unbalanced disarmament campaigns; selective anti-discrimination campaigns, and the "abuse of legitimate interest in cultural preservation to attack Israel." A coincidence of views between the powerful Secretariat and "a majority of fairly disciplined Third World representatives led by the African group, ensures that it is difficult, if not impossible, to achieve substantial modification of the organization's program." In giving many of Unesco's programs a political slant, the Secretariat and its supporting majority had often ridden roughshod over minority points of view represented by democratic countries.

Concerning the budget, the review noted that the United States and other major donors had called on U.N. agencies to restrict program growth. Most had responded by holding growth close to zero. Yet in the budget debate at Unesco's 22nd General Conference, zero program growth had been rejected by a vote of 11 in favor, 101 against and 19 abstentions.

The review examined possible alternatives to Unesco programs in the case of withdrawal. In the case of education, for example, the United

States could perhaps provide grants to Unesco subsidiary organs like the International Bureau of Education, the International Institute of Educational Planning and the Institute for Education. It could finance individual education projects in the Third World through the Unesco funds-in-trust mechanism, and increase funding of bilateral education assistance by the Agency for International Development, the U.S. Information Agency or the Peace Corps. Non-government organizations might provide mechanisms for continued professional contact and financial aid. In the science sector, too, other arrangements could be made. The United States would remain a member of the International Oceanographic Commission, thus continuing to receive valuable marine data. It could continue participation in the International Geological Correlation Program, and the program on Man in the Biosphere. And it could increase support for other multilateral, intergovernmental and nongovernmental scientific organizations. Alternatives to Unesco's social science programs could include more bilateral assistance, greater cooperation between American academic institutions and the developing countries, and increased participation in such organizations as the International Social Science Council and the International Committee for Social Science Information and Documentation. Cultural activities could be maintained, with continued participation in the preservation of cultural antiquities. The United States would remain a party to the World Heritage Convention, through which this work is carried on. The United States would also continue its membership of such institutions as the International Council on Museums, the International Council on Monuments and Sites, and the International Center for Conservation. The United States might also increase its support for American cultural organizations active in the international field. In communications programs, the United States could contribute bilaterally to Third World projects through the International Program for the Development of Communication. In addition, AID and the United States Information Agency (USIA) could devote additional resources to communications training and developmental assistance in their bilateral programs.

Staff Study Mission

A report drawn up by a staff study mission of the House Committee on Foreign Affairs, as mandated by the Beard Amendment (see Chapter 3) was published in February.[17] The study gave a history of problematic issues between the United States and Unesco, a comprehensive summary of the arguments for and against withdrawal, and recommendations as to what U.S. policy should be. It found that there had been a decline in the quality of U.S. leadership in Unesco. Like other multinational organiza-

tions, it had been given a low priority by the State Department after the 1960s as part of a policy of benign neglect of emerging Third World nations. This had an effect on the quality of personnel and policy development relating to Unesco, and led to a lack of long-range strategy for U.S.–Third World relations. The result was that forums had developed where there was hostility and polarization between the United States and other countries, with a consequent decline in U.S. leadership in the world.

The study analyzed the administration's reasons for its decision to withdraw. Politicization, the study said, meant the introduction of highly charged, controversial issues into international debates that tended to polarize parties and promote hostile, confrontational rhetoric. Examples of these were said to be programs dealing with disarmament studies and the education of Palestinian refugees. Also considered politicized were programs emphasizing collective, or "people's" rights, as opposed to individual rights, and those supporting national liberation movements and the PLO. The study's own finding on this issue was that Unesco is a political institution; it held that members must promote international cooperation through bargaining and agreement on political as well as technical issues.

The charge that Unesco favored "statist" policies, the report said, referred to its support of new international orders in economics and communications. Allegations of mismanagement focused on the director general's management style, the appointment of technically incompetent staff, cronyism and nepotism, and the resignation of senior staff of recognized competence. The study found that there did exist an "imbalance of power" between Unesco's Executive Board and its Secretariat. This had occurred as programs had become more numerous and the board had relied more heavily on the Secretariat for information. The board and the Secretariat, the report said, appeared to engage in "intemperate debates" without resolving issues.

Unesco's annual budget, it found, had increased from $6.95 million in 1947 to $208.46 million in 1983, with most of the increase occurring in the 1970s as a result of inflation and currency fluctuations. In 1984, however, the budget had decreased to $187 million, due to a decline in program growth and the strength of the U.S. dollar. (Most Unesco disbursements are made in French francs.)

The study provides a succinct summary of the arguments made for and against withdrawal. Those in favor of withdrawal held:

- Problems in Unesco were endemic and impossible to solve. The United States and other Western nations were in the minority and could not bring about reform;

- If, having threatened to withdraw, the United States did not do so, it would suffer a loss of face;
- The United States could achieve the same objectives through alternative programs, such as bi- and multilateral arrangements;
- Withdrawal could spark reform in Unesco;
- The benefits of staying in and trying to achieve reform would be disproportionate to the expense;
- Withdrawal by the United States and other donors would diminish the value of Unesco to the Soviet Union.
- Unesco had not been faithful to its original purpose, and a U.S. withdrawal would have a salutary effect on the behavior of other U.N. agencies.

The arguments against withdrawal, said the report, included:

- The policy review of Unesco by the administration did not adequately substantiate the decision to pull out;
- Withdrawal was a drastic measure for a superpower to take in foreign diplomacy, and would have serious consequences;
- The U.S. decision was not representative of broad interests and constituencies in the government and the private sector. The administration had not consulted with these;
- So-called politicization was not a valid basis for withdrawal. Unesco was supposed to encourage debate on issues within its jurisdiction, and the U.S. denial of this was contrary to its own democratic principles;
- Unesco had trimmed its budget growth, and the U.S. contribution had declined in 1984 because of the strong dollar;
- The administration's policy review did not evaluate the positive effects of increasing participation and upgrading U.S. relations with Unesco;
- The policy review also did not mention the impact of withdrawal on commercial and trade interests;
- United States participation in Unesco may be more cost effective than withdrawal. The withdrawal might cost government and academic scientists more than the U.S. paid to belong;
- Withdrawal would create an intellectual and political leadership vacuum in Unesco;
- Proposed alternative programs in education, science and culture had not yet been defined;
- The United States would lose an important forum for promoting Western values and combating anti-Western propaganda;
- The timing was bad: the general conference of Unesco would not meet again until 1985, and no reforms could be made until then;

- It would penalize nations that had pledged to work with the United States for change; many had demonstrated a willingness to consider reforms;
- A decision to stay in for now would not preclude withdrawal later.

Based on its investigation, the study mission recommended that a Unesco monitoring panel be set up to define what changes were needed in the agency, and identify those that could be made. It suggested that the State Department lend a budget officer and an Agency for International Development officer to Unesco for the rest of the year. It said that the United States should "concentrate every effort on turning Unesco around," which meant lending support to every part of the organization it was concerned about. It recommended that relevant congressional committees should hold hearings to investigate the planned withdrawal. And the report urged that the United States should not expand its efforts to establish alternatives to Unesco, or encourage other nations to withdraw.

The State Department reported to Congress at the end of February in terms of the Beard Amendment that mandated an end to U.S. funding for Unesco if the organization persisted in efforts to restrict a free press. The report said that marginal gains were made in the communication sector at the 22nd General Conference:

> On the ideological level, our view that any NWICO is "an evolving, continuous process," not an established, defined, order was accepted. Also accepted was our contention that any study of a "right" to communicate must take into account traditional human rights (as opposed to collective, second-generation rights). We successfully introduced new studies to the work program for 1984–85 concerning the "watch-dog" role of the press, the role of the private media, censorship and self-censorship, and ways to strengthen freedom of information. We were also successful in eliminating projects calling for studies of the "tasks" of the media, safety of journalists and grants to journalist organizations to study "codes" of conduct, and implementation of the Mass Media Declaration.[18]

The report concluded that none of the programs included in Unesco's program and budget for 1984–85 "poses any active, direct threat to the press."

GAO Audit Arranged

Toward the end of February, Unesco agreed to let the General Accounting Office (GAO) of Congress conduct a full investigation of its activities and gave the investigators access to its internal documents, budget records and financial reports.[19] The agreement arose out of meetings be-

tween Director General M'Bow and Congressman James H. Scheuer, chairman of the House Subcommittee on Natural Resources, Agriculture Research and Environment, on February 24 and 25 to discuss Unesco programs dealing with the environment and population. Scheuer raised the possibility of a review of Unesco operations. He then put his proposals in writing, suggesting to M'Bow that an effective approach to the various allegations against Unesco would be a "thorough, in-depth and independent review—authorized, funded and executed by the Congress of the United States." M'Bow had agreed, he wrote, "that such a group would have full and unrestricted access to all documents, budgets, and financial reports of the organization as well as unrestricted access to any and all Unesco personnel the group may wish to interview." M'Bow's response, dated February 25, pointed out that Unesco's budget, management operations, financial practices and procedures were "completely open to examination on behalf of member states." If the review was initiated by the United States, M'Bow wrote, he was prepared to ensure full cooperation on the part of the Unesco Secretariat.[20]

The next day, however, Scheuer told a press conference in Paris that he had heard "rumors that files are being destroyed." And UPI quoted "an official close to the U.S. delegation" in Paris as saying that a preliminary congressional review had turned up "outrageous" evidence of inefficiency and mismanagement.[21] M'Bow, protesting that critics had chosen the very moment he had agreed to cooperate with the GAO "for stepping up the campaign which is being waged against the organization and in particular against the honor and dignity of its director general," announced that the probe could go ahead only if the Reagan administration officially requested it. And M'Bow suggested that an internal commission be set up to investigate what he called "untruthful allegations" and a "veritable smear campaign" against him.[22]

MARCH 1984

House Hearings, March 8

Scheuer"s subcommittee of the House Committee on Science and Technology held an oversight hearing on Unesco on March 8. This session focused primarily on political issues with testimony from Rep. James Leach and from Jean Gerard, U.S. ambassador to Unesco.[23] Scheuer, fresh from his discussions with M'Bow in Paris, made his own position clear in his opening remarks. He had requested the General Accounting Office investigation, he said, "because of the widespread rumors of rampant corruption, mismanagement, financial irregularities on a very large

scale, and total corruption of the civil service system of merit appointments." In one of his questions, Scheuer referred to Unesco's "aberrational programs, these viciously anti-western, anti-freedom, anti-western values, going to the heart of our western value structure, going to the heart of what a democracy is all about."

Gerard, in her first appearance at a congressional hearing since the announcement of the withdrawal, was outspokenly critical of Unesco. It had failed, she said, to restrict its activities to those within its constitutional mandate. An example was its entry into peace and disarmament activities. Unesco was not the appropriate forum for this topic, which should properly be dealt with at the Conference on Disarmament in Geneva or in the United Nations General Assembly in New York. In addition to trespassing on the work of other international forums, Unesco's disarmament activism converged dangerously on the goals of the Soviet Union's "peace offensive." A second anti-Western tendency was Unesco's crusade to establish a New World Information and Communication Order. It was true, she said, that Unesco had been foiled in its attempt to draw up an international code of conduct for journalists, but that was only a small part of the story. Unesco's debates, studies and declarations on the subject over the course of more than a decade had "shaken the conceptual foundations upon which rest the western notion of a free press." Unesco had devised a formula that substituted the traditional journalistic responsibility of seeking and reporting facts with a "newly-minted series of social and ethical responsibilities for ridding the world of its evils." This formula left the press open to state intrusion into the content of news. And Unesco's imprimatur on state control had already encouraged some nations to adopt anti–free press policies.

Gerard criticized Unesco's management, citing "widespread inefficiency in program execution" and a "continuous manipulation by the Secretariat of member states." A third serious management problem was Unesco's unwillingness to exercise budgetary restraint. The governing bodies of Unesco no longer worked as they were designed to, she said. Power had been usurped from its representative bodies like the General Conference and the Executive Board and transferred to the director general and the Secretariat, who set the agenda and controlled the pace.

The United States had been in the forefront of efforts over the years to improve Unesco's budgetary, management and program practices. But it had "reluctantly concluded that all our efforts to achieve significant reform were foredoomed by the institutional deficiencies and malfunctioning of Unesco." The United States did not think a turn-around in Unesco was a likely possibility in the short term, and for this reason had not elaborated on conditions that would cause it to remain a member. Although it had no list of conditions for reconsidering withdrawal, there

were a number of possible remedies for complaints about Unesco including adoption of a zero-growth budget and the reduction of program
support for disarmament and the New World Information Order. Unesco
would also have to endorse the primacy of individual rights over "collective" rights and give greater priority to core programs in education,
science and culture. Asked if Unesco had any value at all, Gerard
responded that it had done, and was continuing to do, some very useful
things: "Their programs, for example, in illiteracy are very useful. Adult
education. The cultural heritage programs—even though there I feel they
have become too diffuse."

A very different point of view came from Congressman Leach, who
argued that it was incumbent on Congress to review the administration's
decision carefully and to present alternative perspectives. It was not
clear what other alternatives—short of total withdrawal—had been
considered, nor why they had been rejected in favor of this radical
option. Leach pointed to Unesco's achievements in education, science
and culture. The organization had moderated its stance in such controversial areas as communications and efforts to deny Israel the right to
participate. It was unclear, said Leach, how the United States could
actively defend its own interests, let alone the right of Israel to participate
in Unesco, from an empty chair.

Leach pointed out that earlier administration reports had concluded
that U.S. interests were generally well served by Unesco programs, and
that Unesco was a major forum for U.S. multilateral diplomacy. Why
then had the administration decided to withdraw from Unesco?

> It would appear that strong ideological and/or domestic political
> concerns intervened in a process of what would otherwise have been a
> rational, professional calculation of U.S. interests, benefits and prob-
> lems in Unesco. The language of U.S. criticism to date has been
> exceedingly strong but surprisingly ill-defined. For the administration to
> refuse to produce a detailed case is to acknowledge implicitly that there
> may be holes in that case. And for the administration to refuse to
> submit a laundry list of changes it wants in Unesco procedures is to
> imply ideological hard-headedness and a desire not to be serious about
> reform.[24]

House Hearings, March 15

A week later, on March 15, Scheuer's subcommittee and the House
Subcommittee on Science, Research and Technology held a joint hearing
concerning the impact on U.S. science of the proposal to withdraw.[25]
Three scientists and a librarian gave testimony. Prof. Paul Baker, chairman of the U.S. National Committee for the Man in the Biosphere

program, pointed out that Unesco's contribution to the sciences had to be seen in financial perspective. Unesco, with its $200-million budget, spent less than the average major American university. Baker said there was no way to assess the impact of the withdrawal on American science because no one had been given the funds to gather the necessary information. However, the direct and indirect benefits that U.S. science derived from Unesco would inevitably be damaged by withdrawal "because no substitute mechanisms exist." The deficiencies of Unesco's science programs were related to its administrative policies, said Baker. And the lack of U.S. funds for supporting American scientists working on Unesco-related projects had severely limited the benefits. However, there was strong support for remaining in Unesco, he said. "There is discontent over the way the scientific program is administered in Unesco, but it is generally believed this problem could be resolved if the United States would provide the support necessary for a fuller participation of U.S. scientists."

Baker criticized the "optimistic view" expressed in the State Department's U.S./Unesco Policy Review, released on February 27. "I did not see included anywhere in the document that the scientific groups consulted believed almost universally that we should stay in Unesco." The review had suggested that the United States could continue to participate in international science and technology at near-present levels without Unesco involvement. "I don't know where this optimism came from," Baker said.

William A. Nierenberg, director of the Scripps Institution of Oceanography, testified that the effect of the withdrawal on U.S. science would be minimal, "provided that the moneys now committed are carefully husbanded and systematically reapplied using new channels." Nierenberg considered the State Department review a "realistic evaluation." He pointed out that the experimental sciences, like laboratory chemistry or physics, stood to gain little from Unesco. But the observational sciences, like oceanography and meteorology, could benefit from the cooperative nature of Unesco programs.

Prof. A. K. Solomon, professor emeritus of biophysics at the Harvard Medical School, stressed the value of scientific training and exchange programs sponsored by Unesco. He cited the Distinguished Fellowships in Science, offered jointly by Unesco and the International Council of Scientific Unions (ICSU). These fellowships were awarded to young scientists of exceptional promise and were tenable for one year in a developed country. "The advantage to the United States is that many of these scientists will carry out their studies in Western nations and will return home with a personal knowledge of life in a democratic society," said Solomon.

On a broader scale, Unesco awarded 300 or more fellowships a year, mainly to younger scientists. Well over half of these fellows were sent to the United States, France or the United Kingdom. In 1982, 183 fellows had come to the United States, and only 19 went to the Soviet Union. Unesco training programs were also effective programs, he said. In 1982, there were 2,637 students in training courses in basic sciences, about two-thirds of them from the developing nations.

Thomas Galvin, chairman of the International Relations Committee of the American Library Association, said it was essential for scientists to have full and easy access to all kinds of scientific and technical data and information. Between 75 and 80 percent of all current research activity worldwide was being done outside the United States. Without access to that ongoing research by other scientists, U.S. science could not progress. Throughout its history, Galvin said, Unesco had worked to improve access to all forms of information, especially scientific information. Among Unesco's major accomplishments in the information field was the Universal Copyright Convention, which protects the rights of authors and publishers, and also facilitates the flow of technical information across international boundaries. Unesco-sponsored agreements eliminating import duties on a wide variety of published materials made it easier for libraries to support the U.S. scientific community. These agreements were also significant to the American publishing industry. In 1982 alone, foreign sales of U.S. scientific, technical and professional books amounted to over $118 million. These accomplishments, said Galvin, "on balance greatly outweigh the negative impact of some of the recent rhetoric on communications issues that have caused us so much concern with respect to Unesco."

Galvin noted that the United States should make certain by its continued presence that Unesco did not adopt international standards that could jeopardize future American access to essential international computerized data banks. U.S. withdrawal could lead to the adoption of norms and protocols for transborder data flow that could imperil important American scientific and commercial interests. "In my judgment, we simply cannot abandon the Unesco forum without jeopardizing our own future access to vital scientific and technical information," said Galvin.

"Crisis in Unesco"

The United States and 23 other developed countries submitted an informal list of proposals for major reform of Unesco to M'Bow on March 14. The countries included the 10 members of the European Common Market, and four neutral countries—Austria, Finland, Sweden and Switzerland. The others were Australia, Canada, Iceland, Japan, New Zealand,

Norway, Portugal, Spain and Turkey. Their 11-page paper, entitled "The Crisis in Unesco," was not made public but was leaked to the press. It was drafted by the Dutch delegation headed by Maarten Mourik.[26] A statement accompanying the list said that the American decision was "a symptom, to be taken very seriously, of tensions that have been building up within Unesco over a long period of time, leading to disappointments and frustrations which wholly or in part are shared by a number of other member states, irrespective of their geographical situation." The paper called on Unesco members to pledge, by signing agreements, not to politicize issues before the agency and to exercise stricter control over its budget and personnel. It proposed that Unesco's voting system be changed to give Western contributors, who provided 85 percent of the agency's budget, greater control over how the money was spent. The joint paper stated that it was "of the highest importance" that the United States should not withdraw, but added that the only way to prevent a pullout was to improve the functioning of Unesco so that the United States could rescind its decision. It suggested that the proposed changes be submitted to Unesco's Executive Board due to meet in May, for approval at the meeting in September.[27]

Arson in Paris

A fire set by arsonists gutted a wing of Unesco's modernistic, Y-shaped headquarters in Paris on March 21. It severely damaged seven of the building's eight above-ground floors before being brought under control. Pointing out that the fire took place just before the planned GAO review, some news reports suggested that documents that could substantiate U.S. allegations of poor management and accounting could have been deliberately destroyed. But Unesco officials stated that "nothing of any possible consequence to these inquiries was involved," and that budget, administrative and personnel files were untouched.[28]

On March 24, the State Department appointed James B. Holderman, chairman of the U.S. National Commission for Unesco and president of the University of South Carolina, to chair a 13-member panel to monitor Unesco's activities in 1984.[29] The panel was to report to the secretary of state at the end of the year on the degree and kinds of change that had occurred, with a view to determining whether the U.S. decision should be reviewed. And on March 25 it was announced that the United States had formally requested an audit by the General Accounting Office. The GAO was asked to review five broad management areas of Unesco: Overall management structure, with an emphasis on how decisions are made; the personnel system, focusing on the employee profile and recruiting methods; program management, to determine how the organiza-

tion plans and evaluates its activities; budget development and presentation; and expenditure controls.

Also in March a conference of Organization of African Unity (OAU)
members meeting in Addis Ababa passed a resolution regretting the U.S.
decision and its consequences for Unesco's mission. The resolution expressed the concern that the withdrawal would "deprive the organization
and its members of valuable representation in the fields of education,
science, culture and communication." It paid tribute to Unesco's assistance to the OAU, and also to African liberation movements and African
refugees.[30]

The Council of the Arab League met in Tunis in March and appealed
to the United States to reconsider its decision "in the vital interest of the
international community as a whole and to avoid a dangerous precedent."
The resolution reaffirmed the council's support for Unesco and its director general, and recommended that Arab states continue to support the
organization.[31]

APRIL 1984

Warning from the United Kingdom

The United States position received support in April with the release of a
letter from Britain's minister of state for overseas development, Timothy
Raison, to M'Bow. The letter accused Unesco of "undue attention to
matters of political controversy" and particularly "increased involvement
with . . . media issues."[32] It warned that the United Kingdom would find
it "increasingly difficult to justify our membership of Unesco unless we
can point to real improvements in its operations."[33]

M'Bow, visiting the United States, told a news conference on April 9
that withdrawing would be costly to the United States because of its
heavy participation in the agency's scientific programs. He said that
the United States participated more in the design, implementation and
evaluation of Unesco programs than any other nation.[34] M'Bow told the
press conference at the United Nations that the idea had emerged in the
minds of some journalists that Unesco was "a menace to the press, a
threat to freedom of information, aiming to impose a code of conduct on
journalists and to license and censor them." Nothing could be further
from the truth. He challenged anyone to find in any of the decisions,
programs or activities of Unesco anything that could substantiate these
allegations. All Unesco programs concerning information and communication were adopted by consensus by members of the organization—
including the United States.

In reply to a question related to Unesco's budget, M'Bow stated that spending by Unesco had grown the least of all the United Nations agencies between 1975 and 1984. With regard to alleged politicization of the organization, M'Bow said that Unesco, like other U.N. agencies, was an intergovernmental organization. Governments were not technical; they were political, and they express their viewpoints.

House Hearings, April 26–May 2

Two subcommittees of the House Foreign Affairs Committee held hearings on Unesco on April 25 and 26, and May 2. The subcommittees on Human Rights and International Organizations and on International Operations, met to explore the problems cited by the administration as reasons for the withdrawal and to examine ways in which U.S. participation in Unesco could be improved. The hearings represent one of the few occasions on which a broad range of opinions by U.S. non-government organizations was articulated. Of the 16 people who gave testimony only three—Gregory Newell and Edward Derwinski of the State Department, and Owen Harries of the Heritage Foundation—spoke strongly in favor of withdrawal.[35]

Rep. Jim Leach, the ranking Republican on the Human Rights Subcommittee and a former foreign affairs officer, pointed out to the panel that the United States had not lost any major debate on communications issues in Unesco and that it had been successful in creating the International Program for the Development of Communication (IPDC). The United States had been able to introduce new studies into Unesco"s work program for 1983–1984, including the watchdog role of the media, the role of private media, and strengthening freedom of information. Conversely, said Leach, the United States had successfully eliminated programs on the protection of journalists, and journalistic codes of conduct. Unesco, he said, did not invent censorship or the idea of a state-controlled press; it was merely a forum for debate on these issues. Leach maintained that the decision to withdraw was based on ill-defined reasons and was as much an indictment of U.S. policy and performance within Unesco as an indictment of Unesco itself.

Edmund Hennelly, general manager of the Mobil Oil Corp. and chairman of the U.S. delegation to Unesco's General Conference in 1983, gave testimony that recognized Unesco's shortcomings but opposed withdrawal. The agency suffered from some endemic flaws, he said. It was politicized, with some states using it as a political platform instead of an organization to further science, education and culture. Some nations tried to implant peace and disarmament issues into every Unesco program. The agency also had a propensity for global controls, said Hennelly, the

most notorious example being the New World Information Order, which was a product of Third World and Communist bloc states.

Hennelly maintained, however, that Unesco's 1983 General Conference in Paris had been the least politicized in recent memory. The United States had been given a fair chance to explain the liberation of Grenada, thereby "effectively depriving the Soviets and Cubans of a propaganda opportunity." If it did not remain a member, he asked, how was the United States to assure that it did not lose by default in the world's main intellectual and ideological arena?

When Rep. Dan Mica, D-Fla., commented that much of the anti–U.S. rhetoric appeared to have come from the director general, Hennelly responded that M'Bow had been helpful in neutralizing controversy. He had lobbied Third World ambassadors to withdraw their votes from a proposal on a code of conduct for transnational corporations.

A former U.S. ambassador to Unesco, Esteban Torres, while acknowledging that "certain administrative problems exist within Unesco," said the decision to withdraw was "damaging to our intellectual, commercial and political interests." Dr. John E. Fobes, former chairman of the U.S. National Commission for Unesco, suggested that a lot more study was needed before a final decision to withdraw. "Drastic changes in [Unesco's] structure may be needed," he said, "but I think America has to get into the act."

Hans N. Weiler, professor of education and political science at Stanford University, referred to problems of poor countries in improving the life of their citizens through education. "The solution of these problems depends critically on the kind of help Unesco is capable of providing," Weiler said. "The United States has not only a moral and political, but also an intellectual obligation to assume its share and to continue its role in this worldwide effort." Keith Geiger, vice president of the National Education Association, testified that "we believe that no substitute program exists to successfully address the educational needs of the world's children in the absence of Unesco. We have, therefore, consistently argued that the United States remain in Unesco while seeking sufficient remedies to any shortcomings which exist."

Dr. Harold Jacobson of the Center for Political Studies at the University of Michigan referred to the benefits to social science of U.S. membership. "I recognize that there are serious problems within Unesco," he said. "I think that Unesco, even with these serious problems, would be vital to social science, and I think that the United States is in a better position to deal with these serious problems and to contribute to the growth and betterment of social science as a member of Unesco."

Walter Rosenblith, foreign secretary of the National Academy of Sciences, said that the costs of withdrawal would be significant for Amer-

ican science, and reported that the academy was undertaking a critical review of Unesco science to determine if there were any alternatives. Terry Morton, head of the U.S. Committee for the International Council on Monuments and Sites, said that withdrawal would mean that Unesco's cultural heritage budget would be reduced by one-fourth, affecting international restoration campaigns, missions of experts and unique exchange of information. Unesco, she said, "is our principal medium through which we can identify with all nations of the world concerned with cultural heritage."

Given the context of this study, the views expressed by Leonard Sussman of Freedom House are particularly relevant. Sussman pointed out that over the past ten years he had been the most persistent critic of Unesco's activities in the communications field. The question, he said, was not whether Unesco has the mandate to examine news and information flows—"it certainly has." The proper question was "whether Unesco has moved beyond the problems and opportunities created by international communications, to the point of framing a normative or universal standard for the content of news and information flows." Delegates from some countries with state-controlled media systems had given the impression that they wanted to extend their press control systems worldwide. But on the same platform, free press advocates were heard, and heard effectively—"so effectively that throughout the decade of bitter communications controversies there has never been a single resolution or program approved at Unesco that supports press censorship, the licensing of journalists or other proposals to harm press freedom." What, then, Sussman asked, had so blackened the name of Unesco that the communications debate had mainly prepared the way for the U.S. withdrawal? "American press coverage has reflected the possibilities of press controls, not actualities."

In a prepared statement to the committee, Sussman noted that U.S. media had reported communications debates at Unesco as though the ultimate goal was censorship: by licensing journalists, establishing codes of journalistic practice, monitoring reportage, and penalizing those who broke the code. "Indeed all of these were mentioned in the debates. Yet never have any of these elements been approved at Unesco. Not a single resolution, not a single statement of a top official at Unesco ever called for licensing, governmental codes for journalists, monitoring of journalistic output, or censorship. On the contrary, Director General M'Bow and his deputy for communications repeatedly decry censorship, even as they call for improved communications infrastructures and better coverage of social and economic developments in the Third World."

Sussman pointed out that the Soviet Union's draft resolution of 1976 tying all the press to government oversight had been defeated.

Yet the memory of that bitter debate remains and blackens the name of Unesco more than the Soviets who introduced the draft. Two years later, another outrageous Soviet draft was personally killed by M'Bow's action, and a bland Western-oriented resolution on the mass media was approved by acclamation. Were there sizable headlines in major U.S. papers hailing the defeat of the Soviet effort? Was there even modest reporting of the killing of other press-control initiatives . . . were there editorials hailing the new Western-oriented programs in communications, such as Unesco efforts to study the watchdog role of the press, the effects of government censorship and self-censorship? You may have guessed the answer. There were no headlines, just small, colorless stories wrapping up the two-week negotiations of communications. The blackened name of Unesco stands undiminished.

Sussman argued that press freedom advocates would have a hard time making their case at Unesco once the United States left. American technologies and American news media would find themselves cut off from sales as well as discussions. Sussman's conclusion: "I believe that the tactic of withdrawing from Unesco before it can be reformed is self-defeating. We should maintain pressure to reform Unesco. It is too valuable to turn over to our adversaries, and it cannot be reformed from the outside. We should stay the course, and if necessary, extend our notice of withdrawal."

James Holderman, chairman of the U.S. National Commission for Unesco, told the panel that the commission, after detailed reviews, had decided that although Unesco had problems, its basic programs were worthwhile, that it would be harder to defend U.S. interests from outside than from within, and that with some effort Unesco could be turned around. A former assistant secretary of state for international organization affairs, Samuel DePalma, asserted that if the decision to withdraw were implemented, it would constitute "another breakdown in our communications with other governments and people." The United States, he said, should increase its participation in the organization. Edwin C. Luck, executive vice president of the U.N. Association of the United States, argued that the problems within Unesco didn't justify withdrawal. And Ruth Robbins of the League of Women Voters stated unequivocally that the league was opposed to withdrawal, which would "abdicate an important leadership role the United States could play in world affairs, and would undercut vital work on science, culture and education throughout the world."

The most critical view of Unesco at the hearing came from Owen Harries, former Australian ambassador to Unesco and a resident associate of the Heritage Foundation, and from a State Department counselor,

Edward J. Derwinski. Harries testified that Unesco was grossly politicized. It had moved toward controversial issues like the new international economic order and disarmament. It had ceased to maintain its neutrality, but had taken on a pro-Soviet and pro–Third World bias, and was anti-Israel. In addition, said Harries, Unesco was badly managed and overspent. Over 80 percent of its budget was spent on its Paris headquarters. There was a lack of priority in its work program, and conferences were poorly organized. Harries criticized M'Bow as being ideologically militant, combative, authoritarian and inefficient. It was a good thing for the United States to withdraw, he said. It would encourage Unesco to reform and force the Third World to rethink its anti-Western propaganda. The only thing that would justify the United States staying in, said Harries, was M'Bow's resignation and the appointment of a new director general.

Derwinski repeated the conclusions of the State Department's policy review of Unesco: politicization; endemic hostility toward the basic institutions of a free society, especially a free market and a free press; unrestrained budgetary expansion and poor management. "During our review of Unesco," he said, "we asked ourselves whether our leaving would deprive us of any benefits that were both invaluable and irreplaceable. If we withdrew would our national interest be affected in any significant way? We concluded that the answer to these questions was no."

Newell, questioned closely by committee members about how the decision to withdraw was arrived at, said at first that "the decision was made by the administration." Asked who in the administration had made it, Newell replied, "The decision was made by the President."

REP. DAN MICA: The President made the decision on his own, without any recommendation?

NEWELL: There was a recommendation from the Secretary of State.

MICA: Secretary Shultz recommended we should get out?

NEWELL: Yes, he did.

MICA: And you had no input in that decision?

NEWELL: Surely, we did, in terms of conducting the [policy] review and then forwarding the results of those reviews to the Secretary.

Newell was questioned further on this topic by Rep. Mel Levine, who asked if it was correct that the administration had recommended the withdrawal.

NEWELL: That is correct, and I represent the administration, Mr. Levine.

LEVINE: Was it also correct that the first recommendation taken within the administration was yours?

NEWELL: Yes, it was my recommendation to the Secretary of State.

LEVINE: And it went from you to the Secretary, and from the Secretary to the President?

NEWELL: Yes. There is one part I think might be valuable to add here. That is it went through Under Secretary of State [Lawrence] Eagleburger.

LEVINE: So it was initially yours, through Eagleburger to Secretary Shultz, and from the Secretary on behalf of the Department, to the President?

NEWELL: That is correct.

Newell conceded that the majority of the organizations he had consulted had opposed the withdrawal, but said that those organizations were "users and beneficiaries of Unesco resources. Consequently, they do have interests which are significant." Their input, he said, was not to advise the administration as to whether it should get in or stay out, but rather to provide a balanced view of Unesco. The pullout was a "foreign policy decision which these associations are not responsible for." Newell said people in positions of responsibility at the State Department were in unanimous agreement with the decision. One could argue that they are all Republicans, he said, "But it is a Republican administration that happens to be well staffed at the State Department."

MAY 1984

Adminstrative Reforms

Unesco's Executive Board began a 14-day meeting in Paris on May 9. M'Bow proposed several reforms, including budget cuts, decentralizing his power to regional offices, restructuring the permanent Unesco staff, and recruiting more efficient personnel.[36] M'bow set up five working groups composed of members of the Unesco Secretariat and outside specialists to evaluate programs and recommend reforms to improve the effectiveness and efficiency of the organization. "We take seriously specific suggestions from some of our major members," said M'Bow, "and we will make every effort to improve where improvement is possible."[37]

M'Bow appointed at least one American with previous experience of

Unesco affairs to serve on each of the five groups. John Fobes, former deputy director general of Unesco, would head the Working Group on Procedures and Staff Management Methods. The group would make recommendations on hiring, promotion and termination of service. Virginia Householder, former inspector general of the Organization of American States, would represent the United States on the Working Group on Budgeting Techniques and Presentation of the Budget. It would propose improvements in preparing budget data for the 1986–87 program. Winthrop Southworth, a former director of the State Department's Personnel Projects staff, would serve on the Working Group on Evaluation Methods and Techniques. It would examine the internal systems that evaluate Unesco planning, programming and budget drafting.

Two Americans were named to the Working Group on Public Information: John Reinhardt, former U.S. ambassador to Nigeria, and Leonard Sussman, vice chariman of the U.S. National Commission for Unesco. The fifth group, the Working Group on Critical Analysis of the Unesco Program, would consist of 21 current and former Unesco staff officers who would clarify goals and priorities within Unesco's various fields and recommend improvements. The five groups would meet in the second half of July and make their recommendations to M'Bow, who would study their reports and make recommendations to the Executive Board in late September.

The U.S. chief delegate, Jean Gerard, responded that M'Bow's reform proposal was "encouraging . . . it showed an effort in discussing that there were some problems." But Gerard cautioned that "politicization is one of our problems that hasn't been touched." M'Bow sparked a new controversy, however, when he warned that the United States might still have to pay about $43 million in Unesco dues in 1985 even if it withdrew at the end of 1984, because the budget was for a two-year period. He said if the United States refused to pay, Unesco's executive board might have to haul the United States before the International Court of Justice in The Hague. Gerard stated she was in total disagreement.[38]

The Executive Board spent three days debating the British letter of April 2 that urged higher priority for programs in education, science and culture, and corresponding reductions in other programs. William Dodd, the British delegate, said certain work in communication offered no chance of agreement. Unesco activities should instead concentrate on core areas where agreement was possible—mainly practical and technical, and mainly concerned with assisting the developing countries. Jean Gerard said there would be "no lack of effort on the part of the United States to contribute to change and reform." The United States had

specific proposals to put forward and would pursue them with the proposed working group. Unesco's surest path to reform and renewal, she said, was to give absolute priority to those cores in education, science, culture and communication where consensus existed for international cooperation. Other Unesco members at the meeting urged the United States not to pull out, contending that the move would harm international coorperation and threaten the United Nations system. France, India and Spain were among those asking the United States to reconsider, and several delegations expressed support for M'Bow.

The Executive Board, by a 33 to 6 vote, formed a Temporary Committee consisting of 13 members of the board to recommend improvements in Unesco operations. The committee was specially mandated to consider criticisms leveled at Unesco by the United States and Britain. It was to report to the next meeting of the board in September.[39]

Leonard Sussman said on May 21 that Unesco needed housecleaning but was too valuable to scuttle. Sussman told the International Association of Newspaper Publishers in Paris that the Reagan administration was persuaded to withdraw from Unesco largely because of press opposition to Unesco's debates over a New World Information Order. The U.S. charges of politicization, mismanagement and lack of budgetary restraint came later, Sussman said.[40] He argued that if Western countries withdrew from Unesco, only the Soviet Union and its allies would gain while moderates in the Third World and developed countries would suffer if Unesco were critically disabled.

Scientists Concerned

Also in May, the president of the U.S. National Academy of Sciences, Dr. Frank Press, said that the academy was concerned about the proposed withdrawal and "its effect on international scientific programs."[41] Members of the American Association for the Advancement of Science, meeting in New York, said there would be serious scientific consequences if the United States withdrew.[42] Dr. Roger Revelle, former director of the Scripps Institution of Oceanography, said the ultimate success of an important 20-year study of world climate was completely dependent on Unesco financing. The only speaker at the meeting to back the withdrawal was Jean Bergaust, deputy assistant secretary of state for international organizations, who repeated assertions that Unesco had become corrupted by politicization, was dominated by anti-Westernism, was extravagant in its budget, and was subject to "atrocious management."

JUNE 1984

Gallup Poll

A Gallup Poll based on interviews conducted nationwide in May was released on June 21. It showed that most Americans who had heard or read about Unesco were against withdrawal. Of the 1,516 adults interviewed, 36 percent were aware of Unesco. Of this aware group, 48 percent said the United States should not withdraw, while 34 percent favored the move (18 percent had no opinion). A plurality of most groups in the sample favored the United States retaining its membership. An exception was Republicans, 42 percent of whom favored the withdrawal, compared to 36 percent who opposed it.[43]

Newell, however, told a news conference at Abidjan, Ivory Coast, on June 30 that the United States was unlikely to change its mind, despite growing recognition of the need for reform within Unesco. He said that Unesco had ceased to carry out the missions outlined in its charter and had devoted itself instead to such tasks as the condemnation of Israel and the promotion of an agenda that he said was largely inspired by the Soviet Union.[44] Newell said that during his 12-day African tour, officials had expressed "understanding for the U.S. decision and regret that the United States was withdrawing."

A conference representing 102 international non-government organizations met in Paris in June and expressed the hope that the U.S. government would reconsider. Delegates reaffirmed their attachment to Unesco's ideals and objectives, and expressed satisfaction with steps taken by the Executive Board and the director general to strengthen and improve the organization. They also declared their indignation at the "slanderous attacks" on Unesco and M'Bow.[45]

JULY 1984

Western Reform Proposals

Specific reforms sought by the United States were first detailed in a letter to M'Bow from Newell and Gerard, dated July 13.[46] These expanded on the concerns expressed by Secretary of State Shultz in his letter of December 28, 1983, announcing that the United States planned to withdraw. Newell's letter delineated the basic changes the United States considered most necessary "if Unesco is to regain the confidence and support of all segments of its membership." Among the American demands were that:

- Unesco should create a mechanism to ensure that all its programs and decisions enjoy the support of all areas, including the Western Group;
- It should strengthen the Drafting and Negotiation Group at the General Conference. This group considers contentious issues in order to structure a consensus position for consideration by the full General Conference;
- Unesco should create a budget procedure requiring an affirmative vote of members who together contribute 51 percent of the budget before the program and budget can be officially approved;
- The agency should return to its original purposes, that is, it should abandon contentious programs and themes such as disarmament, economic theorizing, global standard setting and collective rights;
- It should reassert the authority of member states and governing bodies to ensure that members have real decision-making power, such as the right to eliminate or change programs;
- Unesco should present a zero-growth budget for 1986–87, and simplify the budget format to increase member states' understanding of the programs funded. The new budget should present a rank ordering of major sub-programs;
- It should speed up the recruitment process to attract top-flight talent, and take steps to improve employee morale and the relationship between staff and management.

On July 17, the Netherlands joined the United States and the United Kingdom in formal warning of possible withdrawal. Dutch Ambassador Maarten Mourik handed M'Bow a letter from the Netherlands minister of education and science that reflects the degree of support for the U.S. position from its European allies. The letter refers to the "Crisis in Unesco" document by the Western Information Group and to the letter from the United Kingdom's Timothy Raison urging reform, and notes that the Netherlands agreed with the main proposals made there. Nevertheless, it said, the Netherlands government wanted to put a number of points in its own words. These included:

- *Evaluation:* The government looked forward to concrete proposals from M'Bow on better evaluation of Unesco programs.
- *Politicization:* While Unesco's terms of reference were such that political aspects of a number of subjects could not be ignored, "we have the impression that a disproportionate amount of attention is being devoted to political aspects at the expense of the content of the programme, and that subjects are being placed on the pro-

gramme which have little or nothing to do with Unesco's terms of reference."

- *Budget:* The letter expressed concern "not only with the budget ceiling but with the transparency of the budget itself and the monitoring of expenses."
- *Staffing:* Serious staff problems had reduced the effectiveness of the Secretariat. The government was not convinced that the current staffing policy met the highest requirements as regards specialized professional skills, nor that the policy "is intended to achieve the best possible regional spread when it comes to recruitment and appointment."
- *Program:* The government felt that the program as a whole had lost consistency and concentration on the most important matters. Greater concentration and more selectivity were required. As regards the communication program, "the Netherlands government would stress here again that the NWICO must be regarded as a continuous and evolving process." It remained strongly opposed to "anything which could lead to government interference in the content of information supplied through the media."

The letter noted that Unesco had received concrete proposals for reform from various sides. And it ended with a thinly veiled threat: "if the reforms which are generally agreed to be necessary are not carried out, or are not carried out sufficiently, and in particular if this should lead to the withdrawal of one or more member states, the Netherlands government will again have to review its position vis-a-vis the organization."[47]

The five working groups that M'Bow appointed in May to evaluate procedures and recommend changes to improve Unesco's effectiveness wrapped up their work on July 20. Their findings were given to M'Bow, who would make recommendations to the Executive Board in September. Meanwhile, the Temporary Committee appointed by Unesco's Executive Board held its first meeting in July. And the committee of U.S. scholars appointed by the State Department held an eight-day meeting with Unesco Secretariat members in Paris to discuss progress on the proposed reforms.

House Hearings, July 26

There were further hearings on Unesco by two subcommittees of the House Foreign Affairs Committee on July 26.[48] Three people gave testimony. Charles M. Lichtenstein, a senior fellow of the Heritage Foundation and former U.S. ambassador to the United Nations, focused his

remarks on alternatives to Unesco. The organization, he said, was so deeply and so basically flawed that continued U.S. participation would be a disservice to the national interest. In leaving, the United States was not turning its back on its responsibilities in the fields of education, science and culture. Its efforts and contributions could be used more effectively in "alternative vehicles that are now in existence or that might be brought into existence." The decision to withdraw might well signify a strong reaffirmation of U.S. cultural, economic and scientific activities "undertaken bilaterally or under the aegis of some alternative multilateral vehicle."

Lichtenstein asserted that a good deal of the criticism of the U.S. withdrawal was coming from "what can only be identified as vested interests—from academic and intellectual elites in this country, and in a number of Third World countries. There is some reason to suspect that the concern of these subsidized elites is less 'the life of the mind' than it is the threatened end of the non-stop free lunch at the public trough."

Burton S. Levinson, chairman of the national executive committee of the Anti-Defamation League of B'nai B'rith, welcomed the decision to withdraw. He recalled that the Anti-Defamation League, a Jewish organization based primarily in the United States, had in 1980 and 1981 adopted resolutions calling on Congress "to withhold further subvention of Unesco so long as Unesco continues to politicize its actions by means of anti-western, anti-democratic attacks in violation of its mandate." Unesco had veered from its mandate. Rather than promoting the world's cultural diversity or disseminating scientific advances, it had degenerated into a "highly politicized forum for the Soviet bloc and the Third World."

Levinson said Unesco's unraveling had begun with a decade-long propaganda war against Israel in the late 1960s. "Particularly pernicious was its campaign against Israel's archaeological excavations in the capital city of Jerusalem, which produced lop-sided votes against the Jewish state." Led by the Arab bloc, Unesco's vote in 1974 to exclude Israel from membership of its European regional group was "tantamount to expulsion from the organization, since most Unesco decisions are made at the regional level." It was largely because the United States then with-held funding from Unesco that Israel was readmitted to the European group in 1976. Still, he said, "the anti-Israel, politically charged hysteria within the organization continued unabated." In 1977 Unesco had helped underwrite a film on the Palestine Liberation Orgainzation, "a group whose name is synonymous with international terrorism." Unesco had also supported the Islamic States Broadcasting Association, which disseminated blatantly anti-Semitic programs.

Levinson associated his group with the media critics of Unesco, which he said had "mischievously tampered with our cherished principles

of freedom of speech and freedom of the press by seeking to enact press limitations." Even the name New World Information Order conjured up "an Orwellian chill within those who see in its promotion the hand of the Soviet Union, its client states and those Third World nations which live under authoritarian or totalitarian rule."

Dana Bullen, executive director of the World Press Freedom Committee (WPFC), told the hearing that the WPFC was a "strong, global voice against those who advocate a state-controlled news media, those who seek to deny truth in news, and those who abuse newsmen." One of the committee's objectives was to be a watchdog on these issues. Since its inception in 1976, the WPFC had sent delegations to Unesco and to non-aligned and other conferences where the news media had been under critical scrutiny.

Bullen said there had been some gains for free press principles at the last General Conference, among them inclusion in Unesco's program of a study of the watchdog role of the press and of censorship. But this was only part of the story. Numerous code-word projects were also approved for Unesco's program. These included work on codes of conduct, safety of journalists, a right to communicate, working conditions of journalists, participation in media management, responsibility of journalists, "and similar open-ended, broadly worded code phrases that have meant trouble for newsmen in the past."

It was true, said Bullen, that Unesco had not adopted licensing of journalists, an imposed code of conduct, binding rules for the content of news, or similar restrictive proposals. "But it seems that in too many cases this has been only because member states with a strong free press tradition have successfully fought back such proposals." Even now, he said, Unesco was proposing research on collective rights in the context of new communications technology. And it continued efforts to elucidate principles for a new world information order, and to develop critical public awareness of the news media.

Yet, said Bullen, the WPFC had taken no position for or against a U.S. withdrawal from Unesco. When the United States had announced its intention to withdraw, WPFC chairman Harold Andersen had said: "This decision is based on a number of considerations and was taken by the government, not by the news media. There have been serious problems at Unesco. We hope this sends an important message which, if heeded, might make such withdrawal unnecessary. For our part, we intend to continue to monitor communications issues at Unesco and to vigorously oppose any proposals there that threaten press freedom." Bullen told the House panel: "That continues to be our position." Rep. Dan Mica, chairman of the International Operations subcommittee, expressed his surprise at the WPFC's refusal to take a stand on the with-

drawal. "The information I had as I assumed the chairmanship of this subcommittee earlier this year was that your organization was a leader in the world in trying to stop any moves towards licensing of journalists. That is why I must say . . . yours is the most surprising testimony I have heard. I would have thought that there would have been a very strong position taken by the World Press Freedom Committee either to stay in and fight, so that we don't end up with licensing, or to get out totally because it's a lost cause." Similar sentiments were expressed by Rep. Jim Leach, who said: "I am frankly astonished, Mr. Bullen, that your organization has not taken a position on the withdrawal question, and I would suggest, in the strongest way that I can, that you are abrogating your responsibilities." Bullen's response was that "no one issue should determine a decision of this nature." While the WPFC was concerned with press issues, "it does not mean we necessarily have to take a position on budget issues, on human rights issues, on procedural issues, on staffing issues, on a whole web of issues that have gone into this decision."

M'Bow, visiting the San Francisco Bay area at the end of July, said he would not resign his post because of American pressure, and that Unesco would continue to operate even if the United States quit the agency.[49]

AUGUST 1984

U.S. National Commission Reacts

The strongest domestic criticism of the administration's position was voiced on August 8 when the U.S. National Commission for Unesco called simultaneous press conferences in New York and Washington to denounce the pullout. The National Commission, established in 1946 to advise the State Department on the agency, has 100 members. Of these, 60 represent non-government organizations such as the National Academy of Sciences, the American Academy of Arts and Sciences, the American Library Association, the Institute of International Education, the American Council of Learned Societies, and the American Newspaper Publishers Association. Another 25 represent state and local governments, and 15 are elected at large by the administration.[50]

At the press conferences, the commission released a 30-page report entitled "What Are the Issues Concerning the Decision of the United States to Withdraw from Unesco?" the report said that while many of its members shared the Reagan administration's concern over Unesco, they rejected withdrawal as an improper response. The report argued that the timing of the U.S. decision did not allow for a full assessment. In fact, the

U.S. had served notice of its intention to withdraw "after Unesco had adopted the basic elements of a six-year program with the United States joining in a consensus in its favor." It pointed out that other federal agencies, embassies and consulates, responding in 1983 to the administration review of Unesco policy, did not recommend withdrawal. America's allies and other nations also did not support the withdrawal, and none had followed the U.S. example, choosing instead to work for reform from within.

The document sought to refute the main arguments advanced by the administration for its decision. It said Unesco was no more politicized than other international organizations; only 1 percent of the annual budget was spent on programs that the State Department believed were highly politicized—disarmament studies, the rights of peoples and refugee education. Unesco, it said, did not itself advocate a "statist" approach to issues, although some of its member nations might, and the Soviet Union did not exercise inordinate control over Unesco programs. Only 8 percent of the Unesco staff originated from Eastern bloc countries, compared to 40 percent from Western Europe and North America. It argued that Israel was not being attacked in Unesco, and that at the General Conference in Paris in 1983, anti-Israel rhetoric was muted or non-existent. Services to the PLO and African liberation movements were "small in scale and largely educational." The United States did not fund these programs.

Concerning the New World Information Order issues, the report said that Unesco had taken no action to control journalists or limit press freedom. Proposals threatening the free flow of information had repeatedly been rejected at Unesco, and negotiations at the 1983 General Conference had generally favored the Western free press position. The 1980 Unesco resolution setting forth the elements of a New World Information Order "includes freedom of the press and information, the freedom of journalists and all professionals in the communication media, and removal of internal and external obstacles to a free flow and a wider and better balanced dissemination of information and ideas."

In relation to Unesco's management and budget, the National Commission maintained that the proportion of Unesco's funds used for administration was not disproportionately high, and quoted a study of Unesco's plans and budgets made by the General Accounting Office in 1979, which deemed its management procedures to be "unique and forward-looking compared to other UN agencies examined." The budget, said the report, had shown a small increase, but had risen more slowly than those of the International Labor Organization, the Food and Agriculture Organization, and the World Health Organization.

At the New York press conference, Leonard Sussman, vice chairman

of the National Commission, accused the Reagan administration of using "misleading tactics" and of spreading "distorted information" to support its decision. "On the Unesco question this past year, the facts have indeed been distorted, relevant evidence buried and ideological dogma substituted for honest debate."[51] Sussman also accused Newell of bad faith in having consulted with organizations such as the National Commission when the decision to withdraw had already been made.

Dispute over Funds

A new dispute erupted between the United States and Unesco in mid-August over some $80 million that the agency held in a special "currency fluctuation" account, set up to offset the impact on Unesco of changing exchange rates.[52] Because of the rise in the value of the U.S. dollar, a surplus had accumulated in the account. The U.S. share of the account was $20 million. The United States and several other Western countries called on Unesco to return all the money in the account immediately to member nations. They feared that Unesco could use the $80 million to offset the financial impact of the threatened U.S. withdrawal. There was concern also that Unesco might try to spend the money on controversial programs that it could not otherwise afford if the United States withdrew.

State Department spokesman John Hughes was quoted as saying that "one way or another we're going to get our money back—either by Unesco returning it, or we will withhold that much from our last assessment, due in December."[53] Doudou Diene, the Unesco representative in New York, told a news conference two days later that reports of a dispute over the funds were a "distortion of fact." The only disagreement, he said, was over timing, and he quoted M'Bow as pledging at a May 8 executive board meeting to return the $80 million in full to member states after Unesco's outside auditors closed the books in 1985. "The publication of such false and misleading stories about the Unesco surplus indicates either an international campaign to sow distortion and lies about Unesco or an abysmal ignorance of the facts," Diene said.[54]

SEPTEMBER 1984

Public Relations Campaign

Yet another controversy surfaced in the press in early September with a report that Unesco had hired the Washington Public relations firm of Wagner & Baroody, which had handled the press operations of the Republican National Convention in Dallas, to improve its image.[55]

M'Bow had announced in August that Unesco had sought professional assistance from Wagner & Baroody "in accordance with the suggestions of several member states who believe that Unesco has failed to adequately explain its purposes and publicize its achievements, especially amongst its major financial contributors." A press release from Wagner & Baroody, dated August 7 said the firm had been hired by Unesco to assist in disseminating information about its "purposes, programs and structure." The contract, said the release, "was prompted by recent criticism of Unesco by the United States and other free world democracies, some of which appears to be based on misunderstandings and misperceptions."[56] The contract specified that the firm would "try to generate support for Unesco among policy makers, the media, scientific and educational leaders, and the public." The controversy in the press concerned the propriety of Unesco hiring a firm to influence officials of a member nation and the cost of the service—$15,000 a month plus expenses. This was to be paid for out of a special account for public relations activities, which is filled in part by the sale of publications, recordings, movies and television shows. Questions were raised in the press as to whether the proceeds of sales of certain recordings were not, in fact, intended to be used for other purposes like cancer research or programs for handicapped children.[57]

Critical Analysis

No sooner had this dispute subsided than Unesco came in for more unfavorable publicity. At the Executive Board meeting in May, M'Bow had ordered four reports prepared by Secretariat staff and outside experts—on personnel practices, budget, program evaluation and public information. These were made public on September 12. A fifth report was prepared internally by 21 present and former Unesco staff members. Entitled "The Critical Analysis of the Program," the 60-page report was not circulated, but was leaked to the press, as the *New York Times* put it, "by sources unfriendly to Mr. M'Bow."[58] The report criticized duplication, overlapping and fragmentation in Unesco programs, and suggested that Unesco leave such divisive issues as the rights and responsibilities of journalists to other U.N. agencies or to professional organizations.[59] Gerard Bolla, Unesco's deputy director general, told a press conference in Paris on September 12 that while M'Bow had authority to make management reforms on his own, he did not have the right to change programs. That was the reason, said Bolla, why M'Bow had neither published nor accepted the recommendations of the internal committee. "The lack of publication had nothing to do with its being hostile to the organization," said Bolla.[60]

Not Enough Change

Gregory Newell's testimony to a joint meeting of two subcommittees of the House Foreign Affairs Committee on September 13 focused on two areas: the encouragement of reform in Unesco, and the search for alternatives to Unesco activities.[61] Newell noted that the Executive Board's Temporary Committee on Reform was meeting in Paris and that it had made some good recommendations. "We are disappointed, however, that the recommendations often lack specific provisions for their implementation." He said the United States had worked closely with other Western nations to develop many of the proposals the committee was considering and stated that "if significant and constructive reforms are in fact undertaken, the United States would be in a position to reconsider its withdrawal decision."

Concerning alternatives, Newell said the administration had undertaken extensive consultations with domestic organizations and had received a large number of worthwhile proposals, "many more, in fact, than we will be able to fund, by a factor of three and a half." An experts group had been formed to prioritize the proposals. Asked by Rep. Gus Yatron, chairman of the Subcommittee on Human Rights and International Organizations, how the administration planned to "mitigate Third World mistrust of the United States when we pull out of Unesco," Newell said he believed that with sound management and prioritization of programs, "the Third World can actually benefit through this decision by putting these resources into multilateral, regional and bilateral mechanisms that are more effective."

Newell ruled out the possibility of a one-year postponement of the withdrawal. Asked whether the United States still planned to pull out in spite of Unesco's reform efforts, he responded: "If there are no further changes than we have seen to date, then yes, I would recommend that we hold with the decision." The U.S. policy was criticized by several members of the subcommittees, including Rep. Jim Leach, who called the decision to withdraw "a dangerous precedent" for American membership in other intenational organizations.

Jeane Kirkpatrick, U.S. ambassador to the United Nations, sounded a similar theme to Newell's on September 18 in a television program prepared by the U.S. Information Agency for use in French-speaking African countries.[62] Kirkpatrick said the United States was likely to leave Unesco "unless something dramatic happens." One purpose of Unesco was to strengthen a free press, she said, but instead it had been raising obstacles to press freedom. And rather than promoting education and culture in poor countries around the globe, she said, Unesco was spending too much money on its bureaucracy in Paris.

GAO Report Leaked

On the eve of the Unesco Executive Board meeting, copies of the still-confidential draft report on the agency by the General Accounting Office were submitted to the State Department and some congressmen. Copies of the GAO's "Review of Unesco's Management, Budgeting and Personnel Practices" were leaked to the press in Washington and Paris on September 20. The review did not make specific recommendations, but included "observations on certain management areas it believes need improvement."

According to press reports, the review was strongly critical of Unesco, depicting it as inefficient and badly managed.[63] It said that Unesco's management was "highly centralized with most substantive and many routine decisions being made personally by the director general," which delayed decisions and stifled creativity and innovation. It said that M'Bow had built up the Secretariat at the expense of field operations and had inflated the number of service personnel. It found indications of a need for more effective oversight of the Secretariat by the Executive Board and the General Conference. Outside observers familiar with Unesco's operations, said the review, felt that the General Conference had become too dependent on the Secretariat, which influenced its agenda and drafted many of its resolutions. The review was critical of Unesco's personnel management, especially of delays in recruiting professional staff and a heavy reliance on supplementary staff. It found that some programs were duplicative and suggested that there be a mechanism for coordinating them. It suggested that presentation of the budget could be improved to show clearly how and why it had changed from the previous budget. And it commented that Unesco had no effective system for evaluating the usefulness of its programs.

The review referred to cases where funds had been transferred between accounts in violation of regulations, and said that the agency requires "only minimal assurance from recipients of grants that funds were used for the intended purpose."[64] But it also said that the United States and other Western governments did not exercise adequate control over the director general and his Secretariat. Unesco spokesman Dileep Padgaonkar described disclosure of the confidential report as "psychological warfare" by those who wanted the United States to quit Unesco. "Frankly, we are surprised that a confidential document concerning Unesco should be made available to the press before it was made available to Unesco," he said.[65] M'Bow complained that "this use of the document largely contributed to the presentation of a false picture, not only of the organization's activities, functioning and management, but also of the content of the report itself. . . . It should be emphasized that the report

contains much favorable criticism concerning the management of the organization—criticism that has been systematically ignored in the leaks organized through the press."[66]

Unesco officials professed to find some comfort in a statement by President Reagan to the United Nations General Assembly in New York on September 24. Reagan told the Assembly, "Let me again emphasize our unwavering commitment to a central principle of the United Nations system, the principle of universality, both here and in the U.N. technical agencies around the world." Reagan said that "if universality is ignored, if nations are expelled illegally, then the U.N. itself cannot be expected to succeed." Reagan's comments presumably referred to efforts to suspend Israeli membership. But the statement was welcomed by Deputy Director General Gerard Bolla as "very heartening to Unesco."[67]

Debate on Reforms

Unesco's Executive Board began three weeks of meetings in Paris on September 26 to consider, among other things, the reforms demanded by the United States and other Western countries.[68] On the agenda for its 120th session was a list of proposed administrative changes drawn up by M'Bow based on reports of the working groups he had appointed at the May meeting. Also on the table were recommendations by the Executive Board's 13-member Temporary Committee.

A Soviet position paper added to the agenda criticized the Western demands for changes and said it would oppose efforts to abandon Unesco's involvement in peace and disarmament issues. Dealing with charges that Unesco took positions at variance with traditional Western concepts of a free market and a free press, the Soviet paper sharply criticized multinational corporations and the international news agencies.[69] The letter, signed by Soviet Deputy Foreign Minister Viktor Stukalin, said that any attempt to change Unesco's current medium-term work program, which would run until 1989, was "totally unacceptable." Also circulated to all 51 members of the Executive Board were copies of the General Accounting Office draft report, still officially confidential. The copies were distributed by members of the U.S. mission at the request of Frank C. Conahan, director of the National Security and International Affairs Division of the GAO.[70]

M'Bow reported he had already taken steps to improve the geographical balance of Unesco personnel and bring in "new blood" and to extend in-service training and introduce more rigorous assessment of the performance of new employees. Steps would be taken to provide explanatory material to the budget so that members would find it easier to understand. M'Bow said that he would strengthen mechanisms for eva-

luating Unesco programs to measure better the impact they had, and he said that he would restructure the Office of Public Information to make it more efficient.[71]

M'Bow's proposed reforms were generally well received by the 51-member Executive Board—except by the country they were most meant to impress, the United States. Jean Gerard, the American chief delegate, criticized the "leisurely pace" of the debate on September 28, saying that few agreements had been reached on practical changes. This, she said, demonstrated a "reluctance to change, an unwillingness to face facts, a functional if not deliberate avoidance of responsibility."[72] Gerard said she was not optimistic that the United States would remain in the organization, but vowed to keep working for change that would allow continued membership.[73]

The British member of the board, William Dodd, told the meeting that M'Bow's draft proposals for reform represented "only a beginning" of what was needed. In particular, Dodd said, Unesco must agree to set up "a sensible and efficient monitoring system" to ensure that all changes agreed upon at the meeting were effectively implemented.[74] In addition, the British delegate said that the board should give high priority to altering Unesco's work program—meaning that it should start reducing divisive activities in fields like disarmament and regulation of journalists and concentrate instead on practical steps to help poor countries.[75] But Dodd acknowledged that "progress had been made, and that the ideas produced by the working groups, if fully implemented, could lead to useful improvements."

Karl Moersch of Germany told the board that he was impressed by the suggestions "and in particular by the number of immediate decisions made by the director general."[76] Takaaki Kagawa of Japan, which earlier had expressed strong criticism of Unesco, told the board that he generally agreed with the proposals and was pleased the director general had taken steps to implement them, "since implementation is what really matters." Luis Villoro, speaking for Mexico, characterized the reforms as "serious, careful and thorough work." No one could say that the agency hadn't achieved a change of atmosphere, he said. "There is a will to reform and instruments by which to so so."

Soviet delegate Dimitri Yermolenko supported M'Bow's plans for administrative reforms, but opposed suggestions that Unesco's programs or constitution be changed. Yermolenko criticized the release to the press of the GAO report. "The draft document was strictly confidential," he said. "In some mysterious way it was leaked to the press and became a tool against Unesco . . . such acts constitute an element of psychological warfare.[77] M'Bow voiced a similar criticism a week later, saying that Unesco was the victim of "systematic denigration" in distorted news

dispatches.[78] M'Bow told the board that newspaper articles on Unesco were "changed by editors, or presented with shock or negative headlines that often have nothing to do" with the context of the reports.

OCTOBER 1984

Organizational Changes

The Executive Board approved an 88-page list of recommended organizational changes.[79] The U.S. position seemed ambivalent. Although it joined in approving the reform proposals, Gerard told the board on October 8 that the Temporary Committee had "failed to make the kind of far-reaching recommendations for which we saw the most need" or to propose ways of ensuring that changes it did recommend were carried out.[80] As a result, she said, the United States would soon propose additonal changes in several areas of Unesco's operations. And on October 10 Gerard told the board that the United States might reconsider its decision to pull out if reforms were adopted within the next 10 weeks.[81] "We would take into account any such progress in deciding whether to reconsider our announced withdrawal," Gerard said.

The second set of reform proposals, those submitted by the 13-member Temporary committee, contained 16 groups of recommendations that it had adopted by consensus.[82] Among their suggestions were that the role of the General Conference and the Executive Board should be strengthened. This was in answer to criticisms that in the past too much power had been ceded to the Secretariat and the director general. The committee recommended that Unesco's activities should be decentralized, that programs should be better focused and evaluated, and that recruiting procedures and budgeting techniques be improved. The reforms were unanimously approved by the Executive Board on October 9.[83]

Newell told a press conference in Paris on October 13 that Unesco had not changed enough to prompt the United States to reconsider. He said, however, that the United States would make a "maximum effort and apply maximum pressure" to bring about reform as the Executive Board went into the final week of its meeting. No definite decision had been made on withdrawal, said Newell, "we are not on automatic pilot."[84]

That final week saw a demand from the United States that the Executive Board call a special session in November to consider the GAO report. Gerard reminded members that the United States was contributing one-quarter of the agency's budget and would quit unless major

changes were made. She said that the GAO report was the most thorough review of Unesco's management ever conducted and told the board that it was "frivolous and irresponsible" to dismiss the report because it came from only one member, as M'Bow had suggested.[85] M'Bow told the board that although the GAO report was still in draft form and had no official standing as far as Unesco was concerned, since it had been prepared by the government of a member state, he was willing to consider any positive recommendations it contained. In the debate that followed, several board members said they would be prepared to discuss only the final version of the report and that they needed time to consult their governments. The debate closed without a decision after Georges-Henri Dumont of Belgium declared that he saw no point in discussing a document that did not formally exist.

The United States also proposed a major change in the way Unesco's budget was approved. It recommended that a vote of 85 percent of the membership be required to pass the budget. The budget commonly was approved by consensus, but could be passed by a two-thirds majority of the members, and the change would have given Western countries a virtual veto over spending. U.S. delegates argued that requiring an 85 percent majority would protect the interests and views of minority groups in the organization when there was no consensus. Not one other nation— including those of the Western group—supported the U.S. effort to put the proposal on the agenda, however. Faced with certain defeat, the State Department told the delegation to stop pressing it.

In the event, the board ended its meeting on October 22 by bending to Western demands and adopting a first outline for the organization's 1986–87 program, which Western representatives said met some but not all of their concerns.[86] It approved a series of measures to improve management and recruitment policy, and extended the term of the Temporary Committee. The most significant change was the adoption of a zero-growth budget for 1986–87. Developing nations initially had wanted Unesco to plan for a 2 percent annual growth rate but agreed to the freeze because they hoped it would persuade the Reagan administration to reconsider its decision to withdraw. The budget decision allowed Unesco to take inflation into account, but did not allow for any real growth in spending above the 1984–85 level of $391 million.[87] The recommendations of the Executive Board were to be submitted to the next General Conference in Sophia, Bulgaria, in October 1985.

The board also had before it a report from its external auditor, the United Kingdom's comptroller and auditor general. In accepting the report, the board noted that the auditors had found nothing that could justify accusations of corruption, bad management or negligence.[88]

Heritage Foundation

On October 8 the Heritage Foundation, a conservative policy research organization, asked its members for $75,000 in contributions to counter Unesco's public relations campaign in the United States. Edwin J. Feulner, president of the foundation, claimed in a direct-mail campaign that the U.S. withdrawal was a "direct result" of a Heritage paper written by Owen Harries, listing abuses by the agency. Harries, who was Australia's ambassador to Unesco during 1982–83, had argued in the paper and in newspaper columns before the withdrawal that Unesco was politicized, hostile to Western values and institutions, including a free press, favored the rights of peoples rather than individuals, and was consistently hostile to Israel while supporting the Palestinians. It was also, he wrote, appallingly managed and administered. Feulner, in appealing for funds to continue the Heritage Foundation's anti-Unesco campaign, said M'Bow's hiring of Wagner & Baroody was "just one more proof that Unesco is thoroughly under the control of communist and third world 'diplomats' whose only standard of conduct is raw power."

Final GAO Report

On October 31 the U.S. General Accounting Office released the final version of its report on Unesco.[89] It differed from the version leaked to the press in September in that, while its criticisms remained, it incorporated extensive comments from the Unesco Secretariat explaining or refuting some of the points it made. The report also made reference to recommendations for reform by the working groups set up by M'Bow, and to the proposals of the Executive Board's Temporary Committee, and commented that "the fact that Unesco now recognizes that problems exist in the way that it manages its activities is, in itself, an important step toward solving the problems." It was, however, too early to tell which of these recommendations would actually be translated into concrete actions. The Unesco analysis of the GAO report contested some of its details, but noted that "most of the GAO's major points and recommendations coincide with Unesco's own internal management reform program."[90]

NOVEMBER 1984

The United Kingdom Gives Notice

The United Kingdom had warned Unesco in April that it would reconsider its membership unless there were substantial reforms. The reforms adopted by the Executive Board meeting in Paris were not extensive

enough to persuade Britain to commit itself to continued membership. On November 17 the *New York Times* reported that the United Kingdom had told its principal allies that it intended to leave Unesco in a year unless the agency agreed to further changes. The move gave rise to considerable opposition. Other members of the European Economic Community, including West Germany and the Netherlands, which had strongly criticized Unesco, urged the United Kingdom not to withdraw. So did 41 Commonwealth countries, among them Canada, Australia, and many developing nations, which asked the United Kingdom to remain a member and lead the fight for reform from within. France was strongly opposed to the move. However, Prime Minister Margaret Thatcher told a questioner in Parliament on November 20 that criticisms of Unesco were "abundantly justified." She referred specifically to criticisms about "the direction" of Unesco expenditures and to "the attempts they make from time to time to prevent freedom of speech and freedom of the press."[91] Britain contributed $6.25 million a year, or about 5 percent of Unesco's budget.

The United Kingdom's formal announcement of intent to withdraw came on November 22 when Sir Geoffrey Howe, the foreign secretary, told the House of Commons that the United Kingdom would leave at the end of 1985 unless there was clear evidence of further reform. "We have not been satisfied that value for money has been obtained," said Howe. "Nor are we satisfied that the developing world has been getting value from Unesco. We acknowledge that some progress has been made . . . but much remains to be done."[92] Timothy Raison, the overseas development minister, said British funds earmarked for Unesco would be diverted to educational, scientific and cultural projects in the Third World that the government considered more worthwhile.

Patrick Seddoh of Ghana, chairman of Unesco's Executive Board, responded that he was "not only disappointed but also disturbed" in view of the "tremendous and genuine efforts made by the Secretariat and the Executive Board to improve the functioning of the organization, as borne out by the decisions of the board's 120th session, in which the United Kingdom delegation played a prominent role."[93]

The Dutch Foreign Ministry commented that it had no plans to withdraw. "We are still cautiously positive, still optimistic about Unesco," a spokesman said. In Paris, the French Ministry for Foreign Affairs said it deplored the British decision, especially since "a fruitful cooperation has been established among the Unesco member states and that, thanks to the initiatives taken together by Britain and France, we were able to obtain reforms which are hardly negligible in the functioning of the organization—and others are still on the way." A Third World point of view came from the African Group within Unesco, which said it

was "shocked and surprised" by the British decision. The group noted that many of the reform efforts in Unesco were "essentially the initiatives of the British Government."

Doudou Diene, director of the Unesco liaison office at the United Nations in New York, expressed his regret at the British withdrawal. The United Kingdom, he said, had played a leading role during the past year in efforts to bring about change in Unesco. British proposals had formed the basis of the work of the Temporary Committee of Unesco's Executive Board and of the work of the board itself at its 120th session in September. Proposals for reform which had included the United Kingdom and the United States as co-sponsors had been accepted unanimously. Diene raised the question of "how an intergovernmental body can work if member states, after having their proposals accepted by all other countries, then decide to withdraw." He hoped the British government would heed the appeal of its allies and the Commonwealth nations and reconsider its decision.[94]

DECEMBER 1984

Time for Decision

In December the focus of attention shifted back to the United States where the administration was to make a final decision on withdrawal by the end of the month. The impending decision set off a flood of news agency copy as proponents and opponents of the pullout sought to influence the decision at the last moment. Rep. James Scheuer, who had arranged the GAO review of Unesco, said on December 1 that "the most significant reform" would be to replace M'Bow as director general. M'Bow, however, told the *Washington Post* that there was absolutely no chance of his stepping down to appease his critics. "The director of an international organization cannot give in to pressures like this," he said.[95] Doudou Diene told the editors of the *New York Times* on December 3 that it would be a "dangerous miscalculation" if the United States were to leave. It would then not be able to make its views felt on matters like human rights in debates in the organization. "If the United States participates," he said, "ideas will be discussed in a more moderate way."[96]

Newell repeatedly stressed the theme that although Unesco had made some reforms, they were not far-reaching enough for the United States to remain. He told the *Washington Post* on December 3 "those changes have not occurred . . . any chance of remaining in the organization would appear to be slim." Newell denied rumors that the United States had a "hidden agenda" aimed at forcing M'Bow out. "Our critic-

ism of Unesco deals with substance and not with personalities," he said. "We've been asked by other governments, 'if M'Bow were to go, would we reconsider our decision?' and the answer is emphatically no."[97]

House Hearings, December 6

Newell repeated his message that significant reforms were unlikely at a joint meeting of two House Foreign Affairs subcommittees on December 6.[98] Some advances had been made, he said, but against these must be balanced a number of negatives. First, most of the Temporary Committee's recommendations had no implementing mechanisms; they had to be taken on good faith. Second, a number of changes in management had not gone as far as they could have, or should have. Third, the programs of which the United States was most critical had not been eliminated or even reduced. Fourth, no permanent steps had been taken to protect minority interests. In sum, said Newell, "viewed in relation to its previous performance, Unesco this year has made some movement. Viewed, however, in relation to the concerns we expressed a year ago, an unacceptable gap remains." He said he didn't expect reforms to occur "in the next year, or in the year after that, perhaps. That is why we are withdrawing." Rep. Jim Leach told the meeting, however, that the planned pullout was "an unjustified response to an exaggerated problem." Unesco, he said, was "being sacrificed as one of an array of social compact issues with the so-called New Right." Rep. Dan Mica, D-Fla., said the administration had not properly calculated the financial costs to the United States of carrying on educational, scientific, cultural and communications programs outside Unesco. He was also concerned that the organization was being abandoned to greater Soviet influence. Rep. Benjamin Goldman, R-N.Y., questioned whether the United States was not abandoning its responsibilities to purse its ideals by leaving Unesco instead of staying to oppose the Soviets in ideological debates. But Rep. Gerald Solomon, R-N.Y., declared that "the American people don't want money going to Unesco if it's going to be wasted. Those people were told to clean up their act and they didn't do it . . . I think we ought to pull out."

Senate Hearings, December 10

A hearing before the Senate Committee on Labor and Human Resources on December 10 took as a starting point the assumption that the United States would indeed withdraw.[99] The focus was on what conditions might lead to its eventual return to Unesco. Newell's testimony to the Senate panel was a replay of his remarks to the House panel a week before. He

was accompanied by Jean Gerard, who said that although there had been changes at Unesco, "they were not satisfactory, particularly in that they did not even address the problem that we have had with politicization of the programs." On the management side, there had been more promises than concrete action. Asked to provide a list of reforms necessary if the United States were to return to Unesco after a withdrawal, Gerard submitted a letter citing the need for structural changes, including strengthening the role of the governing bodies of the organization. As far as the program was concerned, she wanted to see Unesco return to its original purpose and a "balance restored between Western, democratic values and statist approaches as advocated by the Eastern bloc and their sympathizers in the Third World." Unesco's inefficient management practices must be corrected, including a credible evaluation effort and improved financial controls. She was, however, "not overly optimistic that the majority of the Unesco member states and, particularly, the present management of Unesco, are ready to take the drastic and bold steps in the near future which would be required to return this organization to a condition where it would enjoy again our wholehearted support."

Owen Harries of the Heritage Foundation also addressed what changes must occur in Unesco in order to justify America's return. First, some way would have to be found to close the gap between program decisions and the financing of those programs. "The present system whereby those who have the votes do not bear the brunt of the costs resulting from their decisions, and those who pay do not have the votes, is an incitement to irresponsibility," he said. Harries suggested that individual countries should have the right to choose whether or not to participate in individual programs, and if they chose not to particpate, their contribution to Unesco would be reduced by their assessed percentage of the cost of the program.

Second, he said, it was crucial that the Secretariat be restored to an impartial, neutral international civil service. The Secretariat had been turned very substantially into a political instrument. Third, there must be change in Unesco's top management. "The reputation of the orgainzation is now so tarnished and lacking in credibility that the appointment of a new Director General and a new team at the top is essential if Unesco's prestige and status are to be restored." Harries criticized the hands-off policy toward M'Bow adopted by the administration, which had introduced "an element of incoherence and illogicality into America's position over the past year." If it was true that Unesco was in an abysmal state, and it was also true that Unesco was dominated by a director general with enormous power, "then it inescapably follows that much of the responsibility for the poor performance belongs to the Director General."

Maxwell Greenberg, national chairman of the Anti-Defamation

League of B'nai B'rith, echoed the complaints about Unesco's anti-Israel policies by Burton Levinson at the House hearings on July 26. The Arab bloc at Unesco, said Greenberg, urged on by the Soviet Union and some of its clients and some Third World nations, had sought repeatedly to undermine Israel's legitimacy, and in vote after vote to support the terrorist PLO. And like Levinson, Greenberg linked Unesco's anti-Israel votes with its communications policies. "The anti-Israel beat of Unesco became a jumping off point for a series of votes, pronouncements and programs which were decidedly against Western nations and democratic nations...this crescendo culminated in the serious discussion of and almost adoption of a so-called New World Information Order, which would have seen the licensing of journalists and state management of the gathering and dissemination of the news."

For the United States to reconsider its decision, Greenberg said, would be to "undo the courageous signals we have been sending to the world community." To agree to stay, despite no concrete moves for reform, "would reward the Unesco administration for its insensitivity, its bent for politics, and its financial mismanagement, and that message would not be lost on the family of nations."

Leonard Sussman proposed to the Senate panel a strategy for reforming Unesco and for a return to Unesco once the reform was accomplished. There would be serious losses to Americans as a result of the withdrawal, he said. With the American withdrawal, it was time to cease the "frenetic assault on the organization, which has not always been based on reason and on fact, and strive instead to preserve Unesco's useful values and programs, while reforming those administrative and programmatic practices that led to the present crisis."

There was a need to compile a list of all the services performed at Unesco, arranged in three categories: those programs that directly benefited Americans; those that indirectly benefited Americans while directly servicing others; and those that had no positive or had a negative effect on American interests. That compilation would be used to determine which Unesco programs should be supported and which reformed by U.S. lights. Sussman suggested that the U.S. National Commission for Unesco, which the State Department had ignored, should be reorganized and resettled outside that department. A new interagency group was needed to reflect the various American interests in Unesco. He called for the appointment of a skilled negotiator, the president's personal ambassador, to meet with the major forces at Unesco and negotiate reforms that would lead to America's return.

International support for Unesco came from the U.N. Gerneral Assembly's Special Political Committee on December 10. It adopted, by a vote of 98 to 6, with 17 abstentions, a resolution expressing strong

support for Unesco and its efforts to promote a new world information and communications order.[100]

Conflicting Recommendations

Two U.S. reports over the next couple of days drew very different conclusions about the withdrawal. The National Commission for Unesco, meeting in Washington on December 13, adopted a resolution saying that the scheduled pullout would occur "before the process of reform with full U.S. participation could be completed." It declared that membership of Unesco was in the U.S. national interest and recommended that in the event of a withdrawal the United States should continue to work for change so that it could "decide to rejoin a reformed Unesco at the earliest possible date."[101] The commission received a report from members who had attended Unesco's executive board meetings in September–October. It stated that the seven-month U.S. delay in spelling out the changes it wanted in Unesco had "greatly hampered" the organization's efforts to reform itself. The report, which had been submitted to Secretary of State Shultz on November 27, also found that major reforms had already begun and cited "a clear gap between the U.S. position and the position of the vast majority of U.S. allies" on the planned withdrawal. It said that member nations at the Unesco board meeting had expressed "anger and frustration" because of a "general belief that no matter what efforts were being made by the other nations, it would not affect the U.S. decision." And it noted that "most of our allies believed that necessary reforms—many of which they also seek—can best be gained from working within the organization."[102]

Monitoring Panel

A report that differed sharply from that of the National Commission was released by Newell on December 13. The 15-page report, prepared by the State Department's official civilian monitoring panel under James Holderman, found that "while there was considerable discussion and some incremental movement" in Unesco during 1984, "there was no concrete change." The document said that most developed countries supported the U.S. position that serious reform was needed in three areas: to depoliticize Unesco programs and reduce their number and scope; to protect the interests of Unesco's major funders, the Western nations who were regularly outvoted by Third World countries, and to decentralize operations to involve more private-sector and intergovernmental bodies. The monitoring group said that "most developing countries resisted fundamental, structural proposals" and "the Soviet Union sought to undermine the

reform process." The Unesco Secretariat, "which openly sides with developing nations on most issues, continued to do so in 1984," it said.[103]

Final Notice

The official announcement of the withdrawal came on December 19, when Newell confirmed that the United States would pull out at the end of the month. He told a news conference at the State Department in Washington that "the circumstances that compelled us last year to announce our plan to withdraw have not changed sufficiently this year to warrant a change in our decision."[104] Newell's statement, a replay of his remarks a year earlier, said that "extraneous politicization continues, as does, regrettably, an endemic hostility toward the institutions of a free society—particularly those that protect a free press, free markets and, above all, individual human rights." Newell said the United States remained committed to "genuine and effective international cooperation" and would continue to support education, science, culture and communication through other existing channels. The United States would continue to promote Unesco's reform—from the outside—by designating a "reform observation panel of independent experts." It would establish an observer mission in Paris to protect American interests at Unesco and to work with like-minded member states on reform measures. "When Unesco returns to its original purposes and principles," he said, "the United States would be in a position to return."

Responding for Unesco, Deputy Director General Bolla said he deeply regretted the departure of the United States, especially in view of the exceptional contribution always made to the organization by American educators, scientists and experts in the fields of communication and culture.[105] "The departure of the United States is all the more regrettable because during the past year the Executive Board of Unesco and the director general have brought many improvements in the functioning and management of the organization. We shall continue our efforts in this direction." Bolla's statement ended with the hope that, as soon as possible, the United States, "which was one of Unesco's founder members and which wanted the organization to be universal, will be able to take its place among the other 160 member states, as it itself has envisaged doing."

NOTES

1. Memorandum from Gregory J. Newell to George P. Shultz, 16 December, 1983. Reports on this memorandum appeared in *The Guardian* (London) on 23 January 1984, and in *Editor & Publisher* on 4 February, 1984.

2. *What Are the Issues Concerning the Decision of the United States to Withdraw from Unesco?* (New York: U.S. National Commission for Unesco, 15 June 1984).

3. U.S. National Commission for Unesco, Resolution on U.S./Unesco Relations, 16 December 1983.

4. *The Guardian,* London, 30 January 1984.

5. National Security Council Memorandum, 23 December 1983.

6. Shultz's letter to M'Bow is reprinted in the *Journal of Communication,* 34 (Autumn 1984), p. 82.

7. Associated Press, 29 December 1983.

8. U.S. Department of State transcript, "On the Record Briefing on United States Withdrawal from Unesco by the Hon. Gregory Newell, Assistant Secretary of State, Bureau of International Organization Affairs," 29 December 1983.

9. M'Bow's letter to Shultz is reprinted in the *Journal of Communication,* 34 (Autumn 1984), p. 83.

10. *New York Times,* 1 February 1984.

11. Unesco Press, "Main Events Since U.S. Announces Decision to Withdraw from Unesco," Information Note No. 7, (Paris, September 1984).

12. Harley's memorandum is reprinted in the *Journal of Communication,* 34 (Autumn 1984), p. 89ff.

13. McFarlane's letter to Shultz is reprinted in *Assessment of U.S.–Unesco Relations, 1984,* Report of a Staff Study Mission to Paris-Unesco, to the Committee on Foreign Affairs, U.S. House of Representatives (Washington, D.C.: Government Printing Office, January 1985), p. 33.

14. Associated Press, 15 February 1984.

15. U.S. Department of State, "U.S./Unesco Policy Review" and "Executive Summary of U.S./Unesco Policy Review" (Washington, D.C., 29 February 1984).

16. "The Case of the Revolving Report, or Who Peeped at the Purloined Letters," *Chronicle of International Communication,* 5, no. 1 (January–February 1984).

17. *U.S. Withdrawal from Unesco,* Report of a Staff Study Mission, February 10–23, 1984, to the Committee on Foreign Affairs, U.S. House of Representatives (Washington, D.C.: Government Printing Office, April 1984).

18. *Congressional Record,* 98th Congress, 2nd session, 9 May 1984, p. H3644.

19. *New York Times,* 1 March 1984.

20. The texts of the letters were released to the media in Unesco Press Information Note No. 13 (Paris, 7 March 1984) and United Nations press release UNESCO/2451 (New York, 7 March 1984).

21. United Press International, 2 March 1984.

22. United Press International, 14 March 1984.

23. Oversight Hearings on Unesco, Subcommittee on Natural Resources, Agriculture Research and Environment, Committee on Science and Technology, U.S. House of Representatives, 8 March 1984.

24. *Congressional Record,* 98th Congress, 2nd session, 9 May 1984, p. H3646.

25. Hearing on Impact on U.S. Scientific Research of Proposal to Withdraw

from Unesco, Subcommittee on Science, Research and Technology, joint with Subcommittee on Natural Resources, Agriculture Research and Environment, U.S. House of Representatives, 15 March 1984.

26. *Washington Post,* 15 March 1984.
27. *New York Times,* 15 March 1984.
28. Associated Press, 22 March 1984.
29. Associated Press, 24 March 1984.
30. Unesco Press Information Note No. 7 (Paris, Septmeber 1984).
31. Ibid.
32. United Press International, 6 April 1984.
33. *New York Times,* 6 April 1984.
34. Associated Press, 9 April 1984. The text of M'Bow's remarks was released by Unesco Press, No. 29-LD (Paris, April 1984).
35. "U.S. Withdrawal from Unesco," Hearings before the Subcommittee on Human Rights and International Organizations, joint with the Subcommittee on International Operations, Committee on Foreign Affairs, U.S. House of Representatives, 25, 26 April and 2 May, 1984.
36. United Nations press releases UNESCO/2453 and UNESCO/2455 (New York, 10 and 17 May 1984) and UNESCO press release (Paris, 10 May 1984).
37. Associated Press, 23 May 1984.
38. United Nations press release UNESCO/2458 (New York, 23 May 1984).
39. The nations represented on the committee were Algeria, Brazil, the United Kingdom, France, Guinea, Iceland, India, Jamaica, Japan, Nigeria, the Soviet Union, Tunisia and Yugoslavia.
40. Associated Press, 21 May 1984.
41. *New York Times,* 2 May 1984.
42. *New York Times,* 29 May 1984.
43. *Los Angeles Times,* 21 June 1984.
44. *New York Times,* 1 July 1984.
45. Unesco Press Information Note No. 7 (Paris, September 1984).
46. Newell's letter is reprinted in "Recent Developments in Unesco and Their Implications for U.S. Policy," Hearings before the Subcommittee on Human Rights and International Organizations, joint with the Subcommittee on International Operations, Committee on Foreign Affairs, U.S. House of Representatives, 26 July 1984.
47. The letter from the Netherlands Government is reprinted in "Recent Developments in Unesco," 26 July 1984.
48. "Recent Developments in Unesco and Their Implications for U.S. Policy," Hearings before the Subcommittee on Human Rights and International Organizations, joint with the Subcommittee on International Operations, Committee on Foreign Affairs, U.S. House of Representatives, 26 July 1984.
49. *Peninsula Times Tribune,* Palo Alto, 23 July 1984.
50. U.S. National Commission for UNESCO, *What Are the Issues Concerning the Decision of the United States to Withdraw from Unesco?* (New York, August 1984), p. 25.

51. *New York Times,* 8 August 1984.
52. *New York Times,* 15 August 1984.
53. United Press International, 16 August 1984.
54. Associated Press, 16 August 1984.
55. *New York Times,* 2 September 1984.
56. "Unesco Retains Public Affairs Counsel," press release, Wagner & Baroody, 7 August 1984.
57. *Los Angeles Times,* 22 September 1984.
58. *New York Times,* 7 September 1984.
59. Associated Press, 9 September 1984.
60. *Los Angeles Times,* 13 September 1984.
61. "Recent Developments in Unesco and Their Implications for U.S. Policy," Hearings before the Subcommittee on Human Rights and International Organizations, joint with the Subcommittee on International Operations, Committee on Foreign Affairs, U.S. House of Representatives, 13 September 1984.
62. Associated Press, 19 September 1984.
63. *New York Times,* 20 September 1984.
64. U.S. General Accounting Office draft report, "Review of Unesco's Management, Budget and Personnel Practices" (Washington, D.C., 17 September 1984).
65. *New York Times,* 22 September 1984.
66. Unesco News, UNESCO/NYO, 28 September 1984.
67. Unesco News, UNESCO/NYO/84-9d (New York, 26 September 1984).
68. United Press International, 26 September 1984.
69. Associated Press, 26 September 1984.
70. *New York Times,* 27 September 1984.
71. United Nations press release UNESCO/2460 (New York, 28 September 1984).
72. *New York Times,* 28 September 1984.
73. United Press International, 28 September 1984.
74. *New York Times,* 27 September 1984.
75. Associated Press, 28 September 1984.
76. Unesco press release "Member Nations Praise Unesco Reforms," 1 October 1984.
77. United Press International, 5 October 1984.
78. United Press International, 10 October 1984.
79. *New York Times,* 8 October 1984.
80. United Press International, 10 October 1984.
81. Associated Press, 15 October 1984.
82. United Nations press release UNESCO/2463 (New York, 11 October 1984).
83. Associated Press, 9 October 1984.
84. Associated Press, 13 October 1984.
85. *New York Times,* 19 October 1984.
86. *New York Times,* 23 October 1984.
87. Reuter, 23 October 1984.
88. United Nations press release UNESCO/2465 (New York, 22 October 1984).

89. U.S. General Accounting Office, "Improvements Needed in Unesco's Management, Personnel, Financial, and Budgeting Techniques," GAO/NSIAD-85–32 (Washington, D.C., 30 November 1984).
90. The text of M'Bow's comments on the GAO Report was obtained from the Unesco Liaison Office in New York.
91. *Washington Post,* 21 November 1984.
92. *New York Times,* 22 November 1984.
93. Unesco press release "British Announce Intention to Withdraw from Unesco," (New York, 23 November 1984).
94. Unesco press release UNESCO/NYO/84-11C (New York, 26 November 1984).
95. *Washington Post,* 30 November 1984.
96. *New York Times,* 4 December 1984.
97. *Washington Post,* 5 December 1984.
98. "Recent Developments in Unesco and Their Implications for U.S. Policy," Hearings before the Subcommittee on Human Rights and International Organizations, joint with the Subcommittee on International Operations, Committee on Foreign Affairs, U.S. House of Representatives, 6 December 1984.
99. "Human Resources Impact of U.S. Membership in Unesco," Senate Committee on Labor and Human Resources, 10 December 1984.
100. Associated Press, 10 December 1984.
101. Associated Press, 13 December 1984.
102. *Washington Post,* 13 December 1984.
103. *Washington Post,* 14 December 1984.
104. *New York Times,* 19 December 1984.
105. Unesco press release No. 94 (Paris, 20 December 1984).

CHAPTER 4

The News Agencies

Our experience has been that when government officials, even those elected in a democratic process, control news reporting there is an overwhelming tendency to portray the government and its actions favorably and to discredit opposing viewpoints.
— *Jerry W. Friedheim, general manager, ANPA*

METHOD OF ANALYSIS

What follows is a quantitative and qualitative analysis of five types of coverage of the withdrawal:

1. Reports transmitted by the Associated Press, United Press International, the New York Times News Service, and the Washington Post/Los Angeles Times News Service
2. Reports that appeared in the press from these sources
3. Newspaper editorials
4. Columnists, syndicated or otherwise
5. Network television evening news broadcasts

The period covered in this content analysis is from December 1983, when the United States announced its intention to withdraw from Unesco, to December 1984 when the withdrawal formally took place. Material for the analysis was obtained from several sources. Reports from the four news agencies that provided the bulk of the coverage were obtained

from the wire services sent to metropolitan newspapers. Material that actually appeared in the press was collected by a commercial clipping agency, Press Intelligence, Inc., of Washington, over the period from December 1983 through December 1984. Press Intelligence clips about 1,400 daily papers, about 4,000 weeklies and most trade publications. It also subscribes to 29 regional clipping services. It claims comprehensiveness for U.S. print media. The clippings file yielded almost 4,000 published news stories, editorials and columns about the Unesco withdrawal over the year. Its coverage was checked by matching the clippings it collected with files in two newspaper libraries, one in Seattle and one in San Francisco, and with the Index to the *New York Times*. Everything in those files was clipped by the service. Comparison of the Press Intelligence items with those of a competing clippings service, however, indicates that in some instances the number of items that appeared in smaller newspapers may have been underestimated. About 2 percent of the clippings had to be discarded because they were duplicates or because their labels were illegible. Material for analysis of the television news reports came from videotapes, from the Vanderbilt University Television News Index and Abstracts, and from transcripts of CBS News programs.

Two kinds of analysis were used. First, in order to determine the extent of the coverage, every agency report, every newspaper story, editorial and column was entered into a computer data base, with fields specifying the date of publication, the name and circulation of the newspaper, the city and state in which it is published, the source, and the first sentence of the item. This made it possible to sort the random order of the clippings files to determine patterns of coverage. Articles in the data base could be sorted on any combination of fields. Matching the first sentences, for example, allowed researchers to check how many papers carried a specific news report even if the source was not given in some newspapers. Likewise, each newspaper's total coverage of the withdrawal could be determined, as could the coverage in a given city, state or region.

Second, a large sample of each type of article was analyzed to determine the orientation of their coverage. In the case of the television coverage, all 13 news reports broadcast over the year were analyzed. The unit of analysis was the theme. Any statement of fact or any assertion about Unesco was treated as a theme. Thus a sentence in a news report asserting that "American officials blasted the agency's deepening involvement in political activities prejudicial to the West and favorable to Marxist countries" would be coded as having three themes: (1) that Unesco was politicized, (2) that it was anti-West, and (3) that it was pro-Soviet. The source for each would be "U.S. officials." Altogether 189 different themes were identified.

The 189 themes were aggregated into successively larger categories for analysis. First, the individual themes were clustered into one of 16 different topics. Thus such themes as overspending, poor personnel practices, inefficiency and complaints that too much was spent on the bureaucracy were combined into a topic called Mismanagement. Themes asserting that Unesco was anti-Western, anti-American, anti-Israeli, pro-Soviet and pro–states rights, among others, were aggregated into the topic Politicization. On the other hand, themes asserting that the United States should not withdraw, that it would be a mistake to do so, that the pullout was not in the national interest, that it should work for reform from within, among others, were combined in the topic Criticism of Withdrawal.

Finally, the topics were combined into one of three categories we have called orientations. The first, Anti-Unesco/Pro-withdrawal, contains all the criticisms of Unesco and its officials or programs, plus expressions of support for the pullout. The second, Pro-Unesco/Anti-withdrawal, includes all expressions of support for Unesco, for the value of its programs, and also opposition to the withdrawal. The third category, Looking Ahead, focused on what would happen next. This category included issues relating to the future of Unesco, the future U.S. relationship with Unesco, and alternative programs proposed by the United States in lieu of participation in Unesco.

For the most part there was no difficulty in assigning items to the different categories. One possible exception was mentions of the fact that the United States paid 25 percent of Unesco's budget. This was coded as being anti-Unesco, because it was often reported in the context of statements to the effect that the United States was not getting value for its money, that U.S. funds were being used against its own interests, or that the one who paid the piper should call the tune.

The reports were coded also to identify the date on which they appeared, the dateline, the agency, the reporter (if identified; otherwise the report was attributed to the agency as such), and the source quoted for each thematic statement. The sources, in turn, were clustered into larger categories we called "origins." Statements attributed to related sources, like a U.S. State Department official, or to "the Reagan administration" or simply to "American officials," were included in the origin, "U.S. Government." Other typical origins, derived from clusters of sources, included "Western Governments" (excluding the United States), the "Soviet Bloc," and the "Third World." Non-government organizations (NGOs,) like the Heritage Foundation, Freedom House, the B'nai B'rith and academic and scientific organizations like the National Academy of Sciences were grouped into the origin "U.S. NGOs."

This technique enabled us to analyze the coverage at different levels,

from the very general (orientation) to the specific (theme), and to do cross-tabulations of any of the coded variables with each other. The data were analyzed at the University of Washington's Center for Social Science Computation and Research. Coding was done by graduate students in the School of Communications at the University of Washington. Inter-coder reliability, after training, was better than 80 percent. All reported findings are significant at the 0.05 level or better.

AGENCY COVERAGE

News-agency coverage was analyzed from a sample of agency reports received by metropolitan newspapers over the year. The sample comprised about half the reports transmitted to newspaper subscribers in the United States. It included 54 reports from the Associated Press, 56 from United Press International, 44 from the New York Times News Service, and 19 from the Washington Post/L.A. Times News Service. The 173 news agency reports in the sample yielded a total of 1,945 themes, an average of about 11 themes each.

Most of the agency reports were filed in December 1983, when the United States gave Unesco notice of its intention to withdraw, and in December 1984, when it confirmed that decision. These two months between them accounted for one-half of all the reports filed. The third peak period for agency coverage was March 1984, when Unesco agreed to permit the General Accounting Office to examine its records, and Rep. James Scheuer told a press conference of rumors that files were being destroyed. March also was the month in when 24 Western nations submitted their "Crisis in Unesco" paper calling for reforms. These events were was covered by all the agencies. The biggest news story that month, however, was the arson fire at Unesco headquarters on March 21; it was covered in several agency reports. November had the fourth highest number of agency reports, largely because that was when the United Kingdom gave notice that it also planned to withdraw, and the final version of the GAO report was released.

The fifth-biggest news month was September 1984. It opened with a flurry of reports about Unesco hiring a Washington public relations firm to improve its image. Soon after, the report by 21 present and former Unesco staff members entitled "The Critical Analysis of the Program" was leaked to the press and enjoyed wide encoverage. Then, as Unesco's Executive Board met in Paris to discuss reforms, copies of the draft GAO report that criticized Unesco as inefficient and badly managed were also leaked to the press.

Lesser peaks in the coverage came in April, when the United King-

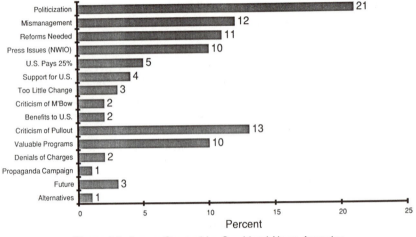

Figure 4.1. Issues Covered by Combined News Agencies

dom first announced that it might join the United States in withdrawing, and in May, when the Unesco Executive Board met and there was a dispute over whether the United States would still have to pay Unesco dues in 1985 even if it withdrew at the end of 1984.

CONTENT ANALYSIS

Taken as a whole, news-agency coverage was strongly anti-Unesco and supportive of the U.S. withdrawal. More than two thirds of the themes were critical of Unesco; only a quarter were favorable toward the agency and critical of the withdrawal. A small proportion focused on the future. The first column in Table 4.1 shows the combined coverage for all four agencies over the entire year.

Anti-Unesco/Pro-Withdrawal

Politicization. Of the themes critical of Unesco, the most common complaint was that the agency was politicized (Table 4.2). This issue included general assertions of politicization; statements that Unesco was anti-Western, anti-American and anti-Israel, and that it supported the enemies of Western values. Thus, for example, on December 12, 1983, UPI quoted State Department spokesman John Hughes as saying that Unesco "seems to be incredibly partisan and opposed to the forces of freedom, and certainly to the United States." Newell was quoted by the agencies in

December 1984 as accusing Unesco of "extraneous politicization" and of "endemic hostility" towards the institutions of a free society.

Mismanagement. The second-largest cluster of criticisms centered on allegations of mismanagement, both financial and organizational. The topic "mismanagement" included themes relating to increases, mismanagement and inefficiency in Unesco's budget; references to the General Accounting Office audit that criticized Unesco in this regard, and allegations that too much was spent on bureaucracy. Also included in this issue were criticisms of Unesco's organization: that it was too bureaucratic, that its staff was concentrated in Paris, and that it favored Third World personnel. Other criticisms under this heading included rumors that Unesco staff had destroyed files before the GAO review. Thus a UPI report quoted Rep. James Scheuer on March 2, 1984, as saying "we have heard rumors that files are being destroyed" and quoted "diplomats" as saying a preliminary inquiry had turned up "outrageous" evidence of inefficiency and mismanagement in Unesco.

Reforms Needed. The third-ranked issue critical of Unesco concerned the need for reform and demands that it should mend its ways. Most of the themes relating to the need for reform were stated in very general terms—the United States would withdraw unless there was "significant" or "radical" change. Britain was reported to have told M'Bow that it "is increasingly difficult to justify our membership in Unesco unless we can point to real improvement in its operations." Newell, according to a *New York Times* report, told a press conference in Abidjan, Nory Coast, that the United States was not seeking any specific measures. "The U.S. has never presented a laundry list, nor would we," he said. Also included in this category were references to the "Crisis in Unesco" paper, drawn up by the 24 Western nations that called for reforms in the agency. Among these was a proposal that Unesco's voting system be amended to give Western contributors greater control over how their money was spent.

Other themes in the "reforms needed" category were more specific as to what Unesco should or should not do. It would, for example, have to improve its management and efficiency, select staff on the basis of merit, hold fewer meetings and publish fewer documents, and take "practical" steps to implement its charter. On the other hand, it would have to stop politicizing issues, stop supporting government control of news media, become less ideological, stop its "diatribes," stop attacking Western values, and curb its bureaucratic growth. Regarding reforms related to the New World Information Order, Unesco would have to stop attacking Western press values and the free flow of information, and quit backing state control of media.

Press Issues. The fourth-largest category comprised press issues. Here Unesco was accused of supporting a New World Information Order, of favoring state control of media systems, of wanting to license journalists and impose codes of conduct on the press. On the other hand, it was said to be opposed to press freedom, and to a free flow of news and information. For example, an AP report said that Unesco had supported a new information order "which Western news media and governments see as threatening the freedom of Western journalists and as being an international charter for government press controls."

These three issues—politicization, mismanagement and press matters—together accounted for almost one-half of all the themes critical of Unesco. They often appeared in a single paragraph by way of explanation of the withdrawal. Thus, for example, an AP report on May 18 noted that "in announcing late last year that it would leave Unesco, the United States said Unesco was hostile to Western concepts of a free press and free market. It also said Unesco was increasingly politicized and did not restrain expenditure." There was, however, seldom a corresponding paragraph indicating that these allegations were in dispute.

Too Little Change. Related to the demands for change were themes asserting that although some reforms were promised or occurring, they were too little, and too late, to make the United States change its mind. U.S. Ambassador to Unesco Jean Gerard was quoted by the New York Times News Service and by AP on September 28 as expressing dismay at "how little has actually changed." Many papers carried agency reports of Newell's press conference of December 19, 1984, when he announced that the United States would go ahead with its withdrawal, because "the circumstances that impelled us last year to announce our plan to withdraw have not changed sufficiently this year to warrant a change in our decision." Jean Gerard was quoted by UPI in December 1984 as saying that "I do feel that while there were changes, they were not satisfactory. And Newell was reported as telling a Senate subcommittee on December 6 that reforms made by Unesco "fall short of those needed to reverse the U.S. decision."

Criticism of M'Bow. Director General M'Bow was the target of some personal criticism. He was accused of being anti-American and anti-Israel, and conversely of being pro-Soviet and pro–Third World. He also was accused of mismanagement, of favoring Third World personnel, and of corruption. But criticism of M'Bow himself was far less frequent than attacks on Unesco as an institution. This apparently reflected a State Department policy not to attack M'Bow personally. Some observers suggested that the reason for this policy was that Third World nations

might have interpreted attacks on M'Bow (a Senegalese) as racially motivated, and that this would have pulled defenses around him. Others took a more cynical view. The State Department, some columnists wrote, did not want to force M'Bow out of office because that would have provided a rationale for continued U.S. membership.

United States Pays 25 Percent. More than one-half of the reports mentioned that the United States paid 25 percent of Unesco's budget, and several suggested that the Western nations who provided the bulk of the funds were not getting value for their money. For example, an AP news analysis noted that voting in Unesco was not weighed by monetary contributions. "As a consequence, the U.S. has found iteself paying the piper while the Third World majority picks the tune." Other reports complained that American funds were used to support programs opposed to its interests or for projects in countries hostile to the United States. An AP report in December 1984 said that Reagan was pulling out of Unesco "because it was felt the interests of certain Western nations were being ignored even though the United States was financing 25 percent of Unesco's budget."

Benefits to United States. America's departure was seen as an impetus for reform and as a warning to other international organizations that they had better toe the line. It was argued that the pullout would force Unesco to prioritize its programs and eliminate undesirable ones. Some sources were quoted as saying that it was in America's best interest to withdraw because it would then no longer be perceived as lending authority and legitimacy to Unesco.

Support for United States. These critical themes were given credence by references to support for the U.S. position from other governments. The British withdrawal was reported by all four agencies. Other reports stated that the Netherlands, Japan and West Germany, among others, were reconsidering their membership. On December 28, 1983, for instance, UPI quoted a West German government spokesman as saying that Germany agreed with many of the U.S. criticisms of Unesco, including its finances and its attempts to "restrict the freedom of information" around the world. Later, there were reports that Singapore had decided to withdraw. The Soviet Union was usually quoted as opposing the withdrawal but agreeing with the United States that Unesco's budget needed to be trimmed. One reason for the preponderance of negative themes was that a large proportion of the reports included a paragraph giving as background the information that the United States was withdrawing be-

cause Unesco was politicized, mismanaged, anti-West and anti–free press.

U.S. Credibility at Stake. As the time approached for a final decision, some sources—chiefly in the State Department and the Heritage Foundation—were quoted as saying that the United States would lose its credibility if it changed its mind and did not proceed as planned. Newell, for example, was quoted by AP and UPI on December 10, 1984, as saying that a one-year postponement of the withdrawal had been considered but rejected because "there are sound reasons to believe that such a course would only strike at U.S. credibility."

Pro-Unesco/Anti-Withdrawal

Themes supportive of Unesco appeared far less frequently. They fell into two main categories: those that criticized the United States for withdrawing and those that defended Unesco. The defenses, in turn, comprised two clusters of themes: denials of allegations made against the agency, and affirmations as to the value of its programs.

Criticism of Pullout. A substantial number of themes related to criticism of the U.S. action, whether direct or implied. The largest group concerned the disadvantages to the United States of the pullout. Here the most frequent theme was that the United States would better serve its interests by remaining a member of Unesco and working for reform from within. The New York Times News Service, for example, on August 8 quoted members of the U.S. National Commision for Unesco as arguing that although the organization had serious faults, "strong American leadership within the organization could lead to reforms." The pullout was seen as politically naive in that it deprived the U.S. of a voice in the agency. There were several references to American groups, particularly scientists, who stood to lose international contacts and access to information. The New York Times service reported on May 29 that members of the American Association for the Advancement of Science had "expressed the opinion that there will be serious scientific consequences if the U.S. carries out its proposal to withdraw." On the day the withdrawal was confirmed, the New York Times carried a sidebar to the main report noting that "American scientists, scholars and cultual organizations stand to lose significant benefits through the abandonment of Unesco membership."

A second cluster of themes critical of the withdrawal concerned expressions of regret at the decision, and references to attempts to keep the

United States in Unesco. Several of the reports mentioned the suggestion that the United States delay its withdrawal by one year to give Unesco more time to effect reforms. Also included in criticisms of the withdrawal were themes relating to the impact of the pullout on Unesco. The most common was that it would undermine the agency's utility and universality. On April 10, UPI quoted Jean-Pierre Cot, a French member of Unesco's Executive Board, as saying that "the walkout is against the principle of universality. All major Western governments must participate in international organizations." And an AP report in September quoted Unesco's deputy director general Gerard Bolla as saying that Unesco would be "gravely hampered in its work if the U.S. pulled out." The Netherlands ambassador to Unesco told the AP that the withdrawal could plunge Unesco into a crisis "from which it might not recover for many years to come." There was, however, virtually no mention of the effect that the loss of U.S. funding would have on Unesco programs in the Third World.

Valuable Programs. The affirmations included themes to the effect that Unesco was trying to implement reforms and that it was improving its management and budgetary procedures. Useful programs were mentioned, including Unesco's role in promoting education, science and culture, and its work in facilitating Third World development. Often, however, news reports that mentioned Unesco's useful programs suggested that they were a thing of the past and that since the agency had been taken over by the Soviets and Third World, these programs had been neglected or perverted. International support for the agency— mostly from the Soviet Union and France—was mentioned only half as often as support for the United States position from other Western governments.

Denials of Charges. Several themes concerned denials that the agency was mismanaged, politicized or opposed to press freedom. For example, a UPI report on January 19 quoted Unesco's assistant secretary general Henri Lopes as saying that the United States had provided no details of its complaints and that that some critical news reports were "a tissue of lies, often tendentious and sometimes slanderous." And M'Bow complained in an AP dispatch on October 5 of a campaign of "systematic denigration, insult and calumny." Some reports pointed out that only a few programs were politicized. These denials, however, were outnumbered by criticisms on these issues in the ratio of 20 to 1.

Propaganda Campaign. Another topic coded as being pro-Unesco had to do with allegations that the pullout was politically inspired—a result of

pressures from the New Right, and specifically the conservative Heritage Foundation. An AP report of December 27, 1984, noted, for instance, that the State Department's allegations against Unesco of budget mismanagement and anti-Americanism were "consistent with the views" of the Heritage Foundation. Critics of the withdrawal were also quoted as alleging that the United States was mounting a deliberate propaganda campaign against Unesco and its director general. UPI quoted M'Bow in March as denying the "baseless accusations" against Unesco, which he said were part of a "smear campaign." The *New York Times* reported that Leonard Sussman had told a press conference in New York on August 8 that the Reagan administration had used "misleading tactics" and "distorted information" to support its decision.

Looking Ahead

Future. A relatively small number of themes focused not on the pro- or anti-Unesco arguments, but on the issue of what would happen next. These included the future of the U.S. relationship with Unesco, the future of Unesco itself, and possible alternatives to Unesco programs. More than one-half of these concerned the United States. There were statements that the United States may get back in and that it would continue to strive for reforms even after pulling out. Some officials were quoted as saying that Unesco would survive the cut in funds and that it would continue to promote a New World Information Order.

Alternatives. A handful of themes dealt with using funds that would have been allocated to Unesco for other educational, scientific and cultural projects, although nothing specific was proposed. Newell told UPI in December 1984 that the United States would divert its annual contribution to Unesco to other cultural, educational and scientific projects to help developing countries.

INTER-AGENCY VARIATIONS

A remarkable feature of the coverage by the different agencies was their similarity (Figure 4.2). The AP, New York Times News Service and Washington Post/L.A. Times service all carried almost identical proportions of pro- and anti-Unesco themes, with 72 percent supportive of the withdrawal. UPI was marginally less critical, but two-thirds of its themes were anti-Unesco and in favor of the withdrawal.

Within that general orientation they all stressed the same issues:

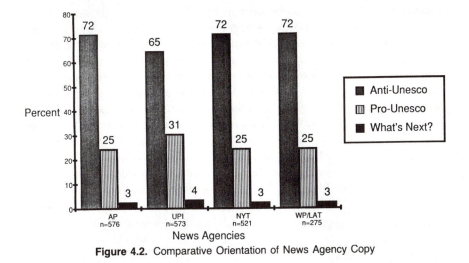

Figure 4.2. Comparative Orientation of News Agency Copy

Politicization, mismanagement, the need for reform and press issues were mentioned most frequently (Table 4.2). The AP coverage came closest to the mean in this respect. These four themes alone accounted for 55 percent of its coverage. Only a quarter of the themes reported by the AP were supportive of Unesco or critical of the withdrawal.

The New York Times and Washington Post services' coverage was very similar to that of the AP. The New York Times was most critical of Unesco's politicization and also placed a strong emphasis on the need for reform. Sixty percent of the New York Times coverage related to politicization, the need for reform, mismanagement and press issues. As in the case of the AP, only 25 percent of the New York Times themes supported Unesco.

The themes mentioned most frequently by the Washington Post were politicization and the need for reform. The Post was less concerned with Unesco's communications policies than the other agencies. It was, however, proportionately twice as critical of M'Bow's leadership than the others, quoting sources accusing him of being anti-Western and calling for his resignation. The top four issues accounted for 53 percent of the Post's news coverage.

UPI differed from the others in that it was significantly less critical and more supportive of Unesco. It was the least critical of Unesco's politicization and management and, conversely, the most critical of the withdrawal. Nevertheless, almost two-thirds of the themes it reported were anti-Unesco.

REPORTERS

Three-quarters of the reports on the four wires came from just 13 sources: those carried by the AP, UPI and the New York Times without a byline, plus those attributed to 10 named correspondents. Nearly half of the reports in the sample from the AP had no byline. Most of the remainder came from two AP correspondents: Harry Dunphy filing from Paris, and Morris W. Rosenberg from Washington. Two-thirds of the anonymous reports also came from Paris, and it is likely that many of those also were written by Dunphy. More than half of the UPI reports had no byline. Most of those that did have a credit were from Aline Mosby in Paris and J. J. Nguyen at the United Nations in New York. All but 16 percent of the New York Times News Service reports in the sample carried bylines. The Times relied on Paul Lewis in Paris for nearly a third of its reports. Also filing from Paris were E. J. Dionne, Jr., and occasionally Richard Bernstein. Most of its reports with a Washington dateline were filed by B. Drummond Ayres and Bernard Gwertzman. These reports together comprise 70 percent of the New York Times themes in the sample. All of the Washington Post reports had bylines. Walter Pincus and Joanne Omang filing from Washington, and Michael Dobbs from Paris, account for two-thirds of the service's coverage.

The major reporters, without exception, were more critical than supportive of Unesco (Table 4.3). At least 65 percent of the themes reported by the major correspondents for all four agencies were hostile toward Unesco. Only Nguyen of UPI came close to balanced coverage, although the reports carried by UPI without a byline also were comparatively even-handed. Nguyen's reports, however, do not appear to have been printed by a single newspaper.

Among the top ten bylined repoters, there was a remarkable degree of unanimity. If one ranks the issues each reported, all 10 had both politicization and mismanagement in their top five categories (Table 4.4). They also emphasized press issues and the need for reform. Several reported a substantial number of criticisms of the withdrawal, and statements supporting Unesco programs. These were, however, outweighed by their overall criticism of Unesco's performance.

The correspondents filing from Paris sent reports with a very similar thematic profile. Apart from a common emphasis on mismanagement and politicization, they put a heavy stress on the need for reform. The Washington correspondents, while also stressing mismanagement and politicization, were less concerned with the need for reform. The reports from New York, while similar in their criticisms, were far more likely than those from other centers to quote critics of the pullout and affirmations of the value of Unesco programs. Only Nguyen, filing for UPI from

the United Nations in New York, put more emphasis on the value of Unesco programs, and denials that it was guilty as charged, than on criticisms of the agency.

The reports that did not carry individual bylines differed from those that did in some significant respects. The AP and UPI reports with only an agency credit were more likely to criticize Unesco's politicization and New World Information Order activities than those from named correspondents.

One might have expected that reporters filing from Washington, where they were usually quoting U.S. government officials, would have been more antagonistic toward Unesco than those filing from Unesco headquarters in Paris. Not so. In many cases the agencies' Paris correspondents took the harder line (Table 4.3). For the AP, Dunphy in Paris was more critical than Rosenberg in Washington. UPI correspondent Mosby in Paris was more critical than other UPI reporters. For the New York Times, Lewis in Paris and Gwertzman in Washington were strongly, and about equally, opposed to Unesco. Ayres, filing from Washington, was the New York Times reporter least critical of Unesco—although his critical themes outnumbered supportive ones in the ratio of 3 to 1. Dobbs, covering Unesco for the Washington Post from Paris, was less critical than Pincus in Washington, but more so than Omang, also in Washington.

Taken as a whole, the reports from Paris were the most critical of Unesco (Table 4.5). Nearly three-quarters of the themes from correspondents there were critical. They tended to emphasize mismanagement and the need for reform more than those from other centers. There also was more personal criticism of M'Bow. The Paris reports carried proportionately little criticism of the pullout.

Reports filed from Washington were marginally less critical than those with a Paris dateline. They stressed the issue of politicization and tended to put more emphasis than those from other centers on what would happen next. The reports filed from New York came closest to giving equal weight to themes supportive and critical of Unesco. These reports differed from those filed elsewhere chiefly in their high proportion of criticisms and expressions of regret at the withdrawal, and support for Unesco programs. This is partly due to the fact that many of the U.S. organizations that opposed the withdrawal did so at press conferences in New York. Unesco's information office in New York was also active in submitting material to the press. The New York reports also included statements from the United Nations that generally were critical of the pullout. The reports filed from London appear to have been the most hawkish of all, but the data are too limited to be reliable.

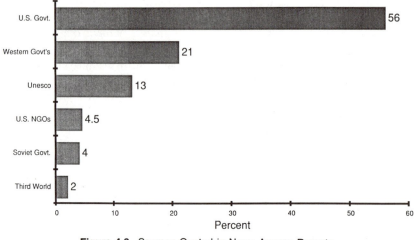

Figure 4.3. Sources Quoted in News Agency Reports

SOURCES

Given the apparent imbalance in coverage of the pro- and anti-Unesco arguments, it is instructive to examine the sources quoted in the news-agency reports (Figure 4.3). Three-quarters of the themes were attributed to a specific source; the rest were simply statements of fact by the reporters with no attribution.

Of the themes that were attributed to specific sources, more than half were from various spokesmen for the U.S. government (first column, Table 4.6). The sources quoted most frequently were officials of the U.S. State Department, who together comprised one-fifth of all sources. Another fifth were attributions to spokesmen for "the U.S. government," "the Reagan administration," "U.S. officials," or simply "Washington."

The second-largest group of sources comprised representatives of various Western governments, who together accounted for another fifth of this group. Spokesmen for the British government, which had also announced its intention to withdraw from Unesco, were quoted most often, followed by France (which opposed the pullout), West Germany and the Netherlands. It is likely that some of the sources identified in dispatches from European capitals as "Western diplomats" or "Western officials" were in fact Americans speaking on condition they not be identified. That would further increase the preponderance of U.S. government sources.

Unesco sources, including M'Bow, accounted for just over one-tenth of the total. The Soviet government, and spokesmen for various Third World governments, each contributed less than 5 percent of the attributions. Non-government organizations in the United States with an interest in Unesco programs, like Freedom House, the Heritage Foundation, the B'nai B'rith, and academic groups like the National Academy of Sciences, were even less visible. Taken together, Western sources comprised 81 percent of the total attributions. Unesco sources (including dissidents) accounted for 13 percent, the Soviet Union for 4 percent, and Third World for 2 percent.

All four agencies relied primarily on official U.S. sources for their information (Table 4.6). The Washington Post, with nearly 80 percent of its attributed statements coming from U.S. government spokesmen, appeared to reflect most closely the official position. Only UPI attributed less than one-half of its thematic statements to U.S. government sources. If one includes spokesmen for other Western governments, then the AP, the New York Times and the Washington Post all relied on Western government sources for more than three-quarters of their attributions. Add the Soviet Union and a handful of Third World governments, and the reliance on government sources rises to above 80 percent for all three. The combined figure for the Washington Post was 91 percent. UPI drew two-thirds of its attributed statements from Western government spokesmen, and three-quarters from government officials as a whole. Sources used by the main reporters appear in Table 4.7.

Orientation of News Sources

Since the sources quoted by the reporters clearly had their own agendas, it is instructive also to analyze their orientation to Unesco (Figure 4.4). U.S. government sources, who provided by far the bulk of the attributed statements, were also the most critical of Unesco at 82 percent pro-withdrawal (Table 4.8). Western government spokesmen were not far behind. Three-qarters of the themes attributed to them were anti-Unesco or favored the U.S. withdrawal. As might be expected, Unesco sources were largely favorable toward the agency, although the views of some disaffected staffers were reported. But Unesco sources were not quoted nearly as often as U.S. and Western government spokesmen, and so had little impact on the overall orientation of the coverage. Two-thirds of the themes attributed to the Soviet government were supportive of Unesco and critical of the withdrawal. The criticisms of Unesco attributed to the Soviets generally had to do with the need to curb its budget.

Themes attributed to Third World figures, and to spokesmen for

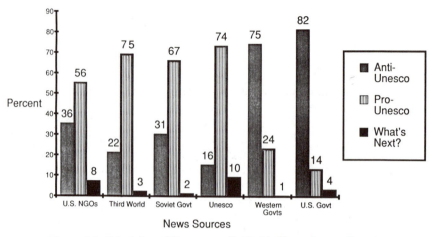

Figure 4.4. Orientation of Sources as Quoted in News Agency Reports

U.S. academic organizations, were chiefly supportive of Unesco, but were too infrequent in the sample to be statistically significant.

Clear differences emerged in the themes attributed to U.S. government spokesmen and those from other sources. For U.S. officials, the most common criticism by far was politicization, followed by allegations of mismanagement, the need for reform, and communications issues (Table 4.9). They also depicted Unesco as being unwilling to undertake meaningful reforms, or of doing too little too late. The criticisms of the withdrawal voiced by U.S. officials comprised for the most part expressions of regret that it was necessary. The affirmations were acknowledgment that Unesco had some useful programs.

Western government spokesmen were quoted most often in the context of statements that they too might pull out if Unesco did not change its ways, and when supporting the U.S. position. Criticisms of Unesco's communications activities came next, followed by charges of politicization. Western government spokesmen were more likely to express criticisms of the withdrawal (especially the French) or regret at the decision, than U.S. officials.

Unesco sources were highly critical of the pullout, spoke strongly in favor of Unesco programs, and denied that politicization, mismanagement or press issues were a problem. They also asserted that the West, and particularly the United States, was waging a propaganda campaign against Unesco and its director general. The news agencies, however, also

reported Unesco officials who criticized its management and programs, and critical internal documents that were leaked to the press.

Non-Attributed Themes

In some significant respects, themes attributed to specific sources differed from those that were not. Taken as a whole, the themes not attributed to a source tended to be more critical of Unesco than those that were (Table 4.10). Thus, of the 334 themes in the sample that were not attributed, 73 percent were anti-Unesco. Of the 1,512 themes that were attributed, 68 percent were anti-Unesco. The unattributed themes were more likely to stress politicization and press issues than the attributed ones, and far less likely to express criticism of the withdrawal. Conversely, however, the unattributed themes were proportionately higher in affirmations as to the value of Unesco programs. This was usually because of "background" information in some reports noting that Unesco carries out educational, scientific and cultural programs.

The AP was the most likely to run themes critical of Unesco without attribution. About 83 percent of its unattributed themes were anti-Unesco or pro-withdrawal, while 69 percent of its attributed themes had that orientation. Criticisms of Unesco's press policies were proportionately higher in the AP's unattributed themes than attributed ones (24 percent to 9 percent) as were allegations of politicization and statements of support for the U.S. position.

CHANGES OVER TIME

The bulk of the news coverage occurred in December 1983, when the United States announced it intended to withdraw, and in December 1984 when it formallly did so. A comparison of the themes reported in those two months shows a change in emphasis over time. The strongly anti-Unesco coverage of the first period moderates somewhat in the second. For the combined agencies, the proportion of anti-Unesco themes drops from about three-quarters in 1983 to about two-thirds in 1984 (Table 4.11). There is a corresponding increase in the second period of themes supportive of Unesco or critical of the withdrawal, and in themes relating to what might happen next.

Charges relating to politicization, press issues and mismanagement are significantly less frequent in December 1984, but there are more reports of support for the U.S. position, and assertions that Unesco had not changed enough for the United States to remain a member. There also is significantly more personal criticism of M'Bow's leadership in the latter period. There is a small increase in December 1984 of criticisms of

the pullout, of affirmations as to the value of Unesco programs, and of denials that the agency is guilty of the sins attributed to it. Themes focusing on what might happen next to Unesco and its relations with the United States are about three times as frequent in the second period as the first.

These aggregate data mask some significant differences between the different agencies. Whereas the AP, New York Times and Washington Post services all moderated their criticism of Unesco over the year and gave more prominence to critics of the withdrawal, UPI coverage remained relatively constant; if anything, it moved in the opposite direction. In December 1983, UPI was the agency least critical of Unesco and most supportive of its activities. By December 1984 it was the most critical and least supportive.

Part of the reason for the change can be found in the sources used by the agencies at different times. In December 1984 the AP, the New York Times and the Washington Post relied less heavily on U.S. official sources than they did a year earlier. Conversely, they were more inclined to quote Unesco officials and Western non-government organizations, who were generally critical of the withdrawal. Despite the more moderate position of these agencies, however, their coverage remained far more critical than supportive of Unesco.

REASONS FOR IMBALANCE

It is clear from the debate that preceded the final withdrawal that the decision was a disputed one; that for every argument in favor of withdrawal there as an equally persuasive counterargument; that for every spokesman for the adminstration's point of view there was one—if not several—who had a contrary opinion. Yet the press agency coverage, while conceding this diversity of opinion, came down heavily on the side of the anti-Unesco position.

This imbalance can be attributed to four main kinds of bias in the coverage. First, as has been demonstrated, there was a strong tendency to rely on sources, particularly the U.S. government, that were hostile to Unesco. Second, there was a tendency to report events that depicted Unesco in an unfavorable light and supported the withdrawal, while playing down or ignoring those with a contrary slant. Third, when events took place about which there was a difference of opinion, or at which conflicting viewpoints were expressed, pro-administration spokesmen usually got the bulk of the coverage. Fourth, when reports that gave both points of view were written, anti-Unesco views were given prominence. The pro-Unesco opinions tended to appear at the end of reports, where

they were likely to be omitted if an abridged version was printed in a newspaper.

Selective Reporting of Events

The news events given the greatest attention by the agencies were almost entirely negative in their orientation toward Unesco. These included the initial announcement of the withdrawal, with an emphasis on the State Department's criticisms; the fire at Unesco headquarters in March; the GAO investigation and its critical report; the British notice of withdrawal; the squabble over whether the United States would have to pay dues for 1985; and confirmation of the withdrawal, again with details of the U.S. reasons for leaving.

This selective reporting of events can be seen throughout the period under review. About two dozen reports were transmitted by the four agencies between the first hint on December 15, 1983, that the United States would withdraw, and the formal announcement two weeks later. Among the events reported were news conferences and interviews with State Department spokesmen Lawrence Eagleburger, John Hughes, Gregory Newell and Alan Romberg. But the fact that the U.S. National Commission for Unesco—an official group appointed to advise the State Department on Unesco matters—had voted against withdrawal on December 16 appeared only in the *New York Times*. Even then, the report on the commission vote was relegated to the end of the article, after nine paragraphs of anti-Unesco statements from Eagleburger and Newell. Ten days after the commission's vote, the *Washington Post* carried a report on telephone interviews with commission members, who were quoted as saying the United States should stay in but insist on reforms.

Another instance of selective reporting occurred in February. Newell's summary of the State Department's policy review of Unesco, with its allegations of politicization, hostility to a free press and mismanagement, was quoted by all four agencies. But the fact that most of the organizations that Newell had consulted opposed the withdrawal was not. Nor did the agencies cover the detailed report of the staff study mission of the House Foreign Affairs Committee, which gave counterarguments and came down on the side of continued membership.

All four agencies carried detailed reports on the "Crisis in Unesco" paper, listing criticisms of the organization by 24 industrialized nations and demanding reforms. Yet only UPI reported that 50 African nations had appealed to the United States to reconsider; only the AP noted that the information ministers of the non-aligned nations had passed a resolution in support of Unesco; only UPI revealed that the Mexican foreign ministry had written to Shultz deploring the withdrawal. The reports on

the Western nations' "Crisis in Unesco" paper also revealed another kind of selectivity. Despite its critical tone, the report stated that it was of the "highest importance" that the United States should not withdraw. This was mentioned in the *Washington Post* report on the paper, but not in the other versions.

More than two dozen separate reports on the United Kingdom's intention to withdraw appeared in the various services. Yet little mention was made of the fact that virtually all the countries in the British Commonwealth and virtually all members of the European Economic Community had expressed their intention of retaining membership and had asked Britain not to withdraw. The findings of a Gallup Poll showing that most Americans who were aware of Unesco were opposed to the withdrawal was carried only by the Los Angeles Times service.

After extensive coverage by the AP, UPI and the New York Times service of conflicts between the United States and Unesco at the organization's Executive Board meeting in September–October, UPI appears to have been the only agency to note that at the end the board had taken steps toward reforms, including a zero-growth budget.

Selective Use of Sources

The second kind of bias, selective use of sources, is also commonplace. As the content analysis indicates, this can be seen in the heavy reliance on U.S. government officials, who contributed more than half of all themes, compared to about 13 percent for Unesco officials, and less than 5 percent each for the Second World and Third World.

The process can most clearly be seen in instances where conflicting opinions about the withdrawal were expressed, but those supporting it were given prominence in the coverage. The hearings by two subcommittees of the House Foreign Affairs Committee in April and May are a case in point. Sixteen people gave evidence before the panel. Three of them, Gregory Newell and Edward Derwinski of the State Department, and Owen Harries of the Heritage Foundation, supported the withdrawal. But 11 witnesses, while acknowledging Unesco's problems and weaknesses, concluded that the bottom line was that the United States should stay in. Two others called for further study. The three days of hearings, most of it pro-Unesco, produced two published reports. The AP transmitted a brief story noting that Esteban Torres had opposed the withdrawal. UPI, in a strange variation of the inverted pyramid style, reported in its lead that "several Democratic and Republican congressmen lashed out at administration plans to withdraw from Unesco, charging that the administration has a preconceived bias." But the second paragraph of the report quotes Derwinski of the State Department. The report then had several

paragraphs giving background information, including the State Department's criticisms. It then went on to quote Newell's testimony at the hearing. Only at the end did it get back to the topic of the lead—comments of three congressmen who accused the administration of acting with ideological bias. Each congressman was allotted one brief paragraph.

Structure of the Reports

It is an accepted convention of American journalism that a news report should be written in the form of an inverted pyramid, with the most important elements at the beginning and the least important tailing off at the end. This makes it easy for newspapers to shorten reports to fit limited space simply by cutting from the bottom. It also implies a value judgment on the part of the reporters and editors when one aspect of a report is presented prominently in the lead, while other aspects are relegated to the end. This kind of bias occurs quite often in the Unesco material, as a few examples will indicate.

The first report that the United States planned to withdraw appeared in the *New York Times* on 15 December 1983. The report quoted State Department officials, specifically Newell, giving in detail the U.S. criticisms of Unesco as reasons for the withdrawal. This occupied the first 15 paragraphs of the 19-paragraph report. The final four paragraphs cite opponents of the withdrawal, and specifically Leonard Sussman, as saying Unesco had been responsive to U.S. concerns and that it would be a mistake to pull out. This report was picked up the next day by the AP, which quoted the *Times* as its source, and repeated Newell's criticisms of Unesco. But the AP version omitted any mention of Sussman or other opponents—even at the bottom of the inverted pyramid.

A UPI report from Paris in December 1983 has as its main theme the contention that "although political squabbles that have dismayed many member countries appear to have been toned down," it may be a case of "too little, too late to salvage U.S. participation." The 20-paragraph article recites the litany of complaints against Unesco—politicization, budget mismanagement and waste, attempts to restrict the freedom of the press, "bureaucratic terrorism" and "total intellectual suffocation." The last two paragraphs, however, note than Unesco "has many useful projects, including teacher-training programs in Africa and Latin America." They refer also to Unesco's campaign to save cultural monuments like Egypt's Abu Simbel temples, and its role as the world's largest publisher of books.

UPI's account of the hearings before the Senate Committee on Labor and Human Resources in December 1984 began by quoting Jean Gerard as defending the withdrawal because there had not been enough

reforms. It then quoted Gregory Newell, who complained that although Western nations provided 75 percent of Unesco's budget, they were not given a major voice in the organization. Next it quoted Maxwell Greenberg, national chairman of the B'nai B'rith, who complained of an anti-Israel attitude at Unesco. The very last paragraph mentioned that Leonard Sussman, vice chairman of the U.S. National Commission for Unesco, had recommended staying to fight for reform from within.

UPI reported in December 1983 that U.S. Ambassador Jean Gerard had informed M'Bow of the decision to withdraw. It quoted administration officials as being unhappy with Unesco because of its "criticism of Israel and proposed curbs on the media." The final two paragraphs noted that a French foreign ministry spokesman said that a U.S. withdrawal would "seriously harm Unesco aims as well as the principle of universality."

NEWS AGENCIES: TABLES

TABLE 4.1. ORIENTATION TOWARD UNESCO OF COVERAGE BY FOUR NEWS AGENCIES (PERCENTAGE)

	Combined agencies *n* = 1,945	AP *n* = 576	UPI *n* = 573	NYT *n* = 521	WP/LAT *n* = 275
Anti-Unesco/ pro-withdrawal	70	72	65	72	72
Pro-Unesco/ anti-withdrawal	27	25	31	25	25
Looking ahead	3	3	4	3	3
Total	100	100	100	100	100

TABLE 4.2. ISSUES COVERED BY FOUR NEWS AGENCIES

	Combined agencies *n* = 1,945	AP *n* = 576	UPI *n* = 573	NYT *n* = 521	WP/LAT *n* = 275
Anti-Unesco/ pro-withdrawal					
Politicization	21	21	18	23	20
Mismanagement	12	14	10	12	15
Reforms needed	11	10	10	12	13
Press issues	10	10	10	12	5
U.S. pays 25%	5	5	6	5	4
Support for U.S.	4	5	5	3	4
Too little change	3	4	3	2	4
Criticism of M'Bow	2	1	1	2	5
Benefits to U.S.	2	2	2	1	2
U.S. credibility at stake	<1	<1	<1	<1	0
Subtotal	70	72	65	72	72
Pro-Unesco/ anti-withdrawal					
Criticism of pullout	13	12	17	11	10
Valuable programs	10	9	10	11	11
Denials of charges	2	2	3	1	4
Propaganda campaign	1	2	1	2	<1
Subtotal	26	25	31	25	25
Looking ahead					
Future	3	3	4	2	2
Alternatives	1	<1	1	1	1
Subtotals	4	3	4	3	3
Total	100	100	100	100	100

TABLE 4.3. ORIENTATION TOWARD UNESCO OF MAJOR AGENCY REPORTERS

	Number of themes	Anti-Unesco/ pro-pullout %	Pro-Unesco/ anti-pullout %	Looking ahead %
Associated Press				
AP (no byline)	281	73	24	3
Dunphy (Paris)	94	72	27	1
Rosenberg (Wash.)	58	67	28	5
United Press International				
UPI (no byline)	342	60	37	3
Mosby (Paris)	114	73	23	4
Nguyen (UN)	25	52	48	0
New York Times				
NYT (no byline)	85	84	15	1
Lewis (Paris)	157	83	16	1
Ayres (Wash.)	41	61	32	7
Dionne (Paris)	37	68	32	0
Gwertzman (Wash.)	47	85	11	4
Washington Post				
Pincus (Wash.)	68	85	10	5
Omang (Wash.)	66	64	33	3
Dobbs (Paris)	47	77	19	4

TABLE 4.4. RANKING OF ISSUES MENTIONED MOST FREQUENTLY BY MAJOR REPORTERS

	Politicization	Press issues	Mismanagement	Reforms needed	Criticism of pullout	Valuable programs
Associated Press						
AP (no byline)	1	3	2	5	4	5
Dunphy (Paris)	3		1	2	5	4
Rosenberg (Washington)	2		3	5	1	
United Press International						
UPI (no byline)	2	5	4		1	3
Mosby (Paris)	3	2	4	1	5	
Nguyen (U.N.)	4	5			1	1
New York Times						
NYT (no byline)	1	2	3	4	2	5
Lewis (Paris)	2	4	3	1	5	5
Ayres (Washington)	1	4	4		2	2
Dionne (Paris)	1	2	5		2	2
Gwertzman (Washington)	1	2	3	5	3	
Washington Post						
Pincus (Washington)	1		3	2		
Omang (Washington)	1		5	3	4	2
Dobbs (Paris)	1		3	2		5

TABLE 4.5. EMPHASIS PLACED ON ISSUES IN REPORTS FROM DIFFERENT CENTERS (PERCENTAGE)

	Paris n = 797	Washington n = 723	New York n = 216	United Nations n = 52	London n = 45
Anti-Unesco/ pro-withdrawal					
Politicization	16	24	18	21	24
Mismanagement	14	12	9	11	11
Press issues	8	9	14	13	13
Reforms needed	16	8	5	8	16
U.S. pays 25%	6	5	3	8	7
Support for U.S.	7	2	1	2	9
Too little change	2	5	1	2	4
Criticism of M'Bow	3	2	1	2	0
Benefits to U.S.	2	2	1	4	0
U.S. credibility at stake	0	<1	1	0	0
Subtotal	73	70	54	71	84
Pro-Unesco/ anti-withdrawal					
Criticism of pullout	10	13	28	11	7
Valuable programs	10	9	14	10	7
Denials of charges	2	2	1	8	2
Propaganda campaign	3	1	1	0	0
Subtotal	25	25	44	29	16
Looking ahead					
Future	2	4	2	0	0
Alternatives	<1	1	0	0	0
Subtotal	2	5	2	0	0
Total	100	100	100	100	100

TABLE 4.6. SOURCES QUOTED BY NEWS-AGENCY REPORTS (EXCLUDING THEMES NOT ATTRIBUTED TO A SOURCE)

Source	Combined agencies n = 1,524	AP n = 472	UPI n = 446	NYT n = 375	WP/LAT n = 231
U.S. Government	56	56	45	54	78
Western governments	21	21	24	22	13
Unesco	13	12	19	9	7
U.S. NGOs	4	4	3	9	2
Soviet government	4	4	4	5	0
Third World	2	3	5	1	0
Total	100	100	100	100	100

TABLE 4.7. SOURCES USED BY REPORTERS (PERCENTAGES)

	Associated Press			UPI		
	AP (no byline) n = 281	Dunphy (Paris) n = 94	Rosenberg (Wash.) n = 58	UPI (no byline) n = 342	Mosby (Paris) n = 114	Nguyen (UN) n = 25
U.S. government	58	37	80	42	38	14
Western governments	19	39	7	27	26	50
Unesco	15	11	0	15	34	27
U.S. NGOs	0	0	13	3	0	0
Soviet government	3	13	0	6	1	0
Third World	5	0	0	7	1	9
Total	100	100	100	100	100	100

	New York Times					WP/LAT		
	NYT (no byline) n = 85	Lewis (Paris) n = 157	Ayres (Wash.) n = 41	Dionne (Paris) n = 37	Gwertzman (Wash.) n = 47	Pincus (Wash.) n = 68	Omang (Wash.) n = 66	Dobbs (Paris) n = 47
U.S. government	71	34	64	60	94	84	86	34
Western governments	12	47	7	15	6	2	8	44
Unesco	6	9	18	7	0	8	6	22
U.S. NGOs	3	0	11	18	0	6	0	0
Soviet government	8	8	0	0	0	0	0	0
Third World	0	2	0	0	0	0	0	0
Total	100	100	100	100	100	100	100	100

TABLE 4.8. ORIENTATION TO UNESCO OF SOURCES QUOTED IN REPORTS (PERCENTAGES)

	Anti-Unesco/ pro-withdrawal	Pro-Unesco/ anti-withdrawal	Looking ahead
U.S. government	82	14	4
Western governments	75	24	1
Unesco	16	74	10
Soviet government	31	67	2
Third World	22	70	3
U.S. NGOs	36	56	8

TABLE 4.9. ISSUES EMPHASIZED BY MAJOR SOURCES (PERCENTAGES)

	U.S. govt. $n = 845$	Western govt. $n = 318$	Unesco $n = 191$
Anti-Unesco/ pro-withdrawal			
Politicization	30	11	<1
Mismanagement	18	9	4
Press issues	11	13	2
Reforms needed	13	22	2
U.S. pays 25%	1	<1	<1
Support for U.S.	1	15	1
Too little change	6	1	2
Criticism of M'Bow	2	3	1
Benefits to U.S.	1	1	4
U.S. credibility at stake	<1	0	0
Subtotal	82	75	15
Pro-Unesco/ anti-withdrawal			
Criticism of pullout	7	19	27
Valuable programs	5	5	23
Denials of charges	1	<1	16
Propaganda campaign	<1	0	9
Subtotal	13	24	75
Looking ahead			
Future	3	1	10
Alternatives	2	0	0
Subtotal	5	1	10
Total	100	100	100

TABLE 4.10. ISSUES EMPHASIZED IN NEWS AGENCY REPORTS (EXCLUDING MENTION OF U.S. FUNDING)

	Attributed themes (%) $n = 1,512$	Unattributed themes (%) $n = 334$
Anti-Unesco/ pro-withdrawal		
Politicization	20	27
Mismanagement	13	13
Press issues	10	14
Reforms needed	13	8
Support for U.S.	4	6
Too little change	4	1
Criticism of M'Bow	3	3
Benefits to U.S.	2	1
Subtotal	68	73
Pro-Unesco/ anti-withdrawal		
Criticism of pullout	15	5
Valuable programs	9	19
Denials of charges	2	1
Propaganda campaign	2	0
Subtotal	28	25
Looking ahead		
Future	3	2
Alternatives	1	0
Subtotal	4	2
Total	100	100

TABLE 4.11. CHANGES IN EMPHASIS OVER TIME (PERCENTAGES)

	December 1983 n = 536	December 1984 n = 548
Anti-Unesco/ pro-withdrawal		
Politicization	29	18
Mismanagement	12	9
Press issues	14	5
Reforms needed	5	7
U.S. pays 25%	5	
Support for U.S.	1	6
Too little change	3	5
Criticism of M'Bow	<1	2
Benefits to U.S.	1	3
U.S. credibility at stake	0	<1
Subtotal	72	60
Pro-Unesco/ anti-withdrawal		
Criticism of pullout	15	17
Valuable programs	9	12
Denials of charges	1	2
Propaganda campaign	0	1
Subtotal	25	32
Looking ahead		
Future	2	6
Alternatives	1	2
Subtotal	3	8
Total	100	100

CHAPTER 5

Published Reports

> *The battle lines are drawn. We should keep ourselves fully informed and support those individuals and organizations whose efforts on our behalf are dedicated to maintaining a free flow of information at all levels.*
>
> *—Tina S. Hills, chairman*
> *Committee on International Communications of the ASNE.*

In addition to the reports distributed by the major news agencies, the study analyzed what actually appeared in the nation's press. Data for this analysis were obtained from the file of press clippings relating to Unesco compiled by Press Intelligence, Inc. Because most of the agency reports appeared in several newspapers, either at full length or more commonly in abbreviated form, there is a large degree of duplication. Few reports appeared in weekly publications, except occasionally in news magazines like *Time, Newsweek* and *U.S. News and World Report*, or in specialist journals like *Editor & Publisher*, the *Library Journal*, and the *Chronicle of Higher Education*. The three major news magazines between them carried nine reports on the topic during the year under review.

PATTERNS OF COVERAGE

Number of Items

Altogether 3,915 newspaper articles relating to the withdrawal were collected by the clipping service during the year. These included 1,950 news reports, 1,363 editorials and 602 editorial page columns. Many of these

items were duplicates—the same agency report or column appearing in several papers. Most of the coverage was concentrated in December 1983, the time of the initial announcement, and in December 1984 when the decision to withdraw was confirmed (Table 5.1). A fairly large proportion of the articles was printed in January 1984. Most were editorials and columns relating to the announcement of the withdrawal late in December. More than one-half of the total coverage dealt with these two official announcements. Of the nation's 1,700 daily papers, about 760, or 46 percent of the total, carried one or more articles about the issue (Figure 5.1).

Coverage of the Unesco story in the press was largely a function of the size of the newspapers: the bigger a newspaper's circulation, the more likely it was to carry news reports, editorials and columns about the withdrawal (Table 5.2). Virtually every one of the 126 metropolitan papers with a circulation of 100,000 or more carried several articles. Because it was the larger papers that carried most material, the combined circulation of those 760 papers amounted to about 80 percent of the 63 million copies sold daily in the United States. Thus 80 percent of daily newspaper readers could have read one or more reports about the withdrawal in their local paper.

Smaller papers showed little interest in the topic. Of the 659 daily papers in the United States with circulations of less than 10,000 copies, only 25 percent carried any articles about the pullout. The small papers that did carry anything had very few: an average of two items apiece for

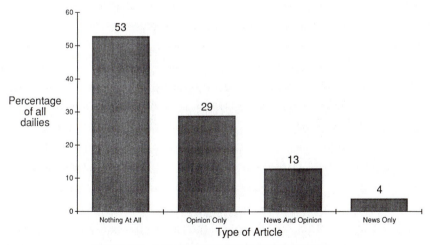

Figure 5.1. Coverage by 1,700 Daily Newspapers

those with a circulation of under 25,000. The top 100 papers, all with circulations of 118,000 or more, ran an average of 16 items each.

Kinds of Items

There was a considerable difference in the kinds of articles that ran in the larger and smaller papers (Table 5.3). The small papers used few news reports about Unesco. If they carried anything, it was likely to be editorials or editorial columns (Figure 5.2). Papers with a circulation of 50,000 or less ran four times as many opinion pieces—columns and editorials— as news stories. Many ran only editorials, or a combination of editorials and columns, with no news reports at all. The large papers used all three types of coverage, with a sharp rise in the number and proportion of news reports as circulation increased. The top 100 papers ran an average of 10 news stories apiece over the year, along with three editorials and just under three op-ed page columns. As far as news coverage was concerned, the cutting point came at roughly the 100,000 circulation mark. Those with circulations of 50,000 to 100,000 carried, on average, a total of six articles, including three news reports. Those with circulations between 100,000 and 150,000 carried an average of 12 articles, including 7 news reports.

People in communities served by the smaller papers, therefore, were likely to be told what to think about Unesco, but not given much factual material by which to judge those opinions. Readers in larger cities were

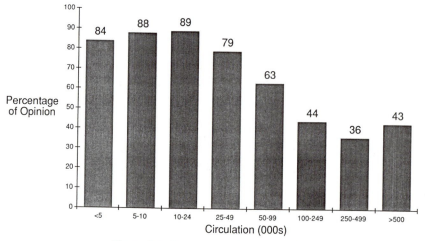

Figure 5.2. Percentage of Opinion by Circulation

exposed to more news, but as will be demonstrated, it tended to give only one side of the picture, and that orientation was reinforced by the high proportion of negative editorials and columns.

NEWS REPORTS

Of the nation's 1,700-odd daily newspapers only 289, or about 17 percent, appear to have carried any news reports at all on the withdrawal (Table 5.4). Seventy-five of those papers had only one report; 21 had two, and 44 had between three and five. Nearly half the papers that carried any news reports at all, therefore, carried five or fewer. Three-quarters carried 10 or fewer. At the other extreme, 13 papers carried more than 20 news reports. These included the Chattanooga *Times* (21 reports), the Columbus, Ohio, *Dispatch* (22), the Hackensack, N.J. *Record* (22), the *San Diego Union* (23), *Newsday* (24), the *Philadelphia Inquirer* (24), the *Kansas City* (Mo.) *Times* (25), the *Toledo Blade* (26), the *Washington Times* (30), the Omaha *World-Herald* (34), the *Washington Post* (41) and the *New York Times* (66).

If the number of papers carrying news about the withdrawal was limited, the number of cities in which it appeared was even more so. Daily newspapers are published in 1,534 cities in the United States. Because many of the 289 papers that carried reports are published in larger cities that have two or more dailies, each of which carried some Unesco stories, readers in only 194 cities, or 13 percent of the total with daily papers, would have gotten news of the pullout from their local daily. The amount of news available to them varied widely from city to city. Of the 194 cities represented, just over 40 percent had a total of between one and five reports over the year (Table 5.5). More than half had 10 reports or fewer, and 86 percent had 20 or fewer. Two cities, Washington and New York, were in a class by themselves. Washington readers, served not only by the *Washington Post* but also by the *Washington Times* and to a lesser extent by *U.S.A. Today*, could have read 81 reports if they had subscribed to all three papers. New York readers, served by the *Times*, the *News*, the *Post* and the *Tribune*, among others, had 89. Other cities with more than 25 reports in their papers over the year included Atlanta, Baltimore, Boston, Chattanooga, Columbus, Denver, Kansas City, Los Angeles, Norfolk, Omaha, Philadelphia, Raleigh and San Diego.

There was a clear correlation between the circulation of the papers and the number of reports they carried (Pearson correlation 0.56). Papers with a circulation of 250,000 or more—just 2 percent of the country's dailies—accounted for nearly 25 percent of the news reports carried. Large circulation was not a guarantee that a paper would carry a sub-

stantial number of reports, however. A more significant indicator was the paper's status as a serious newspaper of record. So, for example, in New York City, the *New York Times* (circulation 905,000), carried 66 reports, but the *News* (1,300,000) had 4, and the *Post* (630,000) had 1. Some large, prestigious papers did not give the issue as much coverage as one might have expected. The *Los Angeles Times* carried 14 reports, the *Chicago Tribune* 11, and the *Detroit Free Press* 8. Other factors influenced the coverage. The Omaha *World-Herald* had more than 30 news reports on the withdrawal over the year (plus several anti-Unesco columns and editorials). Its interest may have been related to the fact that the *World Herald* company's president, Harold Andersen, had been chairman of the American Newspaper Publishers Association and at the time was chairman of the World Press Freedom Committee and a member of the State Department's Unesco monitoring panel. Some smaller papers, in cities were they are the journals of record, had coverage of the Unesco issue out of proportion to their size. These papers generally provided continuous coverage of the controversy as it developed, from the announcement of the intention to withdraw until the final action a year later.

Papers that carried only a handful of the reports generally were smaller, or if large, were those that had no pretension of covering international news. They tended to cover only four events: the announcement of the U.S. intention to withdraw in December 1983; the arson fire at Unesco's Paris headquarters in March 1984; Britain's planned withdrawal, announced in November; and the United States' final decision in December 1984.

USE OF NEWS AGENCIES

Three-quarters of the 1,979 published news reports were credited to one of the four agencies analyzed (Table 5.6). Most of the remainder were also from these agencies but did not carry a specific agency credit. Of all the attributed reports (including duplicates) the largest number by far were from the AP (56 percent of the reports carrying a credit). The New York Times was the second most widely used service (19 percent), followed by UPI (16 percent), the Washington Post/L.A. Times service (7 percent) and Reuter (2 percent). (See Figure 5.3.)

Altogether 1,501 reports used by the press carried the credit of one of the four agencies. These represented multiple uses of just 226 separate news stories. Thus each report was used, on average, in about six newspapers. The most widely used was carried by 54. Some were not picked up at all. The AP provided 91 separate stories that were used, or 40

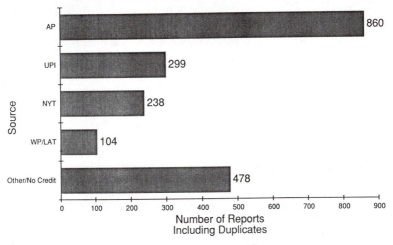

Figure 5.3. Sources of Published Reports

percent of the total. Next was UPI, followed by the New York Times and the Washington Post services (Table 5.7). The AP not only provided most of the reports used, but those reports were used by far more newspapers than the other services. Each AP report appeared, on average, in nearly 10 papers—almost twice as many as the average for the other agencies. Not only did the AP provide the largest number of reports that were used, but its reports appeared in more copies of newspapers than any other agency's. The total circulation of papers carrying the AP reports was in excess of 120 million—about 43 percent of the total (Table 5.8).

Papers carrying reports from the AP or UPI had an average circulation of more than 140,000 copies. The New York Times material was used by papers with an average circulation of nearly 275,000 (including the *Times* itself), while the Washington Post and Reuters were used mainly by the very largest dailies. Because of the large circulation of the papers in which it appeared, the Washington Post reportage actually received more exposure—in terms of the number of copies in which it appeared—than the far more numerous UPI reports that appeared in smaller papers. The New York Times reports, also because of the large papers that carried them, were second only to the AP in total exposure.

CONTENT ANALYSIS

The same content analysis scheme as used for the news agency material was applied to the reports that appeared in the press. The clippings were sorted chronologically and the reports selected for analysis on a random

interval basis. Of the 1,979 news clippings in the data base, about one-quarter were analyzed. Because some reports appeared in a large number of newspapers there is some duplication in the sample. This was intentional since the aim was to examine nationwide exposure.

The number of themes from different agencies that appeared in the published reports was not proportional to the number of reports used from each agency, except in the case of the AP, which accounted for about 44 percent of all the reports used, and for 44 percent of the themes. The reports with no agency credit—23 percent of the total—accounted for only 14 percent of the themes. This is because most of the reports with no agency credit line were very short, often appearing in a "news briefs" or "news roundup" column under a credit such as "from our wire services." UPI provided 16 percent of the reports used, but only 11 percent of the themes, largely because the papers often used shorter, edited-down versions of the agency's material. The Washington Post and the New York Times reports, however, were comparatively rich in themes. Although only 12 percent of the reports used came from the New York Times, they accounted for 23 percent of all the themes. These reports were longer, more detailed and usually ran in papers with a news hole large enough to give them adequate play. This, coupled with the fact that these reports were usually carried in papers with very large circulations, gave these special service reports considerable exposure.

Orientation

The news reports that appeared in the press were even more strongly anti-Unesco and in favor of the withdrawal (76 percent of the themes) than the reports distributed by the news agencies (70 percent), as shown in Table 5.9. As in the case of the news agencies from which the reports were taken, most of the critical themes related to charges of politicization, mismanagement and the need for reform. But each of these categories was more frequent in the printed reports than in the agency files. There was also a higher proportion of expressions of support for the U.S. position, and of statements that Unesco had not changed enough to warrant continued U.S. membership. There was, unexpectedly, somewhat less emphasis on communications issues in the clippings than in the agency reports (Table 5.10).

The increase in the politicization category was due to the publication of more themes accusing Unesco of being anti-Western, anti–free society and anti–free enterprise. There also were proportionately more themes alleging that Unesco favored opponents of the West and that it supported collective as opposed to individual rights. Charges of mismanagement and demands for reform were also slightly higher than in the agency copy.

The decline in the proportion of themes supportive of Unesco was

due to fewer references to the drawbacks to the United States of the withdrawal, or to suggestions that the United States should remain a member but work for reform from within. There were also fewer expressions of regret and criticisms of the withdrawal, or of suggestions that Unesco was in fact making efforts to reform.

Inter-Agency Variations

No matter what agency was used, the reports in the press were more critical of Unesco than the profile for the agency's entire file. This was particularly true of the New York Times reports. While the New York Times file as a whole was 72 percent anti-Unesco and pro-withdrawal, the New York Times reports that ran in the press averaged 81 percent anti-Unesco (Table 6.9). Apart from the greater emphasis on themes critical of Unesco, however, the papers generally followed the agency agenda, both in terms of the news events covered and the way they were covered (Table 5.10).

Changes in Emphasis over Time

Following the cue of the news agencies, the reports in the press moderated somewhat over the year from December 1983 to December 1984 (Table 5.11). But the change was not as marked as in the case of the agencies. Whereas the news agencies moved from 72 percent anti-Unesco in December 1983 to 60 percent in December 1984—a change of 12 percentage points—the newspaper coverage went from 80 percent to 74 percent, a shift of only 6 points.

One remarkable feature of the change in coverage over time is that, as previous studies had shown, before the "year of crisis," press reporting on Unesco focused almost exclusively on the agency's promotion of a new information order. That was the case in the coverage of both the 1980 and the 1982 General Conferences. Once the U.S. government became involved and began to stress Unesco's politicization, mismanagement and need for reform, that quickly became the agenda for the press. Communication issues, in the news columns at least, were downplayed.

REASONS FOR IMBALANCE

The hawkish line that appeared in the press can be attributed to three factors. In the first place, newspapers depended almost exclusively on the news agencies for coverage of Unesco, and, as has been shown, the agency copy was largely hostile to the organization. Second, the papers

tended to run those reports that were more strongly anti-Unesco, while ignoring those that supported the agency or criticized the withdrawal. The third is that some agency reports that gave both sides of the argument were edited to exclude the positive. Usually this was simply a function of the structure of the report. Themes supportive of Unesco often appeared at the end of the agency reports and were omitted when the reports were edited for space or other reasons.

Selection of Reports

There are numerous examples of newspapers selecting from the agency files those reports most critical of Unesco, while ignoring others that supported the organization or opposed the withdrawal. Stories about just ten events—all of them tending to show Unesco in a negative light—comprise 40 percent of all the reports published.

Altogether 240 published reports, based on about 25 different news-agency stories, dealt with the initial announcement in December 1983 that the United States planned to withdraw. These reports, virtually all of which quoted the State Department's criticisms as reasons for the pullout, were strongly anti-Unesco in their orientation.

The most frequently used report on the initial announcement—used by 50 newspapers—was filed by the AP on December 24. It said that President Reagan, acting on the recommendation of Secretary of State George Shultz, had decided to take the first step toward withdrawing. It quoted officials, "who declined to be identified," as saying Unesco had attempted to set press standards, raising concerns of censorship; and of stirring controversy by barring Israel from its activities. The officials also cited poor management and efforts to devise a code for multinational corporations.

The second most frequently used story, based on a dozen different agency reports and appearing in 163 papers, concerned the United Kingdom's announcement in November 1984 that it too would give notice of withdrawal. Half the published reports were based on two AP stories filed from London and Paris. They quoted Foreign Secretary Geoffrey Howe as saying that the United Kingdom would pull out at the end of 1985 unless Unesco made budget and management reforms. Although filed by different reporters in different centers—David Mason in London and Harry Dunphy in Paris—both AP reports carried a virtually identical paragraph stating that "Britain, the United States, the Netherlands and other Western nations have criticized Unesco as being overly politicized, badly managed and often anti-Western." The UPI version, carried by 18 papers, also quoted Howe's criticisms in detail.

The event that drew the third highest coverage was the confirmation

in December 1984 that the United States would withdraw. All the agencies filed reports anticipating the move and on the announcement itself. Of the 150 reports published, the most widely used was an AP story quoting Gregory Newell as saying that the United States would withdraw because Unesco remains "plagued by mismanagement and endemic hostility to Western values," notably a free press, free markets and individual human rights.

Other frequently used reports that put Unesco in a bad light included the fire at Unesco headquarters in Paris, which was depicted as an attempt to destroy records before U.S. congressional investigators could see them. These appeared in 77 papers. The conflict between the United States and Unesco over the return of $80 million in unspent funds was published by 40 papers. A report that the administration would name a panel to monitor changes in Unesco (but that Newell was not optimistic that Unesco would make any changes) appeared in 33 papers. A report by 21 present and former Unesco staff members saying there was duplication, overlapping and fragmentation in its programs, ran in 31. The highly critical GAO report that was leaked to the press made 22 newspapers, and the "Crisis in Unesco" paper, listing criticisms and proposals for reform from 24 Western nations, made 17. Not all agency reports critical of Unesco were used widely by the press; some did not appear at all. But all the most frequently used stories were predominantly anti-Unesco in their orientation.

On the other hand, agency reports that depicted Unesco in a favorable light or that were highly critical of the withdrawal were published far less frequently. When foreign governments, like Britain, joined American criticisms of Unesco, they were widely quoted. When they opposed the pullout, they generally were not. For example:

- At the time of the flood of reports critical of Unesco when the initial announcement was made, UPI filed a story quoting the Soviet Union as saying that the decision was an attempt by Washington to be the "world's self-styled ruler," and quoting a leading West German politician as saying it was "an arrogant example of dollar diplomacy." The report also quoted Luis Ramallo, president of Unesco's Spanish national committee, as saying the U.S. move "is not going to produce any wave of pullouts. It is an infantile tantrum." The report was carried by two newspapers.
- A year later, a UPI report on Newell's press conference giving the reasons for the final decision to withdraw was carried by 22 papers. But another UPI report saying that America's allies, including Canada and Australia, had expressed regret, and said they preferred to work for reform from within, appeared in one paper.

- A UPI report that China had called for an early return to Unesco by the United States was not used at all.

Statements by U.S. organizations and individuals supporting Unesco or critical of the withdrawal proved no more newsworthy to the nation's media gatekeepers. For example:

- An AP report that Esteban Torres, former American ambassador to Unesco, had spoken out against the withdrawal at a congressional hearing in April was picked up by one newspaper.
- A New York Times News Service story in May, reporting that the American Association for the Advancement of Science had said there would be serious scientific consequences if the United States went ahead with the pullout, ran in two papers.
- A New York Times report in December 1984 that American scientists, scholars and cultural organizations stood to lose significant benefits through the abandonment of Unesco membership, made two papers.

News agency reports on the reaction of Unesco or other U.N. organizations were largely ignored, as were reports that Unesco was really trying to implement reforms to avert the pullout. For example:

- A statement in April from M'Bow, filed by UPI, rejecting charges that Unesco was mismanaged and that it sought to put media under government control did not make a single paper.
- Reports in April that M'Bow had proposed sweeping management reforms aimed at improving Unesco's operations was picked up by three UPI subscribers, while two carried the AP version.
- A statement by M'Bow in October saying that Unesco was the victim of "systematic denigration" in distorted news dispatches, made one paper.
- A UPI report in October that the U.N. General Assembly's Special Political Committee had adopted a resolution calling for strong support for Unesco and for a new international information order was not considered newsworthy by a single subscriber.

Structure of Reports

A second reason for the more negative orientation of the stories that appeared in the press was the structure of the agency reports. Following traditional journalistic practice, the reports were structured in the form of an inverted pyramid. The first paragraph, or lead, summarizes the main

items of the news event. Each succeeding paragraph contains supporting details in descending order of importance. While every paragraph in the report is newsworthy, each is less vital than the one before it. The inverted pyramid format allows readers to grasp the main points of the news quickly, and then decide if they want to continue. But it is also useful to newspaper editors, since they do not have to search through a story to find the main point for a headline, and they can shorten it quickly by cutting from the bottom.

An analysis of the most frequently used reports on Unesco shows that this is precisely what they did. Very few papers used the agency reports at full length, and when they shortened them, it was almost always by simply lopping off paragraphs from the bottom. The problem is that even when the agency reports were relatively balanced in terms of the number of pro- and anti-Unesco themes they contained overall, the themes that supported Unesco or criticized the withdrawal tended to be lower down in the reports, and so were often omitted. A couple of examples illustrate this effect.

Altogether 50 papers used the AP report of December 24, 1983, saying that Reagan, acting on Schultz's recommendation, had decided to take the first step toward withdrawal. Only 3 of the 50 papers carried all 18 paragraphs of the agency report. The average number of paragraphs used was 11. Seventeen papers trimmed the story simply by cutting paragraphs from the bottom. Another 25 papers trimmed from the bottom, but also cut one paragraph from the portion they used. Thus 45 of the papers—90 percent of the total—limited their editing to cutting from the bottom of the inverted pyramid, or at most omitting one intervening paragraph. The remaining five papers were more selective. Although they shortened the report, they did so by cutting out two or more paragraphs from the first half and incorporating some material from the latter part to achieve balance.

The structure of the AP report, which included both pro- and anti-Unesco themes but reserved the pro-Unesco themes until midway down, together with the tendency to cut from the bottom, resulted in published reports that were considerably more negative than the original. The first paragraph, used by all 50 papers, reported that Reagan had decided to take the first step toward withdrawal (Figure 5.4). The second, used by 49 of the 50, said that an announcement was expected soon that would set the stage for a U.S. pullout "unless Unesco changes its ways." The third, also carried by 49 papers, stated that Unesco, which was "created to encourage scientific, educational and scientific exchanges," had attempted to set "worldwide press standards" and that it had stirred controversy by "barring Israel from its activities, a move that subsequently was reversed." The fourth and fifth paragraphs, which noted that the United

WASHINGTON – (AP) President Reagan, acting on a recommendation from Secretary of State George P. Shultz, has decided to take the first step towards withdrawing the United States from the U.N. Educational, Scientific and Cultural Organization, an administration official said yesterday. **[50]**

An announcement is expected from the State Department sometime next week that notice to withdraw from the U.N. agency will be filed by New Year's Eve. That will set the stage for a U.S. withdrawal by the end of 1984 – "unless Unesco changes its ways," said the official, who declined to be identified. **[49]**

The agency, which was created to encourage scientific, educational and cultural exchanges between nations, has attempted to set worldwide press standards, thereby raising concerns that it was promoting censorship. It also stirred controversy by banning Israel from its activities, a move that subsequently was reversed. **[49]**

The United States, with a contribution of $50 million, is due to underwrite one-forth of Unesco's 1984 budget of about $200 million. Under U.N. rules, unless notice to withdraw was filed by Dec. 31, the United States could not pull out until 1985. **[47]**

The notice does not require the administration to quit Unesco, however. In fact, the move could be mostly a pressure tactic designed to bring about changes in policy. **[44]**

Among Unesco practices that trouble the Reagan administration besides the press code are efforts to devise a code for multinational business corporations and "poor management," said another U.S. official. He said Unesco spends a disproportionate share of its budget on operations at its headquarters. **[42]**

In a report this year to Congress, the State Department said Unesco "provides the United States with useful opportunities not otherwise available for sponsoring scientific projects of global dimensions." **[42]**

The department cities earthquake predictions, ocean research, and management of the world's forests and water resources as examples. **[35]**

However, the report also said, " there have been a number of recent unsuccessful attempts to distort Unesco's mandate and politicize some of its activities." **[36]**

Like the United Nations itself, Unesco is often dominated by a bloc of countries whose policies collide with those of the United States. **[35]**

Earlier this month, Unesco's director general, Amadou-Mahtar M'Bow, defended the agency against accusations of promoting government control of the news media. In fact, he said, Unesco supports press freedom and diversity. **[26]**

M'Bow said large western news organizations do not provide in-depth coverage to the developing nations. The western press denies this claim. **[19]**

On Dec. 15, John Hughes, the State Department spokesman, said a review of U.S. participation in Unesco had been undertaken in June. "For about 10 years," Hughes said, "there have been serious difficulties, including politicization, mismanagement, attempts to restrict press freedom and to impose economic regulation." **[20]**

Hughes said viewpoints expressed within Unesco "seem to be incredibly partisan and opposed to the forces of freedom and certainly to the United States." **[13]**

In November, the United States cast the only vote against Unesco's two-year $3714.4 million budget, contending it was excessive. **[11]**

In 1977, President Carter had the United States withdraw from the International Labor Organization, saying it was no longer committed to its original purpose of improving the lot of workers around the world. Critics of the U.N. agency had complained it was dominated by the Soviet Union and Third World countries. **[6]**

Carter ended the U.S. boycott in 1980, saying the ILO had taken steps to "reduce its level of politicization." U.S. officials said the ILO's tilt towards the Soviet Union had been corrected. **[5]**

The ILO withdrawal was the only U.S. pullout from a U.N. agency since the world organization was formed in 1945. **[4]**

Figure 5.4. Number of Newspapers Carrying Paragraphs of an AP Report of 24 December 1983 (Numbers in Brackets)

States paid one-fourth of the organization's budget and that the move "could be mostly a pressure tactic," were carried by 47 and 44 papers respectively. The sixth paragraph, concerning Unesco's efforts to derive a code for multinational corporations, ran in 42 papers.

The seventh paragraph, also used by 42 papers, noted that the State Department, in a report to Congress earlier in 1983, had said that Unesco "provides the U.S. with useful opportunity not otherwise available for sponsoring scientific projects of global dimensions." Thirty-five papers used the follow-up paragraph that said the State Department had cited as examples earthquake predictions, ocean research, and management of world forest and water resources. And 36 papers carried the ninth paragraph, quoting the State Department as saying, however, that there had been a number of recent attempts to destroy Unesco's mandate and to politicize some of its activities; and the tenth which said that Unesco is "often dominated by a bloc of countries whose policies collide with those of the United States."

The next two paragraphs quoted M'Bow as defending Unesco against accusations of promoting government control of news media, and saying that large Western news organizations do not provide in-depth coverage of developing countries. This is the point where many papers chose to curtail the report. Altogether 26 papers—ten fewer than used the previous paragraph—carried M'Bow's denial, and only 19 ran his criticism of Western news agencies.

The report then recalled remarks made ten days earlier by State Department spokesman John Hughes, criticizing Unesco for "politicization, budget mismanagement, attempts to restrict press freedom and to impose economic regulation." And it concluded with three paragraphs recalling that President Carter had in 1977 withdrawn from the International Labor Organization in 1977 because it was "no longer committed to its original purpose" and was "dominated by the Soviet Union and Third World countries." These final three paragraphs ran in six papers or fewer.

A similar example of bias introduced by the inverted pyramid form is a New York Times News Service report of December 15, 1983, which noted that "the Reagan administration is seriously considering withdrawing the United States from Unesco." The report devoted the first 16 of its 19 paragraphs to criticisms of the organization by State Department spokesmen, particularly Newell. The 17th paragraph reported that "opponents of the withdrawal say the U.S. made major progress at the 22nd biennial conference of Unesco" and that the withdrawal would "turn the organization over to those who are opposed to U.S. interests." The last two paragraphs quote Leonard Sussman of the U.S. National Commission as saying that the Paris conference showed that Unesco "can

be responsive to Western positions" and that if the United States were to sever its ties, "we would have still less chance of influencing policy consistent with our objectives." Of the 22 papers that carried this report, 19 cut out Sussman's comments.

Precisely the same kind of pattern emerged from an analysis of another widely published story, an AP report of 20 December 1984 that Reagan had confirmed his decision to withdraw. The report ran in 34 papers (a second, slightly modified version of the AP report was used by another 20 papers). Of the 34 papers carrying one version, only three used all 28 paragraphs that the AP transmitted. The average number used was 15—or about one-half of the original. Eleven papers, or nearly a third of the total, cut it to the length they wanted by trimming paragraphs from the bottom with no further editing. Three others cut from the bottom but also omitted one paragraph from the portion they used. Sixteen papers were more selective in their editing, omitting several paragraphs but including material from the latter part of the agency copy for the sake of balance.

The first four paragraphs of the report, quoting Newell as attacking Unesco for "endemic hostility to a free press, free markets and individual human rights," were carried by all 34 papers that used the report. The fifth paragraph, quoting the Soviet Union as saying that the Reagan administration had shown "flagrant disregard for the interests of the international community," appeared in 30 of the papers. But the following paragraph, quoting Tass as saying that the withdrawal had followed a "long and malicious campaign" against Unesco, was used by only 20. Criticism by Newell of Unesco's mismanagement in the eighth paragraph ran in 27 papers; the ninth which referred to the U.S. contribution, ran in 29. A reference to the United Kingdom's threat to pull out made 23 papers.

After that there was a sharp drop. The 19th paragraph, which noted that the U.S. National Commission for Unesco had opposed the pullout, was reported in nine of the 34 papers. Paragraph 20, a statement from M'Bow that Unesco would survive the withdrawal, was carried by 10. Comments by Rep. Jim Leach defending Unesco and criticizing the pullout appeared in nine. A statement by the Heritage Foundation saying that the White House should be commended for its "principled stand," got into 10 papers. And the last two paragraphs, listing Unesco's projects to preserve historical sites, to develop education, media and agriculture in Third World countries, got into only seven.

Occasionally the news agency reports used a variation of the inverted pyramid. A story might open with a paragraph quoting someone criticizing Unesco. The second paragraph would introduce an element of balance, quoting another source who disagreed with the first. Then would

follow several paragraphs expanding on the first paragraph, and finally several paragraphs expanding on the second. When papers trimmed these reports, they often did so by cutting from the bottom the detailed remarks of the pro-Unesco source. Then, to preserve the unity of the report, they would also edit out the second paragraph that introduced those remarks.

In short, there was a close correlation between the position of a paragraph in the agency report and the frequency with which it was used. The inverted pyramid style of writing became self-fulfilling. Given the fact that most papers cut reports from the bottom, efforts by the agencies to introduce balance into their stories by including opposing viewpoints were inadequate because they did not also give those viewpoints sufficient prominence. And very few papers, when trimming reports, made the effort to preserve what balance there was in the original.

TOTAL COVERAGE: TABLES

TABLE 5.1. COVERAGE BY DATE AND TYPE OF ARTICLE

Date	News reports	Editorials	Editorial columns	Totals	Percentage
Dec. 83	415	218	94	727	18
Jan. 84	66	245	170	481	12
Feb. 84	69	45	25	139	4
Mar. 84	219	52	56	327	8
Apr. 84	70	58	24	152	4
May 84	50	50	37	137	4
June 84	3	39	12	54	1
July 84	0	64	8	72	2
Aug. 84	52	78	25	155	4
Sept. 84	159	53	9	221	6
Oct. 84	75	31	12	118	3
Nov. 84	200	100	10	310	8
Dec. 84	572	330	120	1,022	26
Total	1,950	1,363	602	3,915	
Percentage	49.7	34.8	15.5		100

TABLE 5.2. COVERAGE OF UNESCO BY SIZE OF CIRCULATION

Circulation (000s)	Mean circulation	Number of dailies in U.S.	Number that ran articles	% that ran articles
<5	3	230	55	23
5–10	7	429	107	25
10–24	16	524	192	37
25–49	35	261	162	62
50–99	66	141	122	86
100–249	152	79	78	99
250–499	341	29	29	100
>500	778	15	15	100
Total		1,700	760	

TABLE 5.3. TYPES OF ARTICLE BY SIZE OF CIRCULATION

Circulation (000s)	News reports (mean)	Editorials (mean)	Columns (mean)	Opinion (mean)	Total (mean)	Percentage opinion
<5	0.2	0.7	0.3	1.0	1.2	84
5–10	0.2	1.2	0.3	1.3	1.6	88
10–24	0.4	1.6	0.3	1.9	2.3	89
25–49	1.4	1.8	0.5	2.3	3.7	79
50–99	3.3	1.9	1.0	2.9	6.1	63
100–249	8.7	2.9	2.4	5.3	14.0	44
250–499	9.5	2.9	3.0	5.9	15.4	36
>500	13.0	3.1	2.7	5.9	18.9	43

Notes: "Opinion" is the sum of editorials and columns.
"Total" is the sum of news reports, editorials and columns.
"Percentage Opinion" is the percentage of editorials and columns in the total coverage.

NEWSPAPER REPORTS: TABLES

TABLE 5.4. NUMBER OF NEWS REPORTS CARRIED IN DAILY PAPERS

Number of reports	Number of papers carrying reports	Percentage of all dailies	Cumulative percentage
0	1,411	83.0	83
1–5	140	8.0	91
6–10	78	4.6	96
11–15	43	2.5	98
16–20	15	0.9	99
21–25	8	0.5	
26–30	2	0.1	
31–35	1	0.1	
36+	2	0.1	100
Total	1,700	100.0	100

TABLE 5.5. NUMBER OF NEWS REPORTS IN CITIES WITH DAILY PAPERS

Number of reports	Number of cities	Percentage of cities	Cumulative percentage
0	1,340	87.0	87
1–5	76	5.0	92
6–10	34	2.2	94
11–15	29	2.0	96
16–20	27	1.8	98
21–25	13	0.9	99
26–30	9	0.6	
31–35	4	0.3	
36+	2	0.1	100
Total	1,534	100.0	100

TABLE 5.6. SOURCES OF PUBLISHED REPORTS AND THEMES BY AGENCY

Agency	Number of reports (incl. duplicates)	Percentage of reports	Number of themes	Percentage of themes
AP	860	44	1,419	44
UPI	299	16	371	11
NYT	238	12	737	23
WP/LAT	104	5	246	14
Other (or no credit)	478	23	459	14
Total	1,979	100	3,232	100

TABLE 5.7. SEPARATE REPORTS USED FROM EACH AGENCY (EXCLUDING DUPLICATES)

Agency	Reports		Papers Using Those Reports		
	Number	Percentage	Number	Percentage	Average number using each report
AP	91	40	881	57	9.7
UPI	62	27	245	16	4.0
NYT	54	24	306	20	5.7
WP/LAT	19	9	101	7	5.3
Total	226	100	1,533	100	6.8

TABLE 5.8. CIRCULATION OF NEWSPAPERS USING NEWS AGENCY REPORTS ON UNESCO

Agency	Combined circulation	Average circulation
AP	121,126,000	140,844
NYT	82,064,000	274,461
UPI	33,906,000	142,462
WP/LAT	34,328,000	330,067
Reuter	11,411,000	422,629

TABLE 5.9. ORIENTATION TOWARD UNESCO OF COVERAGE BY FOUR NEWS AGENCIES AS USED BY NEWSPAPERS (PERCENTAGE)

	Combined agencies n = 3,232	AP n = 1,419	UPI n = 371	NYT n = 737	WP/LAT n = 246	Other or no credit n = 459
Anti-Unesco/ pro-withdrawal	76	79	71	81	70	70
Pro-Unesco/ anti-withdrawal	21	18	26	18	27	27
Looking ahead	3	3	3	1	3	3
Total	100	100	100	100	100	100

TABLE 5.10. ISSUES COVERED BY FOUR NEWS AGENCIES AS USED IN NEWSPAPERS

	Combined agencies n = 3,232	AP n = 1,419	UPI n = 371	NYT n = 783	Wash. Post n = 246	Other or no credit n = 459
Anti-Unesco/ pro-withdrawal						
Politicization	24	25	21	28	16	19
Mismanagement	13	16	9	13	9	13
Reforms needed	13	12	13	17	10	13
Press issues	7	7	8	10	6	6
U.S. pays 25%	5	5	6	3	5	5
Support for U.S.	6	8	8	5	6	5
Too little change	5	5	4	3	7	5
Criticism of M'Bow	2	1	1	1	10	3
Benefits to U.S.	1	1	1	1	2	1
Subtotal	76	80	71	81	71	70
Pro-Unesco/ anti-withdrawal						
Criticism of pullout	10	9	14	8	12	13
Valuable programs	8	6	10	9	11	11
Denials of charges	2	2	1	1	2	3
Propaganda campaign	1	<1	<1	0	1	<1
Subtotal	21	17	25	18	26	27
Looking ahead						
Future	2	2	3	<1	2	3
Alternatives	1	1	1	1	1	<1
Subtotal	3	3	3	2	3	3
Total	100	100	100	100	100	100

TABLE 5.11. CHANGES IN EMPHASIS OVER TIME (PERCENTAGE)

	December 1983 *n* = 803	December 1984 *n* = 986
Anti-Unesco/		
pro-withdrawal		
Politicization	36	22
Mismanagement	10	13
Press issues	14	6
Reforms needed	6	12
U.S. pays 25%	4	4
Support for U.S.	2	6
Too little change	3	8
Criticism of M'Bow	1	1
Benefits to U.S.	2	2
Subtotal	80	74
Pro-Unesco/		
anti-withdrawal		
Criticism of pullout	10	12
Valuable programs	10	7
Denials of charges	<1	<1
Propaganda campaign	0	1
Subtotal	20	20
Looking ahead		
Future	<1	4
Alternatives	<1	2
Subtotal	<1	6
Total	100	100

CHAPTER 6

Editorials

The editorial writer should discourage publication of editorials pre-pared by an outside writing service and presented as the newspaper's own. Failure to disclose the source of such editorials is unethical, and particularly reprehensible when the service is in the employ of a special interest.

— *Basic Statement of Principles,*
National Conference of Editorial Writers

Like the news reports, editorials for this analysis were collected by Press Intelligence, Inc., over the period December 1983 through December 1984. The file yielded a total of 1,417 editorials relating to the Unesco withdrawal. They appeared in 630 different newspapers, or just over one-third of the 1,700 dailies nationwide. More than twice as many papers carried editorials about Unesco as carried news reports.

States in which the largest number of editorials were published were, in order, New York (with 9 percent of the total), Ohio, Texas, California, Florida and Illinois. Between them these six states—which among them have 38 percent of the nation's population—accounted for more than 40 percent of the editorials published.

More than one-half of the papers that ran editorials (353) printed only one during the year. Another 156 had two; 76 had three; 41 had four; 24 had five and 14 had six. Thus 90 percent of the papers that carried editorials had six or fewer. Just 16 papers had more than six editorials: five had seven; four had eight, and four had nine. The *San*

Diego Union published 10; the San Francisco *Examiner* had 13, and the *San Antonio Light* had 18 (Table 6.1).

The biggest papers—those with circulations of 200,000 and above— published an average of 3.5 editorials on Unesco apiece. This compared to an average of 13 news reports each and 3.4 editorial page columns. Several much smaller papers carried far more editorials than the average for the large papers. Thus, the Ravenna, Ohio, *Record-Courier* (circulation 26,000) had 11; the Elkins, W.Va. (*Inter-Mountain* (26,000) had 10; the Wheeling, W.Va., *Intelligencer* (9,000) had nine; the Woodbridge, N.J., *Tribune* (53,000) had eight; and the Springfield, Ill., *State Journal-Register* (57,000) and the Waukegan, Ill., *News-Sun* (42,000) had seven each. Many small papers carried only editorials about Unesco—sometimes several of them—with no news coverage at all.

The bulk of the editorials were, however, related to news events, usually those that showed Unesco in an unfavorable light. The initial announcement of withdrawal and confirmation of that decision a year later between them gave rise to more than one-half of all the editorials. Consequently, most of the editorials were published in December 1983/ January 1984, or in December 1984. Other news events that spurred editorial writers into action were the British notice of withdrawal, which generally was applauded as being supportive of the American position; the fire at Unesco headquarters, which was typically depicted as an attempt to destroy evidence sought by congressional investigators; and the GAO report criticizing Unesco's management, which was cited as justifying the U.S. action.

Largely ignored by the editorial writers were news events that could be considered favorable to Unesco's cause, such as meetings of its Executive Board that adopted Western proposals for reform; congressional hearings at which witnesses made a case for retaining membership, and the report of the U.S. National Commission for Unesco recommending that the best course of action would be to seek change from within. The emphasis was almost entirely on the negative.

ANTI-UNESCO EDITORIALS

One curious phenomenon that emerged when the computer data base matched the opening sentences of editorials was the high proportion of editorials that were exact duplicates of each other, carried in papers around the country with no indication of their common origin. Of the 1,417 editorials in the file, 377 (or more than one-quarter) appeared in sets of two or more. Most of these "canned" editorials ran in five papers or fewer. But 11 ran in more than 10 papers, and three were used word

for word by more than 30, without attribution and sometimes under headings like "Our Opinion," "In Our View," or "The Way We See It."

Copley Editorial Service

The Copley Editorial Service was by far the biggest source of "canned" editorials on Unesco. Copley distributes about 40 editorials a week to the 600 newspapers that buy its comprehensive news and feature packages, or its Political Cartoons and Editorials package. Most of the editorials it syndicates are from the *San Diego Union* and the *San Diego Tribune*, both of which are Copley papers. But they may also originate from other papers. Twelve separate editorials that could be traced to this service were distributed over the year—nine from the group's flagship daily, the *San Diego Union* (circulation 217,000) and three from the evening San Diego *Tribune* (127,000). Copley-owned newspapers that used its Unesco editorials were the Springfield, Ill., *State Journal-Register* (57,000); the Waukegan, Ill., *News-Sun* (42,000); the Wheaton, Ill., *Daily Journal* (7,000) and the Joliet, Ill., *Herald-News* (48,000). The Copley editorials on Unesco were also used by more than 100 other papers around the nation. Altogether the dozen editorials it distributed ran in 231 papers.

These editorials are significant because of the nationwide readership they reached—the papers were published in 32 states—and because they are typical of the kind of coverage Unesco received in editorial columns. Virtually all the major themes appear in them, and as in the case of the editorials as a whole, they become more critical of Unesco over time.

The first editorial in this group, published in the *San Diego Tribune* on 16 December 1983—the day after the first news report that the United States planned to withdraw—noted that Unesco had been founded to promote development of schools, cultural institutions and scientific discoveries in underdeveloped nations. But in recent years Unesco had become a "bear-baiting ring, with the non-Western majority charging the United States millions of dollars a year in membership fees, to be the bear." The editorial singles out Unesco's press policies: "Third World countries, like Iran, angered by news coverage by the Western media, sought to write rules for international reporting. These rules would amount to U.N.–sanctioned censorship." Yet the editorial quotes Freedom House as saying the United States should remain a member and use its financial leverage to influence Unesco policy. And it concludes that "America should stay in the organization and fight for its values, not pull out and put its head in the sand." The editorial ran in 13 newspapers.

Just three days later, however, a *San Diego Union* editorial, picked up by 10 other papers, noted that there were "sound reasons" for considering a withdrawal, because "the sad truth is that [Unesco] has become

a propaganda forum for attacks on the free world's values and institutions." These included demands by the Third World and communist bloc for a new world information order, "a euphemism for government control of the media."

A January 11 editorial from the *Union*, carried also by eight other papers, called for reforms in Unesco if the United States were to remain a member. "We Americans do not pay our taxes so that the emissaries of 150 nations can dine regularly at restaurants rated highly in the Guide Michelin." Four days later an editorial on "Saving the U.N." said that several of the world organization's agencies had become "shamelessly politicized." Unesco was a case in point. Its "anti-Western bias grew so odious that even the State Department backed the Reagan administration's decision to withdraw from the agency." This was picked up by nine papers.

The fire at Unesco headquarters in Paris sparked one of the more heated Copley editorials. Unesco, said the first paragraph, is "the most notoriously wasteful, inefficient and anti-American branch of the United Nations." This lead was remarkably similar to the first paragraph of a Heritage Foundation "backgrounder" by Owen Harries, distributed to the press earlier. In it Harries called Unesco "the most virulently anti-American—and most inefficient and wasteful—member of the United Nations system." The Copley editorial accused the agency of being a "forum for rabid communist and Third World denunciation of the United States and its principles," of being a "hornet's nest of Soviet spies," and of supporting a New World Information Order "that would license journalists and prohibit them from criticizing communist and Third World governments." Noting that the fire in Paris had been set shortly before the General Accounting Office was to begin examining Unesco documents, the editorial averred that "no one has yet directly accused Unesco of torching its own building, but if the charges of fraud against Unesco are true, the fires certainly would have been convenient." This editorial appeared in 16 newspapers with a combined circulation of about a half-million copies.

In April, 27 papers around the nation ran a Copley editorial that asserted that while Unesco had originally been created to promote literacy, education and culture, "ever since the communists came aboard during the 1960s, the organization has specialized in anti-Western diatribes." It complained that "Unesco's 2,500 bureaucrats are constantly ventilating anti-Western themes, completely ignoring communist outrages proceeding apace. The crowning insult is that the Western nations pay the lion's share of Unesco's tab."

Britain's announcement that it intended to withdraw if Unesco did not reform engendered a Copley editorial noting that the move "greatly

strengthens the hand of the United States in demanding such reforms." The United States, it said, "should make good its threat to withdraw from the organization," then, if there was meaningful reform, it could return later. Unesco could serve a useful purpose "if it stays out of international politics, if it serves its original goals, and if it spends less money on administrative overhead." Until then, "we should walk out and pocket our checkbook."

The confirmation in December 1984 that the United States would indeed withdraw was praised in a Copley editorial that ran in 34 newspapers, with a combined circulation of nearly a million copies. It noted that Unesco's "bloated bureaucracy will have to make do now without the U.S. contribution of $47 million, which is 25 percent of the organization's annual budget," and that this would not be easy for the "Paris-based bureaucrats who have become accustomed to five-star hotels, four-star restaurants and limousines." Nor was Unesco's irresponsibility limited to "unbridled extravagance." During M'Bow's reign, "the organization has condemned Israel, denounced the free-enterprise system, called for a redistribution of the world's wealth, and advanced state censorship and manipulation of international news." The U.S. departure, it said, "should have a salutary effect on Unesco which continues to resist significant internal reforms."

While the Copley Editorial Service was by far the largest supplier of canned editorials on Unesco, several other sources provided editorials to a number of papers, usually members of a chain. Although none of these sources reached as many newspapers as did Copley, some were significant because of the large circulations of the papers in which they appeared. Thus while a Copley editorial might appear in 30 newspapers with a combined circulation of about a million copies, a Scripps-Howard or a Hearst editorial could reach as many readers through fewer but larger papers.

Scripps-Howard News Service

Scripps-Howard was the second-largest distributor of canned editorials. Six editorials that appeared in up to a dozen papers each can be traced to this source. These included major metropolitan dailies that are part of the Scripps-Howard chain: the *Cincinnati Post* (circulation 190,000); the *Pittsburgh Press* (272,000); the Denver *Rocky Mountain News* (231,000); the Memphis *Commercial Appeal* (200,000); the Columbus, Ohio, *Citizen-Journal* (112,000); and the Knoxville, Tenn., *News-Sentinel*, among others. Some papers that are not members of the chain also used these editorials. Altogether 14 papers in nine states carried one or more.

The first, appearing in the *Cincinnati Post* and four other papers in December 1983, had a moderate tone. It noted that the Reagan administration was seriously considering withdrawing from Unesco. It quoted State Department officials as saying that Unesco had become a "costly, wasteful, anti-democratic propaganda shop unworthy of further U.S. support" but also quoted the U.S. Commission for Unesco as warning that the pullout would end American influence in the body and favoring staying in and fighting for reform. "Both points of view have merit," it said. "We believe the administration should give notice of withdrawal . . . if during the year Unesco becomes less politicized and profligate, the United States can simply cancel its letter of withdrawal."

Another Scripps-Howard editorial, at the end of December 1983, after the United States had announced its intention to withdraw, took a somewhat harder line. It said that Reagan had acted sensibly in giving notice "unless the agency mends its wasteful and anti-democratic ways." Unesco's original goal was fostering literacy and education in poor nations, but "unfortunately, it later was hijacked by communists and radical Third Worlders and turned into a propaganda vehicle against democratic ideals and values." And in recent years "the communist–Third World majority and a costly, high-living secretariat in Paris have schemed to control and censor the press and news agencies and to license journalists so they will write according to Unesco guidelines." The U.S. move would be a useful warning to other U.N. agencies that had strayed from their original purpose. This editorial ran in 11 different newspapers, with a combined circulation of more than 1 million copies.

The next widely used Scripps-Howard editorial appeared in November 1984 and was picked up by nine papers. By then the moderate tone of the earlier editorials had largely disappeared. It noted that Reagan was scheduled, within a few weeks, to review his decision to withdraw. Unesco, it said, had been pushing the concept of a new world information order "that is ostensibly aimed at improving the communications systems of developing nations." But its most controversial feature was an attempt, under the guise of protecting the working conditions and safety of journalists, to license reporters. "This is anathema to Western journalists, who correctly view it as a leftist-inspired scheme to legitimize government control of the press that is practiced in communist and most Third World nations and to expand it on an international scale." President Reagan, said the editorial, should "go ahead with his decision to take the U.S. out of Unesco, which has become hopelessly inefficient, wasteful and biased against free institutions."

Confusion in the public mind between Unesco and UNICEF—the U.N. children's fund—which suffered a loss of donations as a result of the criticism of Unesco, led to a Scripps-Howard editorial in December

1984 that sought to set the record straight. UNICEF was worthy of support, as opposed to Unesco, a "communist and Third World-run club that spends much time bashing the United States, the West, Israel, private enterprise and a free press." Also, Unesco had become "unbearably costly and wasteful, spending too little money on illiteracy in the field, and too much on its wasteful bureaucracy in Paris and on useless conferences in pleasant surroundings." Reagan, "properly disgusted by Unesco's antics," had served notice that the United States would withdraw unless the agency mended its ways: "There has been no meaningful improvement."

This theme was elaborated in another Scripps-Howard editorial a week later after the United States had confirmed its decision. Unesco, it said, had made only cosmetic moves to reform. The ideologues and bureaucrats who control its Paris headquarters liked what they were doing and they doubted that Reagan would flout world opinion by leaving: "Now Reagan has their attention." The loss of U.S. funding "might even cause the early departure of Director General Amadou Mahtar M'Bow of Senegal, who lives like a king on money that could be used to teach African children and runs the place like a dictator." This editorial appeared in eight major Scripps-Howard papers.

Hearst News and Feature Service

The New York–based Hearst News and Feature Service distributed canned editorials to newspapers owned by the Hearst Corporation. Ten editorials appeared in two or more Hearst papers during the year. It is likely that more were transmitted: the *San Antonio Light* (circulation 125,000) alone carried 18 editorials on Unesco, nine of which appeared also in other papers. Among the regular users of the Hearst editorials were the San Francisco *Examiner* (157,000) and the Albany, N.Y., *Times-Union* (86,000). Less frequent users were the Midland, Texas, *Reporter-Telegram*, the Baltimore *News-American* and the Seattle *Post-Intelligencer*.

The first multiple-use Hearst editorial ran in mid-December 1983 when the State Department was considering notice of withdrawal. The editorial quoted "several good reasons" for the proposal, including a budget that has "ballooned to $374.4 million," a bureaucracy that "also has ballooned and become so cumbersome that some State Department officials smell mismanagement," and efforts to tamper with freedom of the press: "Third World and Soviet delegates have been trying for several years to create a New World Information Order. What they want to do is license journalists and empower Unesco to decide who gets the licenses, all of which add up to censorship."

Once the decision to withdraw had been announced, a Hearst editorial focused on the U.S. contribution to Unesco's budget. The Reagan administration, it said, was "fed up with an outfit that wastes money on a top-heavy bureaucracy, may of whose members are not only anti-American but opposed to a free press." The funds the United States had been contributing to Unesco "could well be spent by helping needy nations directly without wasting dollars supporting Unesco officials who enjoy a good life in and around their Paris headquarters."

Press issues were the primary focus of an editorial published by three major Hearst papers in February. It said that U.S. officials hoped that Unesco would "come to their senses and initiate reforms," but "significant reform would be almost a miracle" in view of the direction Unesco had been going in the past five years. "A Unesco decision to support freedom of information, and keep governments off the backs of the press, would do a lot to restore America's faith in this agency." But, the editorial cautioned, "the best counsel is, don't hold your breath."

The free-press theme reappears in another Hearst editorial in April. Unesco, it said, ought to work toward championing a free press throughout the world rather than working toward limiting it. Such a policy would not necessarily mean that the United States would change its mind about withdrawing, "but it would eliminate one of the biggest bones of contention." And two weeks later the same papers editorialized that if Unesco "had a genuine interest in education, science and culture throughout the world, it would stand up and be counted on the side of a free press."

The announcement in July that the Netherlands had warned Unesco that it might quit if there were no reforms, triggered another Hearst press-freedom broadside. The Netherlands and the United States had similar complaints about Unesco's anti-Western attitudes, it said. "One such attitude involves freedom of the press. Many Unesco leaders have talked for years about getting governments involved in gathering and dissemination of news. This is a concept totally foreign to leaders in The Hague as well as Washington, and to governments throughout the Free World."

There was little doubt as to the official Hearst line on the withdrawal. As the Albany *Times-Union* editorialized toward the end of 1984, "at the end of the week, the United States will quit its role in Unesco, and it is right to do so."

Other Chains

Other newspaper chains also distributed canned editorials to their member papers. These included Gannett, Thompson, Newhouse, and California's McClatchy Newspapers, although none matched the groups

mentioned above in terms of the number of editorials or the number of papers that published them.

Several small chains of small newspapers were remarkably active in editorializing against Unesco. Freedom Newspapers, Inc., distributed editorials to about a dozen papers in seven states. These included some fairly substantial papers like the *Sioux City Journal* (circulation 59,000) and the Lima, Ohio, *News* (40,000). These papers also used some editorials from the Copley Editorial Service. A curious phenomenon here is that of these papers only the *Sioux City Journal* appears to have carried any news reports relating to Unesco in addition to its editorials (five editorials and three news reports). The others carried only editorials. Thus the *Lima News* ran eight editorials blasting Unesco, but no news reports; the Marysville, Calif., *Appeal-Democrat* had four editorials but no news, and the Crawfordsville, Ind., *Journal-Review* and the McAllen, Texas, *Monitor* had only three editorials apiece.

These editorials were uniformly antagonistic toward Unesco. One, carried soon after the initial announcement, declared that the withdrawal was long overdue. "The only puzzle is why U.S. diplomats chose to give Unesco a year to get its act together (with at least $70 million of U.S. taxpayers' money) instead of withdrawing forthwith." It quotes Owen Harries of the Heritage Foundation as saying that Unesco "represents a worst-case model of the U.N. system" with its "consistent and malignant anti-Western bias."

An editorial carried by nine Freedom newspapers in June asserted that Unesco is "an organization of irresponsible Third World politicians and bureaucrats (few beholden to anything resembling a democratic process) who find in Unesco a marvelous way to substitute anti-American rhetoric for second thoughts about the repressive policies of their own governments that keep their people impoverished."

Another small chain with strong views about Unesco was the West Virginia–based Ogden Newspapers. Again, its editorials command attention because they enunciate themes typical of the editorial coverage. Six of the chain's papers, all with circulations of 30,000 or less, carried several canned editorials during the year. Most of these appear to have originated at the Wheeling, W.Va., *Intelligencer* (circulation 24,000), flagship of the chain. That paper ran nine editorials that were repeated verbatim by other papers in the group, including the Parkersburg, W.Va., *Sentinel* (21,000), the Martinsburg W.Va., *Journal* (18,000), the Marion, Ohio, *Star* (20,000) and the Jamestown, N.Y., *Post-Herald* (29,000).

All these editorials strongly favored withdrawal, with a recurring theme that the United States should not provide financial support to an organization that opposed its interests. Just before the first announcement of the intention to pull out, a Freedom editorial argued that the United

States, by far the greatest single supporter of Unesco, had "cast the only vote against increased spending by this international bureaucracy." This, it said, "furnished just one more good reason to declare the time has come for us to leave Unesco." American taxpayers, it declared, "should no longer be required to subsidize this wasteful U.N. bureaucracy whose only major accomplishment has been to provide a forum from which we may consistently be attacked by our enemies."

By April, the chain was arguing that fundamental reforms requested by the United States as a condition of retaining membership were not likely to come about. "We need now to stick to our original decision and not be satisfied with only cosmetic changes."

When California Congressman Esteban Torres voiced his opposition to the withdrawal in April, papers in the chain complained that "some of our congressional wimps have begun their moaning at the announced decision." A statement by Edmund Hennelly, who had headed the U.S. delegation to Unesco, that the agency had "got the message," was dismissed in the editorial with the question: "What guarantee has the United States that these contemplated changes are [not] merely cosmetic facelifts being performed to keep us and our money in the organization?" For the United States to remain in Unesco it should demand that M'Bow be ousted, that the Unesco budget be reduced by 20 percent, "and that all political bias against the West be suppressed."

The Soviet Union's criticism of the pullout was seen by another canned editorial as a justification for the U.S. action: "If any further reassurance were needed that the decision of this country to withdraw from Unesco was correct, it is provided by this opposition from the Soviets." At the time the Reagan administration had decided to withdraw, said the editorial, "we applauded the move. We still do, and urge the president to stick by the original decision."

In September, referring to documents distributed by Unesco, an Ogden chain editorial complained that "American taxpayers had to foot 25 percent of the bill for disseminating this garbage all over the world. December can come none too soon, when we can leave this left-leaning agency to its own devices, and happily, be relieved of our current obligation to support financially an outfit which has been doing its level best to cut our throats."

The news in November that Britain had served notice of withdrawal prompted an editorial welcoming its decision. If Unesco felt "it must persist in constant denunciation of Western values, there is no reason whatever for the principal targets of those attacks to pay for the forum from which they are mounted." America's final withdrawal was welcomed in an editorial in December 1984 which noted that "we are delighted that

the Reagan administration has followed through on the original decision, since no meaningful improvements have been made."

THE ELITE PRESS

The *New York Times*

Editorials in the "elite" press played a significant role in the withdrawal debate, not only because of their large and influential readership, but because they often set the tone and direction for editorials in smaller papers, and sometimes were reprinted as "guest editorials." The New York Times News Service syndicates between one and three editorials a day to about 540 newspaper subscribers. A *New York Times* (circulation 905,000) editorial of 16 December 1983 is widely regarded has having given the Reagan administration the green light to announce the withdrawal, secure in the knowledge that it would have the backing of the "liberal" press.

The editorial enunciated themes that were to recur in other papers throughout the year: at its inception Unesco had set out to support literacy, education, science and culture. But these constructive purposes had been overwhelmed after the 1960s when the Communist nations joined the agency, after which "every meeting became an anti-Western rally." An American withdrawal, or threat to withdraw, "would not harm any democratic cause or global understanding. If fairly explained, it might even promote scientific and cultural values."

When the State Department named a panel to study the decision, the *Times* ran an editorial that stated—then refuted—the main arguments for remaining a member. There was no point in staying in and using American influence to keep Unesco from becoming even shriller in its anti-Western bias, because it was only under the threat of withdrawal that Unesco had begun to give urgent attention to Western complaints. The argument that Unesco had abandoned its "single most objectionable effort"—to interfere with press freedoms internationally—was flawed because although Unesco had backed down on proposals for licensing journalists or legitimizing censorship, "why should democratic societies ever have to compromise their ideas of freedom with totalitarian governments?" The argument that, despite its failings, Unesco had done much good, notably through its literacy campaigns in poorer nations, was seen as "reason enough to keep the question open." If Unesco showed a willingness to "add to this body of work and abandon the rest, it could again make Americans eager and generous participants."

Just before the final decision was due, the *Times* came out in favor of withdrawal in an editorial which stated that although there had been a distinct change in the attitude at Unesco since the previous December, "the policies that provoked the threat have not really changed." And until they did, "President Reagan ought to keep up the pressure by vacating America's seat and diverting its $50 million in dues to selected Unesco and other global projects."

The *Washington Post*

The *Washington Post* (circulation 726,000), at the time withdrawal was being contemplated, argued that the "idea of withdrawing, or at least of withholding dues, has an undeniable appeal." Unesco, at its founding, "embodied prized values of openness and tolerance," and had run valuable programs. "Then it got hijacked by a Third World-communist collective seemingly interested less in running good programs than in engaging in ideological disputations and living the high life." M'Bow, said the *Post*, "is identified prominently with both of these tendencies." For the administration the question was whether to keep paying in order to work from within, or announce its intention to stop paying in the hope that the agency would be jolted into reforming itself: "We think the jolt of an announced intention to withdraw is indicated."

Toward the end of the year, the *Post* seemed to come down in favor of the United States delaying its decision by a year in order to "fall in with Britain and the other European countries that may follow its lead." It was not clear whether Unesco's "politicization and rampant mismanagement" had been halted. Things were better but not conclusively better. "The argument has shifted to whether they can still improve and, specifically, whether they can improve while Unesco remains under Amadou Mahtar M'bow, the man from Senegal whose leadership style is at the heart of the Unesco dispute."

The *Wall Street Journal*

The *Wall Street Journal* editorials took aim even more squarely at M'Bow. One, published in January 1984, asserted that M'Bow's efforts to "fetter the free press finally succeeded in turning even the most liberal Western news media into critics of his Paris-based playpen." The editorial charged that M'Bow had on his personal staff three KGB spies. When they were kicked out by the French government, he did not fire them; "in fact he gave them raises." He was accused of using a slush fund to "get friendly people into jobs and keep others in line" and of appointing his wife's cousin as personnel director.

The *Journal*'s assault on M'Bow continued in September in an editorial concerning the draft GAO report, "which says in effect that Unesco is the personal fiefdom of its director-general." After accusing M'Bow of paying employees without confirmation that they had actually worked and of violating Unesco's financial rules, the editorial concludes that "we can only assume that the United States will make its withdrawal final as scheduled at the end of the year."

PRO-UNESCO EDITORIALS

Editorials favoring Unesco, or opposing the withdrawal, were far less frequent, and almost invariably appeared in individual papers rather than being distributed by chains. These editorials had several themes in common. Almost all acknowledged Unesco's shortcomings—chiefly mismanagement, politicization and hostility to a free press. But they also emphasized its useful programs, including educational efforts like building schools, training teachers and promoting literacy; scientific projects in earthquake prediction, mineral resource studies, forest and water management; and cultural programs like preservation of important historic monuments.

They tended to stress also that significant reforms were indeed taking place and that Unesco had abandoned plans to restrict journalists. Most concluded that the United States should continue to seek reform, but that it should do so from within the organization, not outside. Withdrawal would mean abandoning any chance of influencing debates that might affect U.S. interests. It would also indicate an abdication of America's leadership role in international affairs. As one editorial put it, "America should stay in the organization and fight for its values, not pull out and put its head in the sand." These editorials often reflect, and occasionally quote, the views of members of the U.S. National Commission for Unesco.

Christian Science Monitor

Of the nationally circulated papers, only the *Christian Science Monitor* (circulation 174,000) could find enough value in Unesco's activities to merit continued membership. A series of *Monitor* articles over the year acknowledged Unesco's failings, but emphasized its positive contributions: "It trains teachers for poor nations. It has undertaken projects to save world monuments. It fights illiteracy. It fosters important oceanographic and environmental research." The *Monitor* pressed for continued efforts to improve Unesco, and after the final decision was announced, it

urged efforts "to effect its reform and permit American reentry into a stronger and more effective organization."

The Hartford *Courant*

A similar position was adopted by some large regional papers. The Hartford, Conn., *Courant* (circulation 215,000) argued in a series of editorials that Unesco's weaknesses were not a sufficient reason to pull out, and that the United States would lose influence if it withdrew. As the deadline neared, the *Courant* lamented that the Reagan administration seemed to have discounted progress in reforming Unesco's budgetary and administrative practices. "A powerful signal will be sent if the U.S. walks out in spite of sincere efforts of the organization to clean up objectionable procedures: America is less interested than before in international cooperation." Once the final decision had been taken, the *Courant* argued that the withdrawal should be viewed as temporary, and that if the United States were to remain apart from Unesco, "the result might be disintegration of the agency and a crippling blow to the United Nations itself."

The Cleveland *Plain Dealer*

The Cleveland *Plain Dealer* (circulation 488,000) noted in March that the decision to pull out, "though applauded by some, has been criticized by others who rightly regard it as short-sighted and ill-advised." The need for change in Unesco was apparent, said the *Plain Dealer*, "but so is the need for strong leadership by the United States in multilateral organizations . . . offering constructive change from within—rather than giving up and withdrawing—is how the U.S. should exert its leadership."

In November the *Plain Dealer* urged in a strongly worded editorial that the Reagan administration "call off the Unesco dogs." As a result of U.S. pressure, it said, Unesco had reorganized its bureaucracy, curbed its budget and lessened efforts to limit international press coverage. The United States could not have insisted on these changes had it not been a member of Unesco. If the United States wanted to see these reforms implemented, "it will continue its membership in an organization that, despite its faults, has made major contributions to global well-being."

When the administration reaffirmed its decision to pull out, the *Plain Dealer* argued that it was an "assertion of nationalism at a time when the government should be strengthening its multilateral approach." And it quoted Rep. Jim Leach, R-Iowa, as saying that "given the fact that we have prevailed on every major issue facing Unesco in recent years, it is difficult to know how U.S. views would be better protected from an empty chair."

The *Houston Post*

The *Houston Post* (circulation 300,000) took a somewhat more equivocal, but generally pro-membership line. It was unsparing in its criticism of Unesco's "gimcrack proposals for 'new world orders' that could, among other things, restrict the free flow of information and hamstring the world economy." However, it argued that "while we have solid grounds for complaint, by withdrawing now we will forfeit an opportunity to further influence the debate on the new world information order on which we have already made important concessions." After the U.S. withdrawal had become final, the *Post* commented that, despite all the drawbacks, "the United Nations remains our best hope in an imperfect world."

Other Papers

Other large papers that supported continued membership included the St. Louis *Post-Dispatch* (circulation 235,000); the Akron, Ohio, *Beacon-Journal* (165,000); and the Hackensack, N.J., *Record* 155,000).

The papers favoring continued membership were, however, in a minority. Most of the large regional papers that took a continuing interest in the issue (defined here as those with circulations of 200,000 or more, that carried four or more editorials over the year), spoke strongly in favor of the pullout. These included the Phoenix *Arizona Republic* (circulation 264,000); the *San Diego Union* (217,000); Denver's *Rocky Mountain News* (322,000); the *Detroit Free Press* (631,000); the *Detroit News* (633,000); the *Indianapolis Star* (217,000); the St. Louis *Globe-Democrat* (260,000); the Memphis *Commercial Appeal* (206,000); the *Dallas Morning News* (317,000) and the *Boston Herald* (317,000).

CONTENT ANALYSIS

A sample of the editorials was analyzed using the same content analysis scheme as applied to the news agency reports and the news stories that appeared in the press. The editorials were sorted by date, and one-fifth selected on a random-interval basis for analysis. The sample comprised 272 editorials, which between them yielded 3,348 themes, or an average of about 12 themes apiece.

Orientation

The editorials proved to be significantly more critical of Unesco and supportive of the withdrawal than the news copy. Of all the themes in the editorials, 84 percent were anti-Unesco or pro-withdrawal (compared to

70 percent for the news agency copy, and 76 percent in the published reports). Just 14 percent of the editorial themes acknowledged the merit of Unesco's programs, or argued against the pullout, and just over 2 percent focused on what the future might hold. The high proportion of negative themes is due to the fact that even the editorials that advocated continued membership almost invariably listed a litany of complaints about the agency before concluding that U.S. interests would better be served by seeking reform from within.

As can be seen in the examples above, the editorials generally expressed the same themes as the news coverage, but with a stronger emphasis on topics critical of Unesco. The editorials as a whole were more critical of Unesco's politicization than either the news agency reports or the published stories, focusing specifically on allegations that Unesco was anti-Western and biased in favor of the Soviet Union and the Third World (Table 6.2).

The editorials also paid more attention to press issues than the news reports did. There were proportionately twice as many references in the editorials to Unesco's support for a new information order, to its support for state control of news media, and to proposals for licensing journalists. Thus while the news reports tended to reflect the administration's concerns about Unesco—primarily politicization and mismanagement—the media's own preoccupation with press freedom is expressed in the editorials. Many editorials stated quite explicitly that Unesco's efforts to curb the press were the major justification for the withdrawal. Criticism of M'Bow's leadership, which accounted for only two percent of the themes in the news reports, was twice as frequent in the editorials.

Conversely, the editorials included only half as many themes critical of the withdrawal and fewer affirmations as to the value of Unesco's activities in promoting education, science and culture. The editorials also expressed less interest than the news reports in the need for reforms in Unesco or in the fact that reforms were taking place. The biggest difference between the news coverage and the editorials is that a large proportion of the editorials expressed the opinion that withdrawal was the right decision and in the best interests of the United States. This category, representing the views of publishers and editors, rose from less then 2 percent of the themes in the news reports to nearly 7 percent in the editorials.

Attributions

About 77 percent of all the themes in the editorials were not attributed to any specific source and thus were expressions of the newspapers' editorial opinions. There were some significant differences between the themes

attributed to a source and those that were not. The attributed themes placed more emphasis on allegations of mismanagement and the need for reform—essentially the line taken by the U.S. government. The unattributed themes, or expressions of editorial opinion, were twice as likely to mention press issues, especially state control of media and attempts to license journalists, and three times as likely to express the benefits to the United States of a withdrawal (Table 6.3).

Of the thematic statements that were attributed, 58 percent cited U.S. government officials, and another 21 percent cited Western government representatives, who probably included U.S. officials (Table 6.4). Unesco officials were quoted as the source of 8 percent of the themes, with U.S. non-government organizations accounting for 6 percent and American academics for 2 percent. Themes attributed to Soviet or Third World sources comprised just 1 percent each. The sources used in the editorials, therefore, were very similar to those used by the news agency reports. Like the news agencies, the editorials used U.S. or Western government spokesmen for more than 75 percent of their attributed themes. The editorials, however, used proportionately even fewer quotations from Unesco, the Soviet Union and the Third World than did the news agency reports.

In addition to being highly selective in the sources they quoted, the editorials tended to quote from those sources only such themes as supported their orientation (Table 6.4). For example, the themes attributed to U.S. government officials—by far the largest source—were 89 percent critical of Unesco (the news-agency figure was 82 percent). Attributions to Western government spokesmen were not far behind at 87 percent (the news-agency figure was 75 percent). Where the selective use of quotations was most apparent, however, was in those attributed to Unesco sources. In the news-agency copy, 74 percent of the themes attributed to Unesco officials were positive about the agency's programs and critical of the withdrawal. In the editorials, however, themes attributed to Unesco spokesmen were more often negative than positive with respect to the agency (55 to 45 percent). Thus, while Unesco spokesmen were sometimes quoted as affirming the value of its programs and criticizing the United States for pulling out, they were quoted more frequently as being critical of Unesco's politicization, of M'Bow's leadership, and of general mismanagement. Many of these statements came from dissident or disaffected Unesco staffers, often anonymous, who were quoted more often in the editorials than official Unesco spokesmen.

The Heritage Foundation, which supported the withdrawal, was quoted more frequently and at greater length than the U.S. National Commission for Unesco, which did not. The Soviet Union, while seldom quoted, generally was depicted—quite accurately—as supporting Unesco

and criticizing the pullout. The Soviet criticism was, however, used by some editorial writers as a means of justifying the U.S. decision: if the Soviets were against it, we must be doing something right. As one canned editorial put it, "any lingering doubts in the minds of Americans that the U.S. is mistaken in its plan to withdraw from Unesco now has been effectively dispelled. Soviet Premier Andropov has criticized this action. That means we must be right in withdrawing our support from Unesco."

Changes over Time

Unlike the news agencies, which tended to moderate their criticism of Unesco during the course of the year and give more prominence to supporters of the organization, the editorials were consistently hostile. If anything, they were marginally more critical in December 1984 than they were when notice of withdrawal was given a year earlier (Table 6.5). Many of the editorials relating to the initial announcement took their cue from news reports that gave the administration's reasons for the step, but also quoted the U.S. National Commission as favoring continued membership to fight for reform from within. Later, however, this view was largely replaced by administration figures and Heritage Foundation analysts who argued that there had been no meaningful reform, and even if there were, once the United States had announced it would leave, it would lose face if it changed its mind. There were also other differences in emphasis. In later months, the editorials muted their criticism of Unesco's politicization but their more frequent attacks on its management meant that the sum of these two categories remained constant. Criticism of Unesco's press policies declined, becoming more in line with the agenda set by the news agencies. But there was a sharp increase in criticism of M'Bow and in opinions that Usesco had not reformed sufficiently to justify continued participation. While the news agency reports at the end of the year included proportionately more criticisms of the withdrawal and expressions of support for Unesco than at the beginning of the period, these themes both declined in the editorials, which remained adamantly opposed to the organization.

The question of canned editorials was raised in a report in *Editor & Publisher* in July 1984 after Joseph Mehan, Unesco's chief of public information in the United States, complained about the practice, saying Unesco had been "victimized by it several times over the past four or five years." *Editor & Publisher* quotes Copley News Service general manager Charles Ohl as saying that the use of syndicated editorials may be increasing because editors of smaller papers "want to take some sort of stand" on current issues.[1] Most of the syndicated editorials deal with national and international topics; even the smaller papers write their own editorials on local matters.

Thomas Huckle, editor of the Cadillac, Mich., *News*, which used Copley editorials on Unesco but no news reports, told *Editor & Publisher* that his paper used syndicated editorials to get "the benefit of research others are doing that we don't have time to do." And Samuel Cothran, publisher of the Aiken, S. C., *Standard*, which ran six canned Copley editorials criticizing Unesco but no news reports, said his paper uses only editorials that are compatible with its general editorial stance.

NOTE

1. David Astor, "Syndicates: Distribution of Newspaper Viewpoints," *Editor & Publisher*, 7 July 1984, pp. 28–29.

EDITORIALS: TABLES

TABLE 6.1. NUMBER OF EDITORIALS CARRIED IN DAILY PAPERS

Number of editorials	Number of papers carrying editorials	Percentage of all dailies	Cumulative percentage
0	1,020	60.0	60
1	353	20.8	81
2	156	9.2	90
3	76	4.5	95
4	41	2.4	97
5	24	1.4	98
6	14	0.8	99
7	5	0.3	
8	4	0.2	
9	4	0.2	
10	1	0.1	
11	0	0.0	
12	0	0.0	
13	1	0.1	
14	0	0.0	
15	0	0.0	
16	0	0.0	
17	0	0.0	
18	1	0.1	100
Total	1,700	100.0	100

TABLE 6.2. ISSUES COVERED BY NEWSPAPER EDITORIALS (PERCENTAGE)

	$n = 3,348$
Anti-Unesco/	
pro-withdrawal	
Politicization	28
Mismanagement	13
Reforms needed	9
Press issues	10
U.S. pays 25/	5
Support for U.S.	3
Too little change	3
Criticism of M'Bow	4
Benefits to U.S.	7
U.S. credibility at stake	<1
Subtotal	84
Pro-Unesco/	
anti-withdrawal	
Criticism of pullout	6
Valuable programs	7
Denials of charges	0
Propaganda campaign	<1
Subtotal	14
Looking ahead	
Future	1
Alternatives	1
Subtotal	2
Total	100

TABLE 6.3. ISSUES EMPHASIZED IN EDITORIALS (PERCENTAGE)

	Attributed themes $n = 799$	Unattributed themes $n = 2,549$
Anti-Unesco/ pro-withdrawal		
Politicization	23	29
Mismanagement	18	12
Press issues	7	12
Reforms needed	16	7
U.S. pays 25%	1	7
Support for U.S.	8	2
Too little change	4	4
Criticism of M'Bow	3	4
Benefits to U.S.	3	8
Subtotal	83	85
Pro-Unesco/ anti-withdrawal		
Criticism of pullout	8	6
Valuable programs	6	8
Denials of charges	<1	<1
Propaganda campaign	<1	<1
Subtotal	14	14
Looking ahead		
Future	1	1
Alternatives	2	0
Subtotal	3	0
Total	100	100

TABLE 6.4. SOURCES QUOTED BY NEWSPAPER EDITORIALS AND ORIENTATION OF THOSE SOURCES (PERCENTAGES)

Sources	Attributed themes ($n = 1,217$)	Anti-UNESCO/ pro-pullout	Pro-UNESCO/ anti-pullout	Looking ahead
U.S. government	58	89	8	3
Western governments	21	87	13	0
Unesco	8	54	44	2
U.S. NGOs	8	90	8	2
Soviet government	1	11	89	0
Third World	1	63	37	0
U.S. academics	2	19	81	0
U.S. media reps.	1	75	25	0
Total	100			

TABLE 6.5. CHANGES IN EMPHASIS OVER TIME (PERCENTAGES)

	December 1983 $n = 441$	December 1984 $n = 970$
Anti-Unesco/ pro-withdrawal		
Politicization	34	22
Mismanagement	6	17
Press issues	19	6
Reforms needed	3	9
U.S. pays 25%	7	5
Support for U.S.	2	5
Too little change	1	7
Criticism of M'Bow	1	5
Benefits to U.S.	8	7
U.S. credibility at stake	<1	<1
Subtotal	81	84
Pro-Unesco/ anti-withdrawal		
Criticism of pullout	9	6
Valuable programs	9	5
Denials of charges	<1	0
Subtotal	18	11
Looking ahead		
Future	<1	2
Alternatives	1	3
Subtotal	1	5
Total	100	100

CHAPTER 7

Editorial Page Columns

There is cause for alarm. The New World Information Order may not have achieved any great success, but it is far from dead.
—Leonard H. Marks, secretary-treasurer, WPFC

Altogether 608 columns relating to Unesco were clipped from the U.S. press over the year by Press Intelligence, Inc. These columns appeared in 258 different newspapers across the nation—or about 15 percent of all dailies. Sixty-one of these papers ran only columns about Unesco, with no related news reports or editorials. Nearly one-half of the papers used only one column during the year—with or without news reports or editorials—while four had as many as seven and one had nine (Table 7.1). The average number for all papers that published columns was 2.24. The largest dailies—those with circulations of 200,000 or more—published an average of 3.4 columns each.

SYNDICATED COLUMNISTS

These published columns consisted of single or multiple uses of just 173 unique articles written by 145 individual columnists. Two-thirds of these appeared in only one newspaper each, and 95 percent ran in five papers or fewer. But a handful of columns reached enormous audiences: three ran in more than 30 papers each, and three others were used by between 40 and 70 papers each.

The coverage was dominated by a small group of nationally syndicated columnists (Table 7.2). Columns by the five most frequently used writers accounted for nearly one-half of the total number used. And the top 10 columnists were responsible for 57 percent of the total. George Will wrote two columns on Unesco that ran in 109 papers with a combined circulation of more than 17 million copies. Flora Lewis wrote four, which appeared in 86 papers with a combined circulation of nearly 15 million. One column by William Buckley ran in 36 papers with a total circulation of about 7 million. James Kilpatrick was published by 50 papers reaching 6 million subscribers. Four columns by Don Graff appeared in 24 papers with a combined circulation of just over 3 million. These five columnists alone accounted for nearly one-half of the total circulation of papers that carried columns about Unesco. Other widely used writers included Richard Reeves, Patrick Buchanan, William Safire, Owen Harries, William Pfaff, Phyllis Schlafly and Garry Wills. Together with the top five, these writers among them accounted for nearly 60 percent of the total circulation of papers that carried columns relating to the withdrawal (Table 7.2).

The content of the columns was analyzed in three ways. First, a data base containing information about every column and its related publication information was set up to determine patterns of usage. Then the columns were subjected to the same content analysis procedure as used for the news agency material, the published news reports and the editorials. First, to get a handle on the overall orientation of coverage by columnists, all the columns in the clippings file were sorted by date and every second one selected for analysis. These data are therefore comparable to those for the news coverage and the editorials. In addition, the output of each columnist was analyzed separately to determine their individual orientations.

Anti-Unesco Columnists

George Will. Columnists who were critical of Unesco and favored the withdrawal were in the majority. Among them was George Will, whose column is syndicated by the Washington Post Writers Group. Will wrote two pieces on Unesco that appeared in 45 and 64 newspapers respectively, including some of the largest and most influential.

The first, written in December 1983 before the official announcement of the intention to withdraw, asked what better way there was to greet 1984 than by "repudiating an organization devoted to Orwellian corruptions." Unesco's "elephantine bureaucracy," said Will, proposed to spend $374 million over the next two years, one-quarter of it contributed

by U.S. taxpayers. "We are subsidizing the steady inoculation of the world with degraded political language manipulated by America's enemies." Unesco had recently received a bad press because it had offended the press: "It has toyed with what it calls a 'new world information and communications order.' That is U.N.-speak for regulation of communication by Third World dictatorships."

Leaving Unesco would be a shot across the U.N.'s bow, a warning that there were limits to U.S. tolerance. "And leaving would help Americans get used to the idea of leaving the United Nations." The U.N. had forfeited moral authority by 1974, Will wrote, when it "roared approval of Yassir Arafat—the head of a terrorist organization pledged to the destruction of a U.N. member—as he went to the podium carrying a pistol." If the United States decided to leave Unesco, 1984 could be the year for weighing the costs, financial, political and moral, of continued participation in the U.N. "By now, surely, the burden of proof is on those who say that participation serves U.S. interests."

A second column by Will, written a year later and just before the administration was to confirm its decision to pull out, ran in more than 60 papers—a larger number than any single news agency report or canned editorial. In it, Will quotes from a Unesco document on communication—"an exquisite example of U.N.-speak"—that "is an example of your tax dollars at work, America. You pay 25 percent of Unesco's bills. For that, the better restaurants and boutiques of Paris thank you." But on January 1 black crepe would go up in the boutiques because "that's when the U.S. withdraws from Unesco. Happy New Year."

Will quotes an opponent of the withdrawal (columnist James Traub) who blamed the action on "radical conservatives" for whom "willingness to debate as equals amounts to defeatism." But, Will wrote, "members of Unesco are not equals. They are not equally civilized. Only a tiny minority of member nations have preserved admirable traditions of education, science and culture. Why should they 'debate' as equals, which they are not?" Another opponent of the withdrawal had said that "virtually every American organization that works with Unesco, including federal agencies, has come to its defense." Of course, said Will: "Threaten the trough where the intelligentsia feeds and folks will fly to their typewriters."

But the mere fact that Unesco had engaged in "an unrelenting assault on the moral foundations of the West" was not sufficient to get it into hot water, until it committed the tactical blunder of suggesting a new world information order and regulation of journalists. "At last the rascals had gone too far." Unesco had been tolerable when attacking everything else. It was one thing to revile the United States, "but to be disrespectful of journalists . . . well! I mean, the nerve."

Flora Lewis. The position taken by Flora Lewis, whose column is distributed by the New York Times Syndicate, was more ambivalent. The majority of the themes in the four widely used columns she wrote about Unesco were critical of the agency. She was particularly critical of its politicization and mismanagement, and of M'Bow's leadership. But she also considered that Unesco could be genuinely useful if reforms were implemented. And when it appeared that there was a possibility of genuine change, her column voiced the concern that the Reagan administration was determined to withdraw no matter what reforms were implemented, and that this would be a "shoddy trick."

In a column in December 1983, before the intention to withdraw was formally announced, Lewis wrote a column on the "Voices of Freedom" conference in Talloires, France. Media representatives were concerned, she wrote, because Unesco had been pressing a campaign to expand government controls on information. For a long time, the Western press had paid little attention, "but there is a growing recognition that the defense of freedom is too important to be left to diplomats and soldiers."

Shortly after the initial announcement, a Lewis column carried by 19 newspapers took as its theme the failure of the United Nations to serve its primary function. "It does a lot of useful things, but not its first job of policing peace." Typical of the degradation of the U.N. system was Unesco, which was not only totally politicized, but often vengeful and abominably managed. "My own view is that it has been too thoroughly deformed to be reformed. The best cure would be to break it up and start over." The U.S. notice of withdrawal probably would not heal Unesco, but would draw attention to its failure. "It is vital to give the right reason, not votes against the United States and Israel, scandalous as the anti-Israel campaign has been. The reason is Unesco's abandonment of its function and its effort to pre-empt the parent United Nations' rightful monopoly of international political hackery."

This sense of betrayal is developed further in a column carried by 35 papers in March 1984, and based on M'Bow's agreement to let Congress investigate his "woefully mismanaged, boondoggling operation." Unesco had been founded as a sister body of the United Nations where the humane, non-political side of international relations would be advanced. However, "years ago it bogged down into a politicized, demoralized bureaucracy whose chief concern is to provide cushy jobs for politicians unwanted at home and a forum for attacking the very concepts Unesco is supposed to serve—human rights for all, press freedom, unrestricted access to culture." The organization could provide good and valuable services, promoting literacy, preserving the artistic heritage of many cultures, spreading knowledge. Without reform, however, "its peevish politicking overrides its genuine usefulness."

By May, Lewis' sense of disillusionment had spread to the Reagan administration. In a column carried by 22 papers, she hinted that the administration was determined to quit Unesco even if reforms were made. The simplest, central reform had to be the removal of M'Bow. Yet the U.S. delegate to Unesco (Jean Gerard) had been instructed by Washington that whatever attacks she made on Unesco's performance, she was not to criticize M'Bow. And others "interested in salvaging what ought to be a useful, inspiring world organization have been unable to pin down the State Department on what the United States considers reforms sufficient to change its mind about leaving." This, said Lewis, reflected the view of Gregory Newell, assistant secretary of state for international organization affairs, who had told visitors he had a mandate from President Reagan to cut down on the number of intergovernmental organizations to which the United States belonged. "Therefore, he doesn't want to push M'Bow aside, the visitors concluded, nor go into details about reforms lest American demands be met." This, Lewis said, was not the position of the congressmen involved, nor of other countries supporting what they believed to be an America effort to restore Unesco to its original purpose.

James Kilpatrick. James Kilpatrick devoted just one column to Unesco in the year under review, but it ran in 50 newspapers, large and small, Kilpatrick's column, distributed by the Universal Press Syndicate in January 1984, establishes its anti-Unesco tone in the first paragraph: the Reagan administration had taken "a splendid first step in foreign affairs" when it formally advised "the tinpot tyrant who runs Unesco that the United States is getting out of Unesco. High time! We should have withdrawn long ago."

The column quotes extensively from an essay prepared by Owen Harries for the Heritage Foundation in October 1983, which had elaborated on Unesco's drift into a "consistent and malignant anti-Western bias." The area of communications was an example. Under M'Bow, the original idea of free communication had been summarily dumped. "Now the idea is to have each nation control its own press. Reporters and editors would be licensed. Those who failed to write constructively of their governments—those who were not 'responsible'—would have their licenses revoked. So much for objectivity, truth, and the free exchange of ideas and knowledge."

Echoing Harries, Kilpatrick accuses Unesco of exalting an economic order imposed by governments, of promoting collective rights at the expense of individual rights, and of leaping into areas of arms control and disarmament "that are far removed from education, science and culture." Reagan's notice of withdrawal would put a damper on the fun and games: "the happy prospect is that a year hence, when the actual secession takes

place, Unesco's raucous and insulting voice will dwindle to an almost inaudible yelp."

Kilpatrick saw the withdrawal as setting "all kinds of pleasant ideas in motion." If the United States could get out of Unesco, how about focusing on a larger target? "The time may not be ripe for getting the United States out of the United Nations, but we ought to think seriously about getting the United Nations out of the United States."

William Buckley. William Buckley, like Kilpatrick, saw the withdrawal from Unesco as the first step toward getting out of the United Nations itself: "We are off to a good start in voting [sic] to pull out of Unesco. But there is more to be done." Buckley, in a column distributed by Universal Press Syndicate that appeared in 36 papers nationwide in January 1984, repeats Newell's stated reasons for the pullout: hostility toward the basic institutions of a free society, extraneous politicization and "unrestrained budgetary expansion." His column also offers a clue as to why Democratic presidential candidates had not "landed on Reagan in protest for pulling out of an outfit deemed integral to postwar idealism." The answer: Unesco had become one of the most militant of the anti-Israel units in the United Nations, and "presidential candidates are not about to criticize a diplomatic step that is objectively, or psychologically, pro-Israel."

William Safire. To William Safire, whose column from the New York Times News Service was used by 14 influential papers, the Unesco pullout was "a major foreign policy achievement of the Reagan administration," ranking with its torpedoing the Law of the Sea Treaty. The American announcement, he wrote in December 1983, was a decade overdue. Unesco had started out to promote literacy and facilitate scientific communication, but "its takeover by communist stooges and Third World demagogues led to a perversion of its aims." In recent years it had become a "hotbed of rhetorical disparagements of Western industrial democracies and a center of attempts to delegitimize Israel."

For years, accommodationists in the United States had argued that it would be wiser to remain within Unesco in hopes of reforming the wayward institution. But the "Unescocrats" had overplayed their hand with the new world information order, "a power play to bring all foreign correspondents under the control of local dictators." When that came before the editorial board of the *New York Times*, said Safire, the newspaper

laid a pox Americana on the offending institution: "A United States withdrawal would not harm any democratic cause or global understand-

ing." That did it. "We had been concerned about more charges of know-nothingism," a high-level diplomat tells me, "and we don't need blasts at right-wing ideology being behind our decision making. But when that editorial appeared in the *New York Times* we had a free pass. Nobody in the Reagan administration wanted *The Times* to get to the right of us." And so the page opposite the Op-Ed page did for a withdrawal from Unesco what Richard Nixon did for an opening to Red China: made possible what had previously been politically unthinkable.

The wonder, concluded Safire, is that "this magnificent reassertion of good sense . . . was accomplished without much of a struggle."

Patrick Buchanan. Patrick Buchanan's column in December 1983, distributed by the Tribune Company Syndicate to 15 newspapers with a combined circulation of more than a million copies, quotes Owen Harries at length. Unesco had been converted into "a major subsidiary of the worldwide Hate America movement." It engaged in a systematic assault on Western institutions, Western values, Western beliefs. It parroted the Soviet line on peace and disarmament, and opposed the Western belief in the inherent rights of individuals against state oppression.

Press issues were a major focus of Buchanan's criticisms. Unesco, he said, was reaching for a system of worldwide licensing of journalists, which would "quickly evolve into a system where favorites of the communist and Third World would be given access and assistance, and 'irresponsible' journalists would travel at their own risk." The West, Buchanan wrote, was being asked to underwrite a competing system of news distribution, to rival AP and Reuters, to provide the government view of events to the West. That is, "U.S. dollars would be used to hire journalists to transmit Fidel Castro's view of the Cuban Revolution back to American capitals."

Why not use a little imagination, Buchanan asked. "For that $100 million Unesco contribution, the United States could put into orbit satellites that would soon provide direct-to-home transmission of American networks." Terrified of the prospect, Moscow had sought to use Unesco to block it: "with good reason. Those Uzbeks and Tadziks in South Central Asia would go wild over 'Dallas.'"

Owen Harries. Columns by Owen Harries, Australian ambassador to Unesco in 1982–82 and later a public policy analyst at the Heritage Foundation, did not reach as many readers directly as did the major syndicated columnists, although his ideas were parroted by the conservatives. Harries' columns, distributed by the Heritage Features Syndicate, ran in the *Washington Times* (circulation 115,000) and the *New York Tribune* (52,000), both owned by News World Communications, which is

associated with the Unification Church. One column, in December 1984, also ran in six other papers, including the Cleveland *Plain Dealer* (487,000). One column was published by the *Houston Post* (419,000). In addition, the *Reader's Digest* (17,750,000) published an article by Harries entitled "Why Unesco Spells Trouble" in its October 1984 issue.

Particularly significant here is a Harries column published in the *New York Times* on 21 December 1983, a few days before the State Department announced its plan to withdraw. Like the *New York Times* editorial of December 16, it could be seen as a signal to the Reagan administration that a pullout would not be opposed by the "liberal" press. In the column, Harries argued that Unesco was in a bad state, "worse than the rest of the United Nations or any other specialized agency associated with it." It was thoroughly politicized, dedicated to attacking fundamental Western values, interests and institutions. "It attacks and seeks to circumscribe the free Western press . . . it attacks the free market economy and multi-national corporations. It seeks to downgrade individual human rights in favor of nebulous and proliferating rights of peoples." Unesco, Harries wrote, was also appallingly managed and administered. It had strenuously resisted curtailing its budget. Given these characteristics, "it seems to be that the U.S. should withdraw from Unesco." It was politically and morally wrong for it to lend authority and legitimacy—and to provide $50 million a year—to such an organization. Above all, he wrote, a decision to withdraw would have a good effect on the United States itself: "A country that takes its ideas and values seriously cannot, without doing damage to its sense of itself, afford to subsidize an organization that systematically undermines its ideas and values."

Harries noted in a column in the *New York Tribune* on 27 December 1983 that the decision to withdraw had been remarkable, in that while virtually every component of Reagan's foreign policy had been subject to strong domestic criticism, this one had received bipartisan support. "The *New York Times* and the *Washington Post* supported it before the event and Fritz Mondale supported it afterwards." The liberal press in particular was "incensed by Unesco's threats to curtail the freedom of the Western communications media; had that special factor been absent it is doubtful whether their ire would have been nearly as robust."

Harries, like Flora Lewis, suggested that the State Department's policy of not criticizing M'Bow directly was a deliberate attempt to avoid his replacement, and thus lessen the justification for withdrawal. "Many of those who welcome the U.S. decision are quite happy to have him stay in his present position, in the correct belief that this would guarantee that serious improvements within Unesco would not occur and that therefore the American decision would stick. He has, after all, become the symbol of a politicized and inefficient Unesco."

A Harries column in the *Houston Chronicle* repeated the contention that the United States, having announced its intention to withdraw, would suffer loss of credibility if it changed its mind. If it did not pull out after the State Department's recommendation, "the view generally prevalent in Unesco—that the U.S. is a paper tiger—will be greatly strengthened and the United States' credibility there will be extremely low." Unesco, Harries wrote, in addition to attacking Western values and interests, sought to circumscribe the free Western press. It attacked the free-market economy and multinational corporations. It sought to downgrade individual human rights in favor of nebulous "rights of peoples." It was consistently hostile to Israel and provided political and financial support to the PLO. Unesco was also appallingly managed and administered. M'Bow himself was thoroughly politicized and anti-American. Given these characteristics, Harries concluded, it was essential that the United States should withdraw.

In December 1984, Harries urged that the government implement its decision. It should do so for three reasons, he wrote in a column that appeared in eight newspapers. It was important to make clear that the United States was not prepared to tolerate, and pay for, attacks on its fundamental values and institutions. Second, America could exert more effective pressure for reform of Unesco from outside than from within— as had happened when it withdrew from the International Labor Organization in 1977–79. Third, "even apart from the merits of the case," the fact that the United States had taken a decision to withdraw was "in itself a compelling reason for not retreating from it or delaying its implementation." The U.S. government should "move quickly to put the matter beyond any doubt or speculation."

It did.

Phyllis Schlafly. Like Safire, Will and Harries, Schlafly believed Unesco had brought disaster upon itself when it incurred the wrath of the press. In a syndicated column in March 1984, she wrote that there was nothing new about Unesco being a "menace to America and our values." The organization had long been attempting, through the school system, to belittle patriotism and promote world government. Unesco had "even been encouraging Third World governments to put restrictions on the Western press and to endorse the notion that governments had the right to control information for their own purposes." That was its mistake. "All the years that Unesco was peddling the liberal-internationalist line to American schoolchildren, it enjoyed fulsome support in the U.S. media. But when Unesco started meddling with freedom of the press, that was going too far, even for liberals."

In another syndicated column in May, Schlafly declared that Unesco

had departed from its three principal mandates: the eradication of world illiteracy, the preservation of historic monuments and the pursuit of scientific exchange. But Unesco didn't seem to be very interested in teaching the world's illiterates how to read and write, she said. Instead it preferred to "spend its time promoting controversial political goals." The column draws attention to Unesco programs to promote disarmament, thus becoming "a conduit for Soviet propaganda." No wonder the Reagan administration had concluded that salvation for Unesco was hopeless, and that the United States should stop feeding this monster with American dollars.

Pro-Unesco Columnists

Syndicated columnists who favored continued membership in Unesco were few in number, ambivalent in their support, and largely ignored by the press. Like the editorials that supported Unesco, they hedged their backing with criticisms of the organization. Even though the pro-Unesco writers argued for continued membership, content analysis of their articles shows that in most cases nearly one-half of their themes were critical of Unesco. While they praised the agency's successes—or potential for success—they also acknowledged its deficiencies. Most of the anti-Unesco columnists, by contrast, used themes that were almost exclusively hostile to the organization and pro-withdrawal. Of the dozen most widely published columnists, nine were hostile to Unesco, among them the four most frequently used: Will, Lewis, Buckley and Kilpatrick. Pro-Unesco writers in the top dozen ranked fifth (William Pfaff), seventh (Richard Reeves) and eighth (Garry Wills) in terms of the total circulation of the papers in which their Unesco columns were published.

William Pfaff. William Pfaff, a Paris-based commentator on international affairs, had the greatest exposure of columnists who appreciated Unesco's achievements and regretted the withdrawal. Three columns by Pfaff ran in three or four fairly large papers each. A compilation of these appeared as a separate article in *Newsday* (circulation 507,000). Altogether, the Pfaff columns appeared in papers with a combined circulation of more than 3 million.

Pfaff's columns took the long view, seeking to explain in historical and philosophical terms the genesis of Unesco, and the geopolitical forces that had led the United States to withdraw. His column in January 1984 pointed out that the United States had largely been responsible for the creation of the U.N. system, based on the principle of one nation, one vote. It had also pressured European imperial powers to set free their colonies. "But now the United States doesn't like it. The majority votes

in the U.N. and Unesco are hostile; Washington wants to be rid of these infuriating organs of world opinion." This world opinion had proven to express "not the lofty idealisms of liberated mankind as imagined by Americans, but the tawdry reality of international life." It proved to be anti-American, anti-Israeli, anti-Western. The Reagan government was asking why American interest should be served by remaining in, and financing, such institutions. In repudiating Unesco, however, "the United States repudiates principles which for 50 years have been at the core of the nation's conception of its world role," Pfaff wrote. One was forced to conclude that "absolutely nothing has been thought through."

Pfaff returned to the Unesco issue in a two-part column written from Moenjodaro, Pakistan, in February. Visiting the "Mound of the Dead"— a significant archaeological site being saved with the help of Unesco funds—Pfaff wrote that it was projects like this that made Unesco seem the most important of the U.N. agencies to people in the Third World. "Unesco does useful and visible things which touch upon the pride of Third World countries. It has also made itself a vehicle of Third World hopes, which are often dampened these days, and most of the resentments and frustrations follow from that disappointment."

This was why Unesco had become a bitter battleground between the developed democratic countries and radical developing states backed by the Soviet Union. What had happened to Unesco represented an effort by Asian, Latin American and African countries not only to make the organization serve their interests but to vindicate their grievances. Pfaff questioned whether the U.S. government could "enter far enough into this intellectual and emotional world of the developing countries to deal seriously with them," grasping the force of what lay behind the Unesco crisis.

Richard Reeves. A single column by Richard Reeves in February ran in 17 papers with a combined circulation of more than 2 million copies. In it, Reeves referred to earlier columns by Will and Buckley, which had applauded the Unesco pullout as a first step toward getting the United States out of the United Nations. "It is not difficult to share many of the anti-U.N. frustrations of the conservatives," Reeves wrote. "It is not fun to go over there and listen to people from Byelorussia or Iran attack the United States for oppressing its own people." Nevertheless, wonderful work was being done by the U.N. in fields such as health and agriculture and refugee relief. More important was the role of the United States as a world leader: "We owe more to other peoples—and to ourselves—than to act in splendid isolation as rich bullies so unsure of our own values and accomplishments that we cannot deign to, or bear to, debate and defend them with the least and meanest of the people united as nations."

Garry Wills. A column by Garry Wills, distributed in January by Universal Press Syndicate, was picked up by eight papers with a combined circulation of 1,500,000 copies. In it,Wills argued that the plan to pull out of Unesco had been praised by people "who never wanted us to be involved in the outside world in the first place." Our best case against Unesco, he wrote, was the attempt to use it as an international instrument of censorship. "Third World countries, with revolutions incomplete, want the press to serve their ideological programs—a reaction that occurs in almost all revolutions (including our own)." But how could the Reagan administration say the press should be free of government control? "This is the administration that barred the press from Grenada. Secretary of State George Shultz has said the press is against the 'us' of government, and must be brought around to support 'us.' No Third World potentate could have put it better." Wills argued that "picking up our marbles and going home makes sense only if there is no game possible without us." It was time we learned this was no longer the case: "The world will not go away when we stop looking at it . . . it is here, and we must cope with it."

Other Syndicated Columnists

Among the less widely published columnists, the 10 writers who appeared in five papers or more (but were not among the top 10 already discussed), were largely anti-Unesco.

George S. Benson, in a column published in a handful of smaller papers, saw the withdrawal as a victory in "the struggle between the forces of freedom and the forces of regimentation." The outrageous programs and rhetoric of Unesco had begun to arouse even those who had been generally complacent, Benson wrote. "This is especially true of the media which has had its own ox gored."

John-Thor Dahlburg, an Associated Press correspondent in Paris, wrote a column used by several larger papers (including the *Houston Chronicle*, circulation 339,000), that was highly critical of M'Bow, seen by "many in the West" as an "insecure, short-fused bureaucrat under whose tutelage a once-respected organization has been taken over by a coalition of Soviet-bloc and radical Third World states."

Ralph de Toledano of the Copley News Service wrote a column carried in September by five medium-sized papers, which criticized Unesco's hiring of a Washington public relations firm to counter the attacks being made on it. Unesco, wrote de Toledano, "the United Nations' covert propaganda agency for the Soviet Union and Third World Marxist-Leninists, has now contracted with the public relations firm of Wagner & Baroody to give it a quick coat of whitewash." The idea was to brainwash the American people into forgetting Unesco's "shocking record of politi-

cal activity, the corruption within the organization, and its determined failure to work at its major mandate, the elimination of illiteracy."

Edwin Feulner, president of the Heritage Foundation, in a column reflecting on the U.N.'s failings on the occasion of its 40th birthday in July 1984, averred that Unesco promotes neither education nor science nor culture. Instead, "it promotes the notion that whatever know-how the Western democracies possess they have developed at the expense of the less fortunate of the world and should now 'return' their earnings to their underdeveloped victims." The column was picked up from the Heritage Features Syndicate by five small papers.

Jim Hampton, editor of the *Miami Herald*, complained in a column also carried in several other Knight-Ridder papers in January that Unesco had "long since abandoned its original noble purpose." Under M'Bow, it had become a "bloated, mismanaged, patronage-riddled vehicle for causes alien to Western democracies' beliefs."

Seymour Rubin, a member of several U.S. delegations to U.N. conferences, wrote a column for the *Washington Post* that was syndicated to other papers as well. In it he offered a "cost-benefit analysis" which concluded that a U.S. withdrawal could result in benefits to scientific, educational and cultural projects.

Of the less widely used columns, one of the few critical of the pullout was written by A. K. Solomon, emeritus professor of biophysics at the Harvard Medical School and a scientific member of the U.S. delegation to Unesco. His article ran in such major papers as the *Houston Chronicle*, the Cleveland *Plain Dealer* and the *Miami Herald*. Solomon argued that, whatever its political merits, the withdrawal would deal a serious blow to the U.S. scientific community.

Don Graff of the Newspaper Enterprise Association wrote three columns about Unesco that appeared mainly in a few smaller papers. The first, written in January, said that the issue was never in doubt: "Withdrawal was too compatible with the Reagan administration's ideological crusade against the Soviet imperialists and their evil machinations in the international community for the decision to have been otherwise." There had not been much opposition to this crusade because Unesco was "in a mess."

Graff was one of the few syndicated columnists to pay attention to criticisms of the pullout by the U.S. National Commission for Unesco in August 1984. He quotes the committee as being in essential agreement with the administration's strictures on Unesco's "politicized programs, administrative shortcomings and budgetary extravagance." Reform, he said, is clearly in order. But Graff pointed out that the committee's position was that the withdrawal was too drastic a remedy, and would have damaging side effects for the United States. The United States

would be better advised to stay put, providing constructive leadership in working for reform from within. And Graff quoted Leonard Sussman as saying the administration was "pursuing a well-managed, ideologically motivated campaign of misinformation that is part of a larger challenge to the U.N. system itself." He quoted Sussman as saying that public needed more, and more accurate information on the issue. So far, it had been kept in the dark with a one-sided, incomplete account. "Americans deserve to know more." This column ran in 17 newspapers, with a combined circulation of about 760,000. Much of this was accounted for by one large paper, the *Houston Post* (circulation 299,000).

In December 1984, a Graff column noted that the United States had confirmed its decision because, "although there have been gestures toward reform, Washington has remained distinctly unimpressed." There was a strong impression, he wrote, that "those making the decision aren't seriously interested in a reformed Unesco. They've already got what they want."

David R. Francis of the *Christian Science Monitor* wrote a three-part series on the consequences of the pullout that treated the arguments for and against Unesco in an even-handed manner and was one of the best pieces of reporting over the year. But only two other papers used his articles. And Brooke W. Kroeger of *Newsday*'s United Nations bureau wrote a balanced piece that also ran in two other papers, questioning whether the withdrawal would have the intended result of effecting reforms.

CONTENT ANALYSIS

Themes in the columns were analyzed using the same content analysis scheme as applied to the news reports and editorials. The sample comprised every second column in the clippings file, including duplicates. This produced a sample of 290 columns, containing 4,178 thematic statements.

Orientation

The overall orientation of the columns was heavily critical of Unesco and supportive of the withdrawal. Of all the themes in the columns, 75 percent were anti-Unesco and pro-withdrawal (compared to 70 percent for the news agencies, 76 percent in the published news reports, and 84 percent in the editorials). About 23 percent of the themes deplored or regretted the pullout, or supported Unesco programs. Many of these affirmations, however, related to what Unesco had achieved in the past,

before "diverging" from its original charter. Just 2 percent related to what alternatives the future might hold.

The themes stressed in the columns were very similar to those in the news reports and the editorials (Table 7.3). In all three cases, the most common criticism of Unesco was politicization, followed by mis-management. The columns included a higher proportion of affirmations as to the usefulness of Unesco programs, and marginally more criticisms of the withdrawal. The columns were proportionately less concerned with press issues, with the need for reform, and with support by other nations for the pullout. Like the editorials, the columns placed for more emphasis on advantages to the United States of the pullout than did the news reports.

Attributions

Nearly 60 percent of the thematic statements were not attributed to any specific source and hence were coded as the opinion of the columnist. Of the themes that were attributed, U.S. government sources accounted for nearly 50 percent (Table 7.4). These included references to the Reagan administration, the State Department, and specific officials, most notably Gregory Newell. The second largest source of attributed statements in the columns—15 percent—was Western governments, led by the British government and "Western diplomats." Two-thirds of the attributed state-ments about Unesco in the columns, therefore, came from U.S. or Western government spokesmen. The U.S. National Commission for Unesco was cited, as an organization, about as often as the Heritage Foundation. But Owen Harries of the Heritage Foundation, who favored withdrawal, was mentioned twice as often as Leonard Sussman of Free-dom House, who did not. Unesco sources accounted for 9 percent of the attributed themes, and the Soviet Union, the Third World, and U.S. academics for less than 1 percent each. The themes attributed to U.S. and Western government spokesmen were uniformly hostile towards Unesco, as was the Heritage Foundation. Even Unesco spokesman cited were more critical than supportive of the organization because several col-umnists quoted dissidents on the Unesco staff.

The unattributed themes (the columnists' opinions) differed from those that were attributed in several respects. The unattributed themes were significantly more critical of Unesco and supportive of the withdraw-al than those that were attributed to sources (Table 7.5). The unattri-buted themes were more likely to emphasize politicization, threats to a free press, the benefits to the United States of withdrawing, and criticism of M'Bow. Conversely, they were only half as likely to mention criticisms

of the pullout or denials that Unesco was guilty as charged. The attributed themes had a higher proportion of references to the need for reform and to criticisms of the withdrawal.

Changes over Time

One-half of all the columns about Unesco appeared in December 1983 and January 1984, at the time of the initial announcement. Another 12 percent appeared the following December, when the decision was confirmed. The columns at the end of the year were proportionately less hostile to Unesco than those at the beginning (Table 7.6). This was largely because most of the conservative big guns fired their salvos at the time of the first announcement. Kilpatrick, Buckley, Safire and Buchanan all wrote widely syndicated columns on Unesco only in December 1983 or in January 1984. Will and Harries had columns in both Decembers.

STACKING THE DECK

Papers that opposed Unesco in their editorials did little to achieve balance in their choice of columnists. The 10 largest papers that took a consistently anti-Unesco stance in their editorials reinforced this orientation by publishing anti-Unesco columnists. Among them, these 10 papers carried 33 columns over the year. Of these, 28 were by critics like Buckley, Buchanan, Lewis, Safire and Will. Only five of the columns they carried could be said to be pro-Unesco.

Thus the *San Diego Union*, which was strongly critical in its editorials, also ran columns by Buchanan, Safire and Will, plus a more moderate column by Andrew Radlof. The *Indianapolis Star*, also consistently critical in its editorials, ran columns by Lewis, plus critical columns by Anthony Lejune, a conservative British writer distributed by the Heritage Features Service, who urged his country to follow the American example by withdrawing from Unesco; by Sen. Dan Quayle, who strongly backed the withdrawal; and by Victor Riesel, who quoted Heritage Foundation criticisms of Unesco's spending.

The Memphis *Commercial Appeal* took a hard line on Unesco in its editorials and ran critical columns by Kilpatrick, Lewis and Safire, but also one largely pro-Unesco column by Reeves. The *Dallas Morning News* used Buckley; two columns by Joseph Harriss, who quoted the Heritage Foundation and Unesco dissident staffers; and one column by its science writer, Gayle Golden, who was critical of Unesco's mismanagement but feared that worthwhile science programs would suffer if the

United States left. The *New York Times* ran columns by Lewis, Safire and Solomon, but also one by James Traub, who said Unesco had indeed undertaken reforms, and argued against withdrawal.

The *Wall Street Journal* did not use the widely syndicated columnists, but the four columns it carried all matched the paper's anti-Unesco editorial stance. These included Gordon Crovitz, editorial page editor of the *Journal's* European edition, who was highly critical of the agency; Vermont Royster, who quoted GAO and Heritage Foundation attacks on Unesco's spending; Rep. James H. Scheuer, chairman of a House science and technology subcommittee, who was strongly critical of Unesco and M'Bow; and by staff reporter Robert Greenberger, who criticized waste in Unesco and in the U.N. system as a whole.

The half-dozen larger papers that generally opposed the withdrawal in their editorials were less consistent in their choice of columnists. They carried a higher proportion of pro-Unesco or middle of-the-road columns than those papers with an anti-Unesco editorial line. But the conservative columnists still outnumbered the liberal, perhaps reflecting the papers' editorial ambivalence—and the fact that most of the widely syndicated columnists were conservative. Thus the Cleveland *Plain Dealer*, which had urged continued membership in its editorials, ran columns favoring withdrawal by Harries, Lewis, Rubin, Solomon and Will, and one by David Bell, a staff writer for the *New Republic,* who gave a more balanced appraisal.

The *Hartford Courant*, which had argued in editorials that Unesco's shortcomings were not reason enough to pull out, ran columns by Will; by Lothar Kahn, who repeated the familiar litany of criticisms, and one by Jean-Pierre Cot, the French representative to Unesco's executive council, who argued against the withdrawal. The St. Louis *Post-Dispatch,* which also had opposed the pullout in editorials, nevertheless carried pro-withdrawal columns by Will, Lewis and Evarts Graham, who lamented the decline of international organizations in general and Unesco in particular.

The most consistently pro-Unesco paper was the *Christian Science Monitor.* Over the year its editorials had recognized Unesco's deficiencies, but also stressed its achievements. The *Monitor* ran a series of well-researched columns by David Francis that gave both sides of the argument; one by George Dorsey that criticized Unesco but acknowledged the value of other U.N. agencies; and one by its natural science editor, Robert Cowen, who expressed concern about the impact of the pullout on scientific programs. Two other papers that opposed the withdrawal in their editorials, the Akron *Beacon-Journal* and the Hackensack, N.J. *Record*, carried only Will and Kilpatrick respectively.

EDITORIAL PAGE COLUMNS: TABLES

TABLE 7.1. NUMBER OF COLUMNS CARRIED IN DAILY PAPERS

Number of columns	Number of papers carrying columns	Percentage of all dailies	Cumulative percentage
0	1,441	84.8	85
1	123	7.2	92
2	46	2.7	95
3	35	2.1	97
4	27	1.6	98
5	17	1.0	99
6	6	0.3	
7	4	0.2	
8	0	0.0	
9	1	0.1	100
Total	1,700	100.0	100

TABLE 7.2. SYNDICATED COLUMNISTS

Columnist	Number of columns	Number of papers using them	Combined circulation of those papers
George Will	2	109	17,254,000
Flora Lewis	4	86	14,768,000
William Buckley	1	36	6,698,000
James Kilpatrick	1	50	5,556,000
William Pfaff	3	11	3,414,000
William Safire	1	14	2,973,000
Richard Reeves	1	17	2,541,000
Garry Wills	1	8	1,550,000
Brooke Kroeger	1	5	1,446,000
John Dahlburg	1	6	1,352,000
Patrick Buchanan	1	15	1,342,000
Seymour Rubin	1	8	1,278,000
Owen Harries	4	12	1,260,000
Don Graff	4	24	895,000
Steve Twomey	1	3	772,000
Barbara Tuchman	1	4	754,000
Phyllis Schlafly	2	9	499,000

TABLE 7.3. ISSUES COVERED BY COLUMNISTS (PERCENTAGES)

	$n = 4,178$
Anti-Unesco/ pro-withdrawal	
Politicization	24
Mismanagement	13
Reforms needed	9
Press issues	6
U.S. pays 25%	4
Support for U.S.	3
Too little change	2
Criticism of M'Bow	7
Benefits to U.S.	6
U.S. credibility at stake	<1
Subtotal	73
Pro-Unesco/ anti-withdrawal	
Criticism of pullout	11
Valuable programs	12
Denials of charges	1
Propaganda campaign	<1
Subtotal	24
Looking ahead	
Future	2
Alternatives	1
Subtotal	3
Total	100

TABLE 7.4. SOURCES QUOTED BY COLUMNISTS AND ORIENTATION OF THOSE SOURCES

Source	Attributed themes ($n = 1,659$)	Anti-UNESCO/ pro-pullout ($n = 1,211$)	Pro-UNESCO/ anti-pullout ($n = 398$)	Looking ahead ($n = 49$)
U.S. Government	48	73	24	3
Western governments	15	74	23	3
Unesco	9	45	55	0
U.S. NGOs	26	74	25	1
Soviet Government	1	12	88	0
Third World	1	25	75	0
Total	100			
Unattributed themes ($n = 2,412$)	—	78	20	2

TABLE 7.5. ISSUES EMPHASIZED IN COLUMNS (PERCENTAGES)

	Attributed themes $n = 2,412$	Unattributed themes $n = 1,766$
Anti-Unesco/ pro-withdrawal		
Politicization	26	21
Mismanagement	13	13
Press issues	7	4
Reforms needed	5	13
U.S. pays 25%	6	<1
Support for U.S.	2	4
Too little change	1	3
Criticism of M'Bow	9	5
Benefits to U.S.	8	3
Subtotal	77	66
Pro-Unesco/ anti-withdrawal		
Criticism of pullout	8	17
Valuable programs	13	12
Denials of charges	<1	2
Propaganda campaign	<1	<1
Subtotal	21	31
Looking ahead		
Future	2	2
Alternatives	<1	1
Subtotal	2	3
Total	100	100

TABLE 7.6. CHANGES IN EMPHASIS OVER TIME (PERCENTAGES)

	December 1983/ January 1984 n = 1,279	December 1984 n = 436
Anti-Unesco/ pro-withdrawal		
Politicization	40	12
Mismanagement	13	8
Press issues	10	3
Reforms needed	2	12
U.S. pays 25/	5	3
Support for U.S.	<1	5
Too little change	1	4
Criticism of M'Bow	4	6
Benefits to U.S.	11	5
U.S. credibility at stake	0	1
Subtotal	87	59
Pro-Unesco/ anti-withdrawal		
Criticism of pullout	8	21
Valuable programs	5	15
Denials of charges	<1	3
Subtotal	13	39
Looking ahead		
Future	<1	2
Alternatives	<1	2
Subtotal	<1	4
Total	100	100

CHAPTER 8

Television News

Most Americans say they get their news about national and international events primarily from television. A Roper Organization survey in March 1987 showed that TV was the prime source of news for 66 percent of Americans, and the only source of news for 50 percent. In addition, people believe what they see on the screen. Asked which media are the most credible, 55 percent said TV, while 21 percent favored newspapers. These people would not have learned much about Unesco from watching the evening news, however. And if they believed what they saw, they would have come away with a very one-sided impression.

EXTENT OF COVERAGE

The Unesco issue was not the kind of story that lends itself to television coverage. It had to do with ideas, not action. Apart from the fire in Paris, there was little to photograph other than talking heads. The most obvious news pegs were official announcements by the State Department. The three major commercial networks together broadcast a total of 13 reports on the issue on their evening newscasts between December 1983 and December 1984. NBC carried five reports, with total air time of 7 minutes. CBS also had five reports, totaling 6 minutes. ABC carried three, with a combined air time of 5 minutes and 20 seconds. The networks also carried several reports on their morning news shows, and CBS had a segment devoted to Unesco on its news magazine program, "60 Minutes."[1]

The 13 reports on the evening newscasts focused primarily on just two events: the initial announcement of the withdrawal in December 1983, and the announcement in December 1984 confirming that the United States would pull out. Eight of the 13 reports dealt with the initial announcement. CBS had a brief report on December 21 saying that President Reagan, in consultation with Secretary of State Shultz, was expected to agree to a pullout in the next few days. NBC had a longer report on December 26 anticipating the announcement. On December 28, the day before the decision was formally made known, all three networks reported that it was imminent. And all three carried the State Department announcement the next day confirming that the U.S. planned to withdraw.

A year later, on 19 December 1984, all three networks reported that the State Department had made good on its threat and that the United States would indeed pull out. On that occasion, the bulk of the CBS report was devoted to allegations that the Soviet Union had been using Unesco as a "massive front for espionage." Correspondent David Andelman reported that there was a considerable body of evidence that the Soviets had used their offices at Unesco "to push their policies in the Third World, recruit intelligence agents, and even finance espionage activity."

Only two other events relating to Unesco were carried on the evening news during the year. NBC had a report on March 22 about the arson fire at Unesco headquarters in Paris, noting that it occurred on the eve of the General Accounting Office investigation. And CBS reported on November 22 that Britain also planned to pull out. A report on CBS Morning News referred to the GAO audit in March 1984. David Andelman said that U.S. Congressman James Scheuer had won an agreement that would allow investigators "to descend on Unesco headquarters." The arrival of the auditors, Andelman said "could open a whole snake pit."

ORIENTATION OF REPORTS

Like the press coverage, the television newscasts emphasized criticisms of Unesco and support for the withdrawal, while playing down mentions of Unesco's achievements and opposition to the step (Figure 8.1). Because of the limited time available on TV, the range of issues and the depth of the coverage were much more limited than in the newspapers. Yet, the overall pattern was almost identical. Of the 102 themes coded in the 13 evening newscasts on all three networks, 76 percent were anti-Unesco and pro-withdrawal; 21 percent were critical of the withdrawal and referred to Unesco's useful programs. Just 4 percent dealt with alternatives to

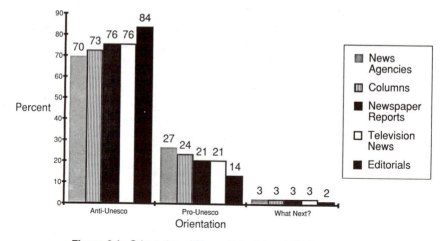

Figure 8.1. Orientation of News, Editorial and TV Reports

the organization, or its future (Table 8.1). The number of themes was too small to make detailed comparisons among the three networks, but on the whole CBS was the most critical of Unesco, while NBC came closest (but not very close) to providing balance.

Of the criticisms, the most common topic, as in the case of the press, was politicization, which accounted for 27 percent of all the themes coded. In announcing the plan to withdraw, for example, CBS's Dan Rather stated that Unesco "is supposed to be a non-ideological United Nations educational, scientific and cultural organization. Increasingly, it has been charged with being zealously anti-American and anti-Israel, dominated by the Soviet bloc ideology and financially corrupt."[2] ABC correspondent Pierre Salinger reported from Paris that evening that the U.S. was withdrawing because "the Reagan administration has become more and more disenchanted with Unesco, portraying the organization as more politicized and anti-American."

Allegations of mismanagement, at 14 percent of the total, were the second most frequent themes. Thus CBS reported that the Reagan administration objected to "Unesco's alleged anti-U.S. and anti-Israel biases, as well as to reported high-level Unesco corruption."[3] Reporting on the United Kingdom's decision to pull out, CBS's Dan Rather said that withdrawal would occur "unless mismanagement and high spending problems are solved. The United States, citing the same reason, already has said it would stop its 25 percent funding of Unesco at the end of the year."[4] The need for reform if the United States was to rescind its decision was the third most frequent topic. Pierre Salinger reported for

ABC that the decision to withdraw "becomes effective in a year and during that time the United States will carefully monitor Unesco's activities to see if it wants to change its mind or carry out its threat to leave."[5] CBS correspondent Bill McLaughlin spelled out what reforms were needed: "But the conditions for a change of American heart are perhaps too tough for Unesco's Third World majority to swallow. They include getting Unesco to stay out of arms control issues, focusing on individual human rights, backing away from efforts to control the press, and an end to anti-free enterprise propaganda and more jobs for American in policy-making positions at Unesco."[6]

As in the case of the press reports, mentions of the U.S. contribution to Unesco were sometimes coupled with statements to the effect that it was not getting value for its money. NBC State Department correspondent Marvin Kalb reported that "Unesco, based in Paris, has 161 member states. But the U.S. pays 25 percent of its 375 million dollar budget, much of that money spent by and in anti-American countries in Asia, Africa and the Middle East."[7] Media issues also figure quite prominently in the TV coverage. ABC's Pierre Salinger noted that Unesco had played a key role in education and science, and in preserving historical cultural sites, but commented that "in recent years Unesco has moved from these primary objectives to create a New World Information Order which would give governments more power over the news and lead to an international licensing of journalists. Western countries have fought this plan bitterly as an attack on the basic freedoms of the press."[8] M'Bow himself was the focus of some of the criticism. NBC correspondent Jim Bitterman commented that Unesco's original ideals

> remain today, but ideology, say many critics, has crept in. Largely, they say, during the tenure of this man, Unesco Secretary General Amadou Mahtar M'Bow from Senegal. As his term began in 1974, Unesco was passing resolutions condemning Israel, and as it continued, the delegates took on such issues as disarmament, human rights, freedom of the press, from perspectives that some say were biased against the West. The personal style of M'Bow was called authoritarian. Numbers of experienced Unesco employees have quit or taken early retirement. Many were replaced by the Director General's personal candidates . . . . Questions have been raised about how Unesco's money, one quarter of which comes from the United States, is spent."[9]

Criticism of America's decision, and appreciation of the value of Unesco programs, each comprised about 10 percent of the themes. One NBC report featured Dr. James Holderman, of the U.S. National Com-

mission for Unesco, saying that "when the commission made its recommendation to stay in, they prefaced it by saying, look, we're not happy with Unesco either. We think a number of things should be done to correct it. But we feel the best way it could be done would be within." The same segment showed Elliott Abel, U.S. member on the MacBride Commission and a former dean of the Columbia School of Journalism, saying: "By walking out the door at this point, somehow brings to mind with me the notion of a spoiled brat who, having been called out on the baseball field, picks up his bat and ball and goes home." The same newscast pointed out that European allies feared that an American walk-out could destroy Unesco.[10] CBS carried a statement by Leonard Sussman, a member of the U.S. National Commission for Unesco, saying that "the United States is as responsible for the bad things happening in Unesco as Unesco itself. We've spent ten years in which we've turned our backs on that organization and we ought now to be spending out time moving in with all of our forces."[11]

Mentions of Unesco's contributions to education, science and culture were few and perfunctory. Marvin Kalb of NBC noted that without America's contributions, Unesco's efforts worldwide would be hurt. "It is involved in scientific projects such as weather forecasting and in cultural exchanges which help in the export of U.S. books, films and records, an estimated one billion dollar business."[12] Pierre Salinger of ABC referred to its "key role in preserving historical cultural sites like the city of Venice and the famed temples of Abu Simbel when the Aswan Dam was built in Egypt."[13] CBS correspondent Bill McLaughlin noted that Unesco was set up in 1946 "to improve education and strengthen cultural ties around the world through better communications."[14] NBC's Jim Bitterman recalled that Unesco was born "in the heady atmosphere of post World War Two idealism." As it grew, so did the hopes of the world's scientists, poets and politicians who were its founding fathers. "Archaeologists studied Bolivian ruins, Egyptian temples were moved and preserved. Byzantine churches were restored. The ideals remain, but ideology has crept in."[15] Frequently, however, these accomplishments were portrayed as something that had occurred in the past, before Unesco had become politicized, corrupt and spendthrift. One would not gather from the coverage that any worthwhile projects were still being undertaken.

There was no reference in the TV coverage to the concerns of U.S. scientists and educators about the effects of the withdrawal; no mention of the impact it would have on essential programs in the developing world; no reference to reforms made by Unesco during the course of the year, apart from a statement on CBS that Unesco had "failed to come up with the improvements this country wanted[16] (see Table 8.2).

SOURCES

The TV reports, with their highly compressed format, attributed proportionately fewer of their statements to specific sources than did the press reports. Of the 102 themes coded from the evening newscasts, only 25 percent were attributed to a particular person or institution. The rest were simply statements of fact by the news anchors or correspondents with no attribution. Two kinds of attribution were used. About half consisted of the news anchor or correspondent quoting a source, for example, "The State Department officially announced today that the United States is making good on its threat of a year ago." The second kind of attribution, known in the trade as a "sound-bite," features a source shown on camera. Of all the sources of either type nearly half were U.S. government spokesmen: George Shultz, Gregory Newell and Alan Romberg of the State Department; congressmen James Scheuer and Dan Mica, and anonymous State Department and administration spokespersons. Western governments were represented on camera by Geoffrey Howe, British foreign secretary, and by references to Britain, France, "diplomatic sources," and "Western governments." U.S. government and Western government sources together accounted for nearly 70 percent of the attributions. Two members of the U.S. National Commission for Unesco, James Holderman and Leonard Sussman, were shown on camera with comments opposing the pullout, as was Elliott Abel, a former U.S. delegate to Unesco. Director General M'Bow appeared on one ABC newscast denying (through a translator) that his organization was dominated by Soviet and Third World politicians. He also was quoted twice in other contexts. The Soviet Union was represented by a defector, Nicolas Poliansky, who said that the high salaries paid to Soviets working for Unesco in Paris financed 120 people at the Soviet embassy; and by the Soviet ambassador to Unesco, Youri Khilchevski, who said in response to allegations that the organization was becoming increasingly politicized: "It is only a pretext to say so, because all international organizations are political." These 14 words were the sum total of the TV coverage of the official Soviet point of view. The Third World was not represented at all unless by U.N. Secretary General Javier Perez de Cuellar, who appeared briefly on one NBC newscast to oppose the withdrawal.

"60 MINUTES"

The most extended treatment of Unesco came, not on the evening news, but in a 15-minute segment on CBS's widely watched news magazine program "60 Minutes" that was broadcast on April 22, 1984. The report

was by CBS correspondent Ed Bradley in Paris. It merits examination because it illustrates the one-sidedness of the coverage. The report is a sustained piece of invective, with Bradley acting like an aggressive prosecuting attorney, calling witnesses to buttress his case and baiting the defendant, Director General M'Bow. As will be shown, problems of translation (M'bow was speaking in French) and highly selective editing produced a distorted version of M'Bow's responses to Bradley's questions and allegations.

Bradley's opening words were the only positive comments on Unesco in the entire 15-minute report. He noted that Unesco had brought literacy to Africa, trained teachers for the Third World, promoted cooperation among scientists and preserved ancient monuments in Egypt and Asia. "Nothing much wrong there, you might think," says Bradley. "But according to Washington, Unesco has now become a politicized, financially mismanaged organization and President Reagan has threatened to pull the U.S. out of the agency."

Bradley, with pictures on the screen of Unesco telephone operators speaking various languages, comments: "Although Unesco has six official languages, it's been said that most of the business here is conducted in a seventh impenetrable language known as Unesco-ese." But, said Bradley, it was not boredom that threatened to drive the United States out. Unesco had become President Reagan's least favorite U.N. agency for a whole lot of other reasons. He then referred to Unesco's rule of one member, one vote: "It doesn't matter if the country is Vanuatu, which has a population of 100,000, or the United States, which has well over 200 million." And no matter what language was spoken at Unesco, said Bradley, the U.S. administration claimed the rhetoric was the same: "It is anti-American and anti-democratic." He then referred to Unesco's budget of $373 million over the next two years, a quarter of that contributed by the United States. Yet, he said, Ambassador Jean Gerard was by no means sure where the money was spent.

Bradley: And as ambassador of a country that contributes 25 percent of the budget, you can't get an answer?

Gerard: I have not got an answer.

Bradley: What does that tell you about the management at Unesco?

Gerard: I would say it is poorly managed.

Bradley then asked Judson Gooding, a former counselor on the U.S. delegation to Unesco, about M'Bow's management style.

Gooding: Unesco's really ultimately run by the Director General. Everybody else is sort of a side boy. . . . It's a one-man show.

Bradley: Well, in a sense, isn't that good if he is a good administrator?
Gooding: Well, I think that when he proves to be a capricious, unpredictable person with a violent temper . . . sometimes he just
absolutely flares. He's brilliant, he has a fantastic memory,
he has a certain smoothness when he chooses to apply it. But
he is also unpredictable and tyrannical.

All the standard criticisms of M'Bow and Unesco are trotted out,
either by Bradley himself or, at his prodding, by Gooding and Gerard.
While critics wouldn't go as far as to accuse M'Bow of embezzlement,
said Bradley, "they do point to internal files leaked recently from Unesco
which indicate that the Director General has been responsible for a
series of financial abuses which benefit member countries from the Third
World." M'Bow is accused of driving out a "significant number of the top
level of Unesco's permanent staff" by creating a "climate of fear."
Despite this atmosphere, staff members wanted to keep their jobs because of the comfortable life in Paris with all its perks: high, tax-free
salaries, subsidized food and shopping, help with school costs and a
six-week vacation every year.
    Bradley referred also to an incident in the spring of 1983 when the
French government charged 47 Soviet diplomats based in Paris with espionage. Nine of these agents were members of the Soviet delegation to Unesco,
and three were on Unesco's permanent staff. All were expelled from
France.

Bradley (to M'Bow): Yet, nearly a year later, those people are still on
                    Unesco's payroll?
        M'Bow: Pourquoi? Vous demandez pourquoi? (Why? You
               ask why?)

M'Bow continues talking in French in the background as Bradley
continues his narrative: "We are indeed asking why . . . the Director General
says he didn't take any action against these three staff members who were
KGB agents because he claims the French government didn't give him any
evidence." The camera then switches to Gerard, complaining that their
salaries were sent to Moscow, which meant that the United States was
helping pay the salaries of Soviet agents.
    Unesco released an official transcript of Bradley's interview with
M'Bow, which was conducted in Paris on February 23, 1983. The transcript
shows that M'Bow gave detailed, lengthy responses to each of Bradley's
questions and allegations. The 37-page, double-spaced typescript shows that
the interview must have run nearly two hours. M'Bow's responses to questions about the Soviet spies alone ran to nearly 2,000 words—which Bradley

summarized in 30 words. Just 2 percent of what M'Bow told Bradley appeared on the program. Three-quarters of the segment was taken up by Bradley's commentary criticizing M'Bow and Unesco. Gooding, who was critical of M'Bow but felt the United States should remain a member, accounted for about 10 percent of the air time. Gerard's comments took another 5 percent. M'Bow—the target of the attack and the only person permitted to speak for Unesco—was given just 10 percent of the segment, or roughly 1 1/2 minutes of the 15-minute segment. And when he was shown it was as responding defensively to hostile questions.

NOTES

1. Details of the network reports about Unesco were obtained from the Television News Index and Abstracts, published by the Vanderbilt Television News Archives; and from the CBS News Index and Abstracts, published by University Microfilms International. The Unesco Information Office in Paris provided transcripts of the "60 Minutes" program, and of M'Bow's interview with Ed Bradley.
2. Dan Rather, "CBS Evening News," 28 December 1983.
3. Ibid., 21 December 1983.
4. Ibid., 22 November 1984.
5. Pierre Salinger, "ABC World News Tonight," 28 December 1983.
6. Bill McLaughlin, "CBS Evening News," 29 December 1983.
7. Marvin Kalb, "NBC Nightly News," 26 December 1983.
8. Pierre Salinger, "ABC World News Tonight," 28 December 1983.
9. Jim Bitterman, "NBC Nightly News," 29 December 1983.
10. NBC Nightly News," 26 December 1983.
11. "CBS Evening News," 29 December 1983.
12. Marvin Kalb, "NBC Nightly News," 29 December 1983.
13. Pierre Salinger, "ABC World News Tonight," 28 December 1983.
14. Bill McLaughlin, "CBS Evening News," 29 December 1983.
15. Jim Bitterman, "NBC Nightly News," 29 December 1983.
16. "CBS Evening News," 19 December 1984.

NEWS AGENCIES: TABLE

TABLE 8.1. ISSUES COVERED BY ABC, CBS AND NBC NEWS (PERCENTAGES)

	Combined networks *n* = 102
Anti-Unesco/ pro-withdrawal	
Politicization	27
Mismanagement	14
Reforms needed	14
Press issues	6
U.S. pays 25/	8
Support for U.S.	4
Too little change	1
Criticism of M'Bow	2
Subtotal	76
Pro-Unesco/ anti-withdrawal	
Criticism of pullout	19
Valuable programs	11
Denials of charges	1
Subtotal	21
Looking ahead	
Future	4
Subtotal	4
Total	100

TOTAL COVERAGE: TABLE

TABLE 8.2. COMPARISON OF ISSUES COVERED (PERCENTAGE)

	News agencies (n = 1,945)	Newspaper reports (n = 3,232)	Editorials (n = 3,348)	Columns (n = 4,178)	TV news (n = 102)
Anti-Unesco/ pro-withdrawal					
Politicization	22	24	28	24	27
Mismanagement	13	13	13	13	14
Reforms needed	9	13	9	9	14
Press issues	11	7	10	6	6
U.S. pays 25%	5	5	5	4	8
Support for U.S.	4	6	4	3	4
Too little change	3	5	4	2	1
Criticism of M'Bow	2	2	4	7	2
Benefits to U.S.	2	1	7	6	—
U.S. credibility at stake	<1	0	<1	<1	—
Subtotal	70	76	84	73	76
Pro-Unesco/ anti-withdrawal					
Criticism of pullout	13	10	6	11	9
Valuable programs	9	8	7	12	11
Denials of charges	2	2	<1	1	1
Propaganda campaign	2	1	1	<1	—
Subtotal	27	21	14	24	21
Looking ahead					
Future	2	2	1	2	4
Alternatives	1	1	1	1	—
Subtotal	3	3	2	3	4
Total	100	100	100	100	100

CHAPTER 9

Coverage after the Withdrawal

Once the withdrawal took effect, media interest in Unesco faded rapidly. It all but disappeared from television news. Only the United Kingdom's withdrawal in 1985 and M'Bow's announcement in 1986 that he would not seek a third term were mentioned on the network evening news programs. In all of 1985, the first year after the United States pulled out, the AP, UPI and New York Times news services distributed fewer than 60 reports among them that dealt with Unesco as their main topic. In 1986 the total dropped to less than 30. Media pickup of those reports was correspondingly low. Clippings collected by Press Intelligence Service showed that in 1985 the daily papers carried a combined total of just over 600 news reports—down from nearly 2,000 during 1984, the "year of crisis." In 1986 this number dropped to less than 400. Editorials and, to a lesser extent, editorial columns continued to comprise a high proportion of the total newspaper coverage. In both 1985 and 1986, opinion pieces comprised nearly one-half of all clippings dealing with Unesco as their main topic. As the conflict between the United States and Unesco became less of an issue, however, a small but growing proportion of the news and news feature reports dealt with Unesco's programs such as attempts to reduce illiteracy or to save cultural monuments.

There was a dramatic spurt in interest in the fall of 1987 when the Executive Board met to nominate a director general at the end of M'Bow's second term. The announcement that M'Bow would, after all, run for a third term, the political machinations that ensued, and the unexpected election of Federico Mayor Zaragoza of Spain as the new

director general, spurred a great deal of news and editorial coverage. American daily papers carried almost 1,300 news reports and some 200 editorials dealing with the nomination process and subsequent election. Once the dust had settled, however, the coverage tapered off again to almost zero.

EVENTS THAT WERE COVERED

In the initial phase after the withdrawal, the focus remained on its aftermath. The AP and New York Times reported in February 1985 that the State Department had named a panel of 10 observers to monitor reforms at Unesco. It was headed by Leonard Marks, treasurer of the World Press Freedom Committee and a former director of the U.S. Information Agency. Its purpose, he said, was "to determine what changes are to be made and whether or not we should return."[1] Other panel members who were on record as favoring the withdrawal included Ursula Meese, wife of presidential counselor Edwin Meese and a former U.S. delegate to Unesco; James Holderman, president of the University of South Carolina; William Korey, director of the Institute for Policy Research of B'nai B'rith, and Edwin Feulner, president of the Heritage Foundation.

Executive Board Meetings, 1985

A flurry of news reports dealt with a five-day extraordinary session of Unesco's Executive Board in Paris in February 1985. They focused primarily on three issues occasioned by the withdrawal: whether Unesco would have to trim programs and seek extra money to meet the financial crisis caused by the end of U.S. funding; whether the United States was still obliged to pay its 1985 dues, since it had pulled out in the middle of Unesco's two-year budget cycle, and whether the United States, although no longer a member, should be allowed to establish an observer mission to monitor developments. Considerable emphasis was given to threats by Japan and Canada that they, too, would withdraw if Unesco failed to adopt radical reforms. In the event, France announced that it would make a special voluntary contribution of $2 million to help ease the financial crunch. And the Soviet Union and several countries in Africa, Asia and Latin America said they would contribute a total of about $6 million by forgoing refunds they would have received from a special Unesco budget used to offset the effect of fluctuations in the dollar exchange rate. Although there was no provision for observer status in Unesco's constitution, the board agreed to allow the United States to

have an observer mission until Unesco's rules on such status could be clarified.

Reports on the special session that the press picked up most frequently included those dealing with observer status for the United States (used by 59 papers); threats of withdrawal by other countries (used by 26), and France's $2 million contribution (used by 23). The *New York Times* report on the French donation noted disapprovingly that "Western delegates expressed surprise and some dismay at the French move, saying it might hamper the effort to use Unesco's present financial problems to force administrative and policy changes."[2]

A notable feature of the editorials published during the first two months of 1985 was their strident criticism of M'Bow's leadership. Other frequent themes in the editorials had to do with "Unesco bureaucrats enjoying the plush life in Paris," references to Unesco headquarters as "a nest of KGB agents," its "anti-Israel policies," and the fact that "80 percent of its budget is spent at headquarters." One dispatch distributed by the Hearst News and Feature Service on February 25 said that "Unesco's controversial secretary general, Amadou Mahtar M'Bow, is reportedly fanning anti-Israeli sentiment to get extra cash from Arab states as compensation for the loss of American financial support." M'Bow's main selling point, said the report, was that the U.S. decision to quit Unesco "was instigated by Israel and the Jewish lobby in America who were angered by the agency's anti-Zionist stance."

The major agencies all carried reports on the opening of the Executive Board's six-week meeting, starting on May 9, to work out a program and budget for the next two years. Both the AP and UPI dispatches from Paris led with efforts by Western nations to have the board discuss the U.S. General Accounting Office report that criticized aspects of Unesco's management. UPI noted that Western governments "lost a bid" to consider the report, while the *New York Times* said the West had "suffered a procedural setback" when the board decided against putting the report on its agenda. AP correspondent Harry Dunphy returned two weeks later and filed three dispatches. One dealt with an announcement by M'Bow that he would have to dismiss 300 staff members because the U.S. withdrawal had left insufficient funds to pay them; the second reported that Western nations had warned Unesco that it would be unwise to renew debate on a New World Information Order, and the third noted that the Executive Board had adopted resolutions condemning Israeli policy on Arab education and culture in the occupied territories. Dunphy also filed a roundup at the end of the Executive Board's meeting on June 21, which reported that although the meeting had begun in "sharp disagreements over what the organization should do to face the crisis covered by the U.S. withdrawal," the Western nations had "avoided

confrontation with the Third World and Soviet Union that would have divided Unesco even more."

The press paid little attention to the meeting. Dunphy's report on possible staff cuts appeared in a dozen newspapers. His story on the New Information Order ran in seven. The *New York Times* carried a roundup and analysis by Richard Bernstein at the end of the session, and three papers carried a *Chicago Tribune* article on possible further withdrawals from Unesco.

The 23rd General Conference, 1985

The 23rd session of the General Conference met in Sofia, Bulgaria, on 8 October 1985 to approve Unesco's budget and program for 1986–87. News-agency coverage was sparse. Harry Dunphy of the AP's Paris bureau covered the first few days of the six-week session and then left, returning to do a roundup a month later. Paul Lewis of the *New York Times* also covered only the opening and closing sessions. UPI apparently was not represented at all, nor was the *Washington Post*. As in the case of previous general conferences, the agency coverage dealt primarily with East–West or North–South conflicts and almost totally ignored any discussion of Unesco's programs. Conference records show that delegates approved more than 100 reform measures put into effect during the previous 18 months and established a special committee to ensure that they were implemented. It adopted a zero-growth budget for the biennium, set up a priority system that emphasized practical projects, and put in place a new mechanism to evaluate the effectiveness of programs.[3] Yet, reports on the opening sessions focused on confrontation: threats by other Western nations to withdraw; on challenges to the credentials of the Israeli delegation; on a proposal by Third World nations, supported by the Soviet Union, to dismiss 130 Americans from Unesco's staff because the United States was no longer a member; and on whether the United States would be allowed to keep its observer status.

The lead paragraph in the *New York Times* roundup at the end of the conference had to do with the United Kingdom "expressing disappointment at the results" and specifically the failure of delegates to agree to eliminate "more politically controversial activities from Unesco's 1986–87 work program, especially in the disarmament and human rights field."[4] The last three paragraphs of the 15-paragraph report noted, however, that in the closing stages the Soviet Union and its Third World allies had taken a generally more conciliatory line, appearing eager to avoid provoking Britain and other Western nations. The lead paragraph in the AP roundup noted that the conference had ended after resolving problems caused by the U.S. withdrawal, and quoted an unidentified

"senior East bloc diplomat" as saying he thought M'Bow should step down when his term ended in 1987. This, the official was quoted as saying, "is necessary for a reconciliation with the Americans."[5] These agency dispatches from Sofia got little play in American newspapers. Press Intelligence found only 74 news reports on the conference in the daily press over its six-week duration, virtually all drawn from the AP and New York Times news services.

Taking Aim at M'Bow

Editorial writers, however, were far more active. In the latter half of 1985 there were more editorials and editorial columns printed about Unesco than news reports. Some were based on news reports that turned out to be distorted or just plain wrong. In August, for example, the Scripps Howard news service distributed to its clients a report from the London Observer Service that alleged that "fistfights have broken out among demoralized, embittered Unesco staffers as the organization scrambles to find ways to cut expenditures." Meanwhile, it said, "Director General M'Bow sits huddled like an ivory Buddha in his split-level Paris penthouse, protected by newly-installed bullet-proof windows and a newly burglar-barred double door with special electrified fittings."[6] The report said that Unesco's staff association, which largely represents Western members, "saw themselves as being taken over by a vast network as M'Bow recruited personal aides from his native Senegal and populated his Cabinet almost entirely with Third Worlders." Even at the height of the crisis, Third World staff "appeared from nowhere to fill posts that popped up to accommodate them." A staff member was quoted as saying, "Everyone is racist here, both black and white." None of these allegations was attributed to an identified source.

The report was not widely used, but it did inspire an editorial that ran in identical form in 23 different newspapers a few weeks later. Alleging that "a siege mentality prevails in the plush offices of Unesco in Paris," the editorial said M'Bow had "installed bullet-proof windows and a double door with electronic locks in his Paris penthouse. Fistfights have broken out between Unesco staff members. Western staff members dominate the staff association, so M'Bow encouraged Third World staff members to form their own staff association. Racism is rampant, with Westerners charging they are being laid off while high-paying jobs are being created for M'Bow's friends from the Third World." The editorials also cited a rumor that "M'Bow has been given a $33,000 raise in his annual salary, while 580 staffers in the lower ranks are being laid off. Third World emissaries continue to visit Paris and stay at the most expensive hotels, where Unesco picks up the tab." All this, it concluded,

"proves the United States made the right decision when it chose to withdraw."

The issue of M'Bow's salary was picked up in another canned editorial that ran in six papers in October. Whatever belt-tightening Unesco was undergoing as a result of the U.S. withdrawal, it said, "has had a perverse effect on the personal fortunes" of the director general. "M'Bow, whose erratic and spendthrift leadership has nearly wrecked Unesco, has just been voted a 26.8 percent pay increase." U.S. tax-payers, said the editorial, could be thankful "that they are no longer putting up 25 percent of the agency's budget and paying a quarter of the director general's new, undeserved $159,115-a-year salary." An editorial in the *Wall Street Journal* on October 21 likewise criticized M'Bow's pay raise.

Criticism of M'Bow's salary appeared to be based on a report from the Washington bureau of the *New York Times* on October 10, which said that

> neither the austerity forced by the loss of 25 percent American contribution nor the Reagan administration's implication that the United States would return to the fold if there was adequate belt-tightening seems to have had much impact on Unesco's leadership. Word is circulating here, in fact, that the agency's director general, Amadou Mahtar M'Bow of Senegal, was recently voted a big pay raise at a closed meeting. State Department officials say M'Bow was given an increase of 26.8 percent, retroactive to January 1, bringing his salary to $159,115.

What had happened, in fact, was that the International Civil Service Commission had recommended that all agency heads and professionals working in the U.N. system should give up their cost-of-living allowances and have their base pay increased by a like amount. Thus M'Bow did not get a raise; his income remained the same. The *New York Times* ran a correction nine days later, and on November 8 the *Wall Street Journal* printed a letter from Joseph Mehan of the Unesco Liaison Office at the U.N., putting the record straight. Ombudsmen for Denver's *Rocky Mountain News* and the *San Diego Union* also noted the mistake. The other editorials were not corrected, however, and the damage was done.

Another canned editorial, one that was also based on a misconception, appeared in 18 different newspapers in August. It dealt with legislation sponsored by Sen. Nancy Kassebaum, which stipulated that unless major contributors to the U.N. were given greater say over spending, the United States would cut its contribution by 20 percent. The second paragraph of the editorial noted that "fiscal horror stories" had already prompted the United States to pull out of Unesco. "And why not? Fully

80 percent of Unesco's budget is going for administrative expenses. And the agency's unseemly extravagances included a lavish conference center in starving Ethiopia." That was disputable on two counts. Unesco maintains that more than 80 percent of its budget is spent on programs directly in member states, but for accounting purposes costs incurred in the field are charged to the headquarters budget. And the conference center in Ethiopia was a project of the U.N. General Assembly, not Unesco. Although one of the 18 papers that ran the editorial printed a letter from Mehan pointing this out, there is no record that any of the others corrected the errors.

The United Kingdom Withdraws

The next development to capture the attention of the media was the United Kingdom's announcement on December 5, 1985, that it would join the United States in withdrawing from Unesco. All the major agencies filed reports on the move, quoting the United Kingdom's minister for overseas development, Timothy Raison, as saying that the organization "had been used to attack those very values which it was designed to uphold" and that inefficient management had "led to programs which contain vague and meaningless studies, and duplication of the work of other agencies," Raison told Parliament that while there had been some reforms, they were not sufficient. The money saved from the British contribution, he said, would go directly to developing countries, particularly members of the Commonwealth, to promote Unesco-type objectives.[7] More than 100 papers in the United States carried reports on Britain's withdrawal, and 49 ran editorials—many of them identical— praising the decision.

A week later, 21 papers carried reports that Unesco staff members in Paris had held a work stoppage to demand changes in the agency's policy on laying off employees and that five staff members had begun a hunger strike to back up demands that their staff association be given greater say in decisions about dismissals.[8] Singapore's decision in December to quit Unesco attracted little attention in the press, perhaps because its stated reasons for leaving were financial, not political. Singapore's ambassador to France, David Marshall, said his nation's decision was made "because of the high level of its annual assessment and not for reasons given by the United States or Britain."[9]

M'Bow Says He Will Step Down

Coverage in 1986 was even more sparse than in 1985 and was dominated by a single event—M'Bow's announcement in October that he would not seek re-election when his second six-year term expired in 1987. The issue

of his re-election was raised earlier in the year. A report from Paul Lewis of the *New York Times* in March that Western nations were trying to block a third term for M'Bow appeared in eight papers. It said that the move marked a shift in Western tactics to introduce administrative and policy changes. Instead of trying to change Unesco's operations, they now agreed that "significant changes are unlikely as long as M'Bow remains."[10] In June Lewis reported that Western members were divided over a strategy for removing M'Bow, with some wanting to force him out by imposing a two-term limit on U.N. executives, while others preferred to concentrate on presenting a good alternative candidate instead of coming out publicly against M'Bow.[11] Several papers also printed dispatches from the New York Times, AP and UPI about the dismissal of 19 senior Unesco employees when the budget cuts took effect. Among them were Dragoljub Najman, a Yugoslav and an assistant director general, and Erwin Solomon, an American and director of the Division of Socio-Economic Analysis. Najman had been a leading critic of M'Bow's leadership, and UPI described the dismissals as a "witch-hunt."[12] There was no formal discussion of M'Bow's re-election at the May meeting of the Executive Board, and the media showed little interest in its proceedings, although a dispatch from Dunphy of the AP recording that the board had decided to grant the United Kingdom observer status was picked up by a handful of papers.[13]

M'Bow's unexpected announcement to the Executive Board on October 6 that he would not seek a third term received extensive coverage. M'Bow recalled that the Organization of African Unity had endorsed his re-election, as had the Council of the Arab League, and that the Non-Aligned Summit meeting in Zimbabwe had adopted a resolution supporting Unesco. However, he said, "I should like you to know that I shall not be seeking a third term of office. I do not wish the interest, the affection even, which I enjoy in many member states to stand in the way of any nomination being put forward."

Nearly 200 papers carried news reports about M'Bow's decision, 91 of them using the AP version and 21 that from UPI. The New York Times dispatch, which ran in eight papers, noted that Western delegates, taken by surprise by the director general's announcement, nevertheless moved quickly to remove any trace of ambiguity from his remarks. They made it clear that they interpreted his speech as a refusal both to seek re-election and to accept a draft from Third World supporters.[14]

In addition to the 198 news reports, M'Bow's announcement spurred dozens of editorials, almost all of them expressing satisfaction that he would not run again. A typical example was an editorial that first appeared in the *San Diego Union* on October 9 under the heading "Good Riddance." This editorial was syndicated by the Copley News Service and

appeared in more than 20 other papers around the country. In fact, five "canned" editorials about M'Bow's decision accounted for 69 of the 122 collected by the Press Intelligence clipping service.

Although the 1985 and 1986 coverage continued to be dominated by the U.S. withdrawal and its aftermath, Unesco did receive some more favorable publicity as well. The AP carried a report in June 1985 on a campaign to save monuments in Bangladesh, while UPI noted in August that year that Unesco had declared Mayan ruins in Guatemala to be World Heritage sites. There also were agency reports on a restoration workshop for African countries and on Unesco efforts to save artwork in Venice from flood damage. The most widely used positive report—carried by 92 newspapers—was an AP story on Unesco efforts to overcome illiteracy in Asia.

Federico Mayor Zaragoza Replaces M'Bow, 1987

The media paid a great deal of attention to the election of a new director general in the fall of 1987. Much was at stake. Virtually every news agency report mentioned that the United States and the United Kingdom had withdrawn from Unesco, and would not rejoin as long as M'Bow was director general. At least nine other Western countries were said to be threatening to withdraw, or not pay their dues, if he were re-elected. Those reported as likely to pull out were Belgium, Canada, Denmark, Japan, the Netherlands, Switzerland and West Germany. Some news reports also mentioned Australia and Sweden. The departure of the United States and the United Kingdom had cut Unesco's budget by almost a third. Those threatening to leave now would account for another third. If they did quit, it was unlikely that the organization could survive.

The director general is elected by Unesco's General Conference for a six-year term. The 50-member Executive Board nominates a candidate to the General Conference, which usually accepts its recommendation but is not bound to do so. The Executive Board members consider nominees, then cast a series of secret ballots until one candidate achieves a clear majority. If, after four ballots, no contender has the 26 votes needed, a fifth ballot is held with members voting only on the two leading candidates.

Before the Executive Board met in September, it was generally felt that, in accordance with unwritten U.N. convention, it was Asia's turn for the director generalship. The Asian candidate was Sahabzada Yaqub Khan, foreign minister of Pakistan and a retired army general. Perceived also as the West's candidate, Khan had support from Executive Board members representing Japan, China, Canada and France. A French foreign ministry spokesman explained that Khan "seems to be the best

candidate for getting people together."[15] This reflected a desire to find a director general who could persuade the United States and the United Kingdom to rejoin Unesco. Since the two countries had left, they had no representation on the Executive Board, but made their preferences known through their official observers and diplomatic channels. The board began its three-week meeting in Paris in late September, preparatory to the General Conference in October.

Although M'Bow had announced a year earlier that he would not run again, he was nominated for a third term by the Organization of African Unity (OAU). The Letter endorsing M'Bow, signed by Zambia's foreign minister, referred to the "outstanding contribution made by M'Bow to the growth and success of Unesco."[16] M'Bow had the backing of most of the 20 members of the Arab League and the OAU represented on the Executive Board, including 10 French-speaking African nations.

Running as an independent candidate was Federico Mayor Zaragoza, a Spanish biochemist who had served a deputy director general under M'Bow from 1978 to 1981. He then became Spain's education minister and later a center-right member of he European Parliament. Mayor had the backing of scores of prominent scientists and intellectuals, including a dozen Nobel Prize winners. He was considered a dark horse, however, largely because some nations opposed having a European head the organization.

Other candidates with at least some support included Nicolai Todorov of Bulgaria, the Soviet bloc candidate; Soedjatmoko (the only name he uses) of Indonesia, who was head of the United Nations University in Japan; Ivo Margan, a Yugoslav and chairman of the Executive Board; Shiela Solomon, the board member from Trinidad and Tobago; Victor Sa Machado of Portugal and Alfonso Barrera Valverde of Ecuador. Not official candidates but waiting in the wings should the call come were Enrique Iglesias, foreign minister of Uruguay and Prince Sadruddin Aga Khan, former U.N. high commissioner for refugees.

The day before the Executive Board's first ballot on October 6, France's representative resigned to protest her country's decision to support Khan. Gisele Halimi, a former Socialist parliamentary deputy and a feminist lawyer, said Khan represented a government "born of a military coup d'etat" that had repeatedly violated human rights, particularly women's rights.[17] She was replaced by Marie-Claude Cabana, the French ambassador to Unesco, who said France would support Khan in the first round because he was the official candidate of the Asian group and offered the best chance of getting the United States and the United Kingdom to rejoin the organization.

M'Bow, with backing from African and Arab members, led the pack with 18 votes in the first round—two or three fewer than expected. Khan,

supported by Western, Asian and some Latin American nations, had 16 votes. Todorov had six—from the board's Soviet bloc delegates, representing the Soviet Union, East Germany, Bulgaria and Mongolia—and also from Ethiopia and Greece. Mayor also had six votes; Soedjatmoko had two, while Margan and Solomon had one each.

Because no candidate received the required majority of 26 votes, a second ballot was held on October 8. M'Bow again led with 18 votes, Todorov retained his East bloc support with six, Soedjatmoko still had two and Margan and Solomon one each. The surprise was that Khan's tally slipped from 16 to 12, while Mayor picked up three votes for a total of nine. One vote was voided. It appeared that some European nations, concerned that Khan could not defeat M'Bow, had switched their support to Mayor.

Once again no candidate had a clear majority, and a third ballot was scheduled for October 9. Just before the vote, however, Khan withdrew from the race. In a letter announcing Khan's withdrawal, Pakistan's delegate Niaz A. Niaki noted that his country was "concerned that a contest between the candidatures of Asia and Africa would be contrary to the interests of both regions and to the tradition of Afro-Asian solidarity."[18] Khan himself was said to be angered by his loss of support from Western nations. France switched its support to M'Bow, a step that was interpreted as a gesture of support for its former African colonies, who strongly favored the incumbent. It was also suggested that France was concerned with keeping French the main language of Unesco: Mayor represented a rival and larger language group, the Hispanics.[19]

M'Bow's opponents, concerned that Khan's former supporters would swing their votes to M'Bow and give him the required majority in the third ballot, persuaded the board to postpone the vote until after the weekend, giving them time to lobby for Mayor.[20] M'Bow did pick up five votes in the third ballot on October 13 for a total of 23, just three short of a majority. Mayor, however, gained nine votes, including those of Japan and China, and doubled his support to a total of 18. Most of the Soviet bloc votes stayed with Todorov, who had five, while Soedjatmoko had three and Solomon got one. Margan of Yugoslavia withdrew as a candidate.

In round four, on October 14, M'Bow's support slipped for the first time—down to 21 votes after 23 in round three. Mayor's total was 19, up from 18 in the previous round. Todorov retained four Soviet bloc votes, and Soedjatmoko also got four. Solomon still had one, and there was one blank ballot. The rules now required a fifth and final round, with delegates having to choose between only the two front-runners, M'Bow and Mayor. In the case of a tie, the president of the Executive Board would draw one of the names from a hat. The Soviet bloc had emerged as the

key swing votes and were reported to be backing Mayor, who also seemed likely to pick up the Asian and Caribbean votes that went to other candidates in earlier rounds.

The fifth and final vote was scheduled for Friday, October 16, but was postponed for 24 hours at the request of African countries, who wanted time to seek a "consensus candidate."[21] Delegates told newsmen that Senegal's representative, Iba Der Thiam, wanted time to arrange for M'Bow to withdraw, thus avoiding a direct defeat of their candidate. A week earlier, Thiam was reported to have angered Western delegates in a speech to the board attacking "the ideology of supremacy of white man" and saying that if M'Bow were rejected it would be a "supreme humiliation for the Third World, for Africa."[22] But East bloc sources told the Associated Press that several delegates, including the Soviet Union's Yuri Khilchevski, met privately with M'Bow to urge his withdrawal.[23]

The next day, as the Executive Board met to choose between M'Bow and Mayor, M'Bow withdrew from the race. In a letter to the board, M'Bow referred to threats by several nations to quit Unesco if he were re-elected. His opponents, he said, "had not hesitated to resort to blackmail, disinformation, as well as pressures and threats of all sorts." By threatening to withdraw or not make their financial contributions, he said, those nations "have perverted and corrupted the democratic process of the election of the director-general."[24] Under the circumstances, he asked the OAU to withdraw his candidacy.

M'Bow's letter set off a 12-hour procedural wrangle on the Executive Board. Some members wanted a fifth ballot, this time between Mayor and the candidates who had tied for third place in round four, Todorov and Soedjatmoko. African states argued that the rules did not allow for only one candidate in the runoff, and wanted to introduce a new candidate to replace M'Bow. Western delegates argued that there should be no fifth ballot, since Mayor was now the only remaining candidate. In the event, after an all-night session the board chose Mayor by a vote to 30 for and 20 against. Those supporting Mayor included most Western nations, many Latin American countries, the four Soviet bloc delegates, plus Japan and China. Most of those opposed were African and Arab nations.

Mayor, who in his election campaign had stressed the need to reform and streamline Unesco operations, told reporters that one of his chief aims was to persuade the United States and the United Kingdom to rejoin. Meanwhile, he would encourage them to participate in concrete projects in some scientific and environmental areas.[25] Mayor also went out of his way to placate M'Bow's African supporters: "My first concern will be for the developing countries, especially Africa," he told a news conference after his nomination.[26] Senegal's Thiam said he would give his "most loyal support" to Mayor.

The focus then shifted to the 24th General Conference, which opened a six-week meeting on October 20, 1987. Its agenda included what to do about a $40 million deficit for the 1985–87 biennium, caused by a decline in the value of the U.S. dollar, the currency in which Unesco dues are paid. Also up for discussion were Unesco's activities in communications, disarmament, human rights and peace. But media attention centered on the vote for a director general, scheduled for November 7. Although the 158-member General Conference traditionally had accepted the nominee of its Executive Board, it was not bound to do so, and there was speculation that M'Bow's African supporters would try to block Mayor's election. Any such intentions were abandoned, however, when the Arab bloc pledged its 20 votes to Mayor, followed by the Third World Group of 77.[27] M'Bow himself, in his farewell speech to the General Conference on November 4, offered Mayor his "warmest wishes for success."[28]

On November 7 the General Conference approved Mayor as the next director general by a vote of 142 to 7. Mayor again told a press conference that he would do his utmost to get the United States, the United Kingdom and Singapore to rejoin. He said he wanted to make Unesco a more creative organization that would emphasize science and the environment. Of particular interest to Western journalists was his view of the New World Information Order. Asked about this, Mayor refused to express an opinion, but said Unesco's constitution called for a free flow of ideas and information.[29]

MEDIA COVERAGE

These events received extensive coverage by the major news agencies. The AP and UPI each filed about 20 separate reports from the announcement in late September that M'Bow would run again until he withdrew and Mayor was nominated a month later. The New York Times News Service distributed about 15 reports over the same period. Just three Paris correspondents were responsible for virtually all the agency coverage: Harry Dunphy of the AP, Steve Holland of UPI and Steven Greenhouse of the New York Times. A handful of American newspapers also used reports from Reuters, or occasionally from the *Washington Post* or *Chicago Tribune*. But the AP, UPI and the New York Times News Service provided by far the bulk of the reports that appeared in daily papers. The AP dispatches being used six times as often as UPI, and ten times as often as the New York Times reports.

Burrelle's Press Clipping Bureau collected almost 1,300 news stories (including duplicates) relating to the nomination that appeared in U.S.

daily papers—a much greater volume than had been published at any time since the U.S. withdrawal became final in 1984. The clippings were not evenly distributed over the period. The announcement that M'Bow would run for a third term, carried by all three agencies, drew a lot of attention. These reports all mentioned that the United States and the United Kingdom had previously withdrawn from Unesco and often placed the blame squarely on M'Bow's shoulders. Thus the *New York Times* version noted that M'Bow had "sharply divided the organization" and that "Western diplomats said that the United States and Britain would probably not return to the group if he remained in office."[30] The UPI report stated bluntly that "Unesco leader Amadou Mahtar M'Bow, whose policies led the United States and Britain to withdraw their funding, was nominated to a third term as director general of the embattled organization."[31]

As the Executive Board began the nominating process, reports on the balloting noted also that other goverments had threatened to withdraw if M'Bow were re-elected. UPI, for example, reported on October 8 that "Japan, The Netherlands, Canada, Denmark, Belgium, Switzerland and Australia have said they might pull out in the event of a new mandate for M'Bow." The AP added Denmark to the list, reporting on October 13 that Danish Education Minister Bertel Haarder had written to his French counterpart that M'Bow's re-election would do "irreparable harm" to Unesco. The agency reports provided little background on the other candidates during the first few rounds of balloting, although Mayor usually was identified briefly as a scientist, former Spanish minister of education and former deputy to M'Bow. Few newspapers picked up the agency accounts on the first four rounds of balloting.

This changed dramatically with the surprise announcement on October 17, just before the fifth-round run-off, that M'Bow had asked to withdraw from the race. Dunphy of the AP filed six reports in a 10-hour period, each updating the previous one with new developments. Holland's report for UPI was topped with a new lead three times. More newspapers used these reports than those of any other single event in the entire Unesco saga. About 150 papers carried the initial AP report of M'Bow's withdrawal. More than 200 carried updated versions with a new lead on Mayor's nomination. Dozens of others picked up the UPI or New York Times dispatches.

The tone of the reporting also changed. Although the agencies cautioned that the United States and the United Kingdom were not likely to rejoin Unesco without further evidence of reform, that clearly had become an option. One AP report after Mayor's nomination quoted the West German foreign minister, Hans-Dietrich Genscher, as saying that Mayor was "a respected scientist whose nomination clears the way for

reforms." AP also quoted British diplomats as predicting that the nomination would pave the way for the United Kingdom's return.[32] The *New York Times* dispatch on October 18 said that not only had the nomination opened the way for the United States and the United Kingdom to rejoin, but that it would persuade nations that had also threatened to quit to remain members. A *New York Times* "Man in the News" feature on Mayor stressed that he had tried to distance himself from M'Bow, that he was "a conciliator and a good listener," a distinguished scientist and an educator who also "writes poetry, studied at Oxford University and is a good friend of King Juan Carlos of Spain."[33] Nowhere was the media preference more clearly expressed than in a dispatch from John Izbicki of the London *Daily Telegraph* that was distributed to clients in the United States. Mayor, it said, was "a man of high academic and intellectual wisdom, a man who would put Unesco back on its once highly-respected feet." He was "an academic through and through, a distinguished member of the Spanish Royal Academy of Medicine. M'Bow, on the other hand, is a self-made man, the son of an illiterate, innumerate peasant. He has had to fight all his life, struggling through school and into college."[34]

Newspaper Editorials

The switch in attitude toward Unesco after Mayor's nomination was even more marked in newspaper editorials. More than 200 papers commented on the nominating process. A third of the editorials ran after the announcement that M'Bow would seek a third term. They were uniformly hostile. According to the *Houston Post*, his "accomplishments during terms one and two included driving the United States out and making Unesco a biased propaganda organ for communist and Third World nations."[35] A *Chicago Tribune* editorial claimed that "in 13 years Mr. M'Bow has turned the organization into a political cartoon. It now functions largely to ensure his personal luxury and promote his goals, which include bringing the world's press under government control."[36] The *San Diego Union*, in an editorial that was syndicated also to several other newspapers, averred that "during the last 12 years, the Senegalese despot has nearly destroyed the agency through his mismanagement." The question was, said the editorial, whether Unesco's members "have the spine to throw the rascal out. Failing that, Unesco's days are numbered."[37] The *Miami Herald* began its editorial as follows: "Ah Surprise! The little tyrant with the Paris penthouse has decided after all to seek a third term as director general of the crisis-ridden Unesco."[38] The Freedom chain of newspapers, in a canned editorial, complained that under M'Bow "Unesco has become a dandy forum for slanderous attacks

on the United States by the Soviet bloc and a haven for high-living diplomats. Unesco has been an international hog trough for years."[39] The *Atlanta Constitution*, in an editorial that began "Be advised to keep an eye on the silver; Amadou Mahtar M'Bow is back at the table," opined that M'Bow was "a triple threat in two terms at Unesco's helm: wasteful, tyrannical and ideologically biased. It was his impossible management that drove the United States and Britain to quit Unesco and could convince Japan, Canada and The Netherlands to do likewise, a trend that could lead to the organization's collapse."[40] The Cleveland *Plain Dealer* was one of the few papers to note that if M'Bow were re-elected, it would be partly a result of the U.S. decision to withdraw: "Rather than staying involved in Unesco and using what influence it had to promote individuals who could take over from M'Bow, the United States simply gave up." The present dilemma showed why the withdrawal was a mistake. Reagan administration policy-makers had dealt themselves out of a direct role in Unesco's future. "They nevertheless can play an indirect part in rebuilding Unesco by lobbying those U.S. allies who still are involved to come up with a replacement for M'Bow."[41]

The editorials also made it clear that one of M'Bow's major sins was his support for a New World Information Order. Of the 125-odd separate editorials (some were reprinted verbatim in several papers), almost one-half referred to Unesco's communications policies as a reason for the U.S. withdrawal. A handful of the editorials acknowledged that the concept of a new information order had some merit, but that the negative aspects had received most attention. Thus the *Christian Science Monitor*, in an editorial that was reprinted in several smaller papers, said that Unesco's goal of improving communications facilities in the Third World "got off track for a time in informal proposals to restrict and license Western journalists. The aim remains valid."[42] An editorial in *The Oregonian* made a similar point: "A particularly serious concern has been M'Bow's backing for a so-called New World Information Order. Its stated purpose is to promote the development of independent news-gathering agencies in Third World countries, but Western journalists opposed it because under the guise of protecting newsmen it would have imposed controls on reporting."[43]

Most references to the New World Information Order, however, omitted any mention of its developmental goals. Instead the focus was entirely on its perceived threat to Western interests—specifically state control of the media, licensing of journalists and censorship. For example, the Fort Lauderdale, Fla., *News/Sun-Sentinel* commented that "another particularly nasty Unesco program is the 'New World Information Order,' a direct assault on the free press and the free flow of news

and information. It would allow Unesco to be the arbiter and licensing agency for international news coverage."[44] The Omaha *World-Herald* said that "under the leadership of M'Bow, Unesco has endorsed a 'New World Information Order,' a thinly veiled attempt to muzzle the world's press through a licensing procedure. The plan could have imposed restrictions on Western journalists while promoting state-sponsored journalism."[45] The *Boston Globe* editorialized that one of M'Bow's "dangerous enterprises" was his sponsorship of the study commission headed by Sean MacBride. "It called for a universal code of conduct for news organizations that included a requirement that journalists obtain government licenses to practice their profession. It also promoted the false notion that Western news organizations such as the Associated Press and Reuters were engaged for imperialistic motives in giving a deliberately unfavorable picture of life in Third World countries."[46]

Once M'Bow withdrew, however, there was a marked change in the tone of the editorials. The first reaction was one of relief: "Good riddance to Amadou Mahtar M'Bow who, at long last, is being replaced," the *New York Post* proclaimed.[47] Under the headline "Bye-Bye M'Bow," the Santa Rosa, Calif., *Press-Democrat* wrote that "our old friend, Amadou Mahtar M'Bow, has finally got what's coming to him." The Santa Rosa, Calif., *Press-Democrat* said that M'Bow "is a great guy if you believe in abolition of press freedom and bashing America."[48] The *Miami Herald* wrote that "a sigh of relief was the world's logical reaction."[49] Like the news reports, the editorials made a point of contrasting M'Bow's failings with Mayor's virtues. Many of the editorials, in identifying Mayor, mentioned that he was a respected biochemist, that he had served as Spain's minister of education, and that he had been Unesco's deputy director general. That link with M'Bow gave rise to the only reservations about Mayor. To the *Wall Street Journal*, his "advantage and disadvantage is that he had served as M'Bow's deputy."[50] And the Pittsburgh, Pa., *Post-Gazette* wondered why he "didn't do more to counter M'Bow."[51] For the most part, however, Mayor's nomination was welcomed by the editorial writers. An example is a syndicated Copley editorial that appeared in more than 20 papers across the country. It began with a typical swipe at Unesco which, it said, was supposed to stand for the United Nations Educational, Scientific and Cultural Organization. "But instead of living up to its high-minded title, it has come to mean the United Nations Extravagant Spending, Squabbling and Cronyism Organization." Nevertheless, Mayor's nomination offered hope that a change in leadership would lure the United States and the United Kingdom back into the fold and set Unesco back on its intended mission. Mayor, the editorial said, was well qualified to restore the confidence Unesco had lost

under M'Bow. "Mayor understands the organization well enough to streamline it. He served as Unesco's deputy director general from 1978 to 1981 and as a special adviser to M'Bow in 1983 to 1984. But he is much more than a United Nations bureaucrat. A biochemist, he has published 75 scientific papers and other scholarly books and articles. He is known as a good listener, an important attribute in an organization that has 158 member nations."[52] Apart from his prowess as a scientist, educator and administrator, Mayor was lauded as a conciliator, a person who is tolerant of opposing ideas. A common theme in the editorials was that Mayor had pledged to reform Unesco, that he would decentralize, streamline, reinvigorate and "reintellectualize" it—in short that he would put it back on the right track. Some editorials depicted him as being pro-Western and his nomination as a victory for the West, although they occasionally noted that his nomination was also supported by the Soviet bloc. The most common theme was that Mayor had pledged to seek the return to Unesco of the United States, the United Kingdom and Singapore. For many editorial writers, the bottom line was that the nomination was a step toward reform and that under Mayor, Unesco could resume its mission of promoting educational and cultural causes throughout the world.

Few papers felt the United States should immediately rejoin Unesco. The prevailing sentiment was that there was no hurry, that it should wait and see if further reforms were made, and rejoin if they were indeed forthcoming. The *Wall Street Journal* said, for example, that Unesco's books "need to be opened to full public scrutiny. Any corruption needs to be punished. Policies need to be put on the right track. It would not be appropriate for Britain and American to talk of returning until these necessary tasks are accomplished."[53] The *Miami Herald*, in an editorial headed "Good Riddance to M'Bow," remarked that Mayor had called for a new start at Unesco and an end to its past divisions and quarrels. "The Reagan administration and Congress should watch this process closely before deciding to rejoin Unesco."[54] In the same vein, the Portland *Oregonian* commented that if Mayor succeeded in promised reforms, "the United States should rejoin the organization for which it formerly supplied one quarter of the budget. The nations of the world have much to teach and learn from each other."[55] Some papers were willing to go further and advocated an immediate return. "Just having Mayor replace M'Bow is reason enough. Washington could do well to dust off its Unesco membership card," wrote the *Atlanta Constitution*.[56] The *Denver Post* said that U.S. withdrawal had served to get Unesco's attention. "Now we have got it. Mayor deserves U.S. support in his reform drive—and the U.S. should give strong consideration to rejoining a revived Unesco."[57]

Newspaper Columns

Two syndicated columns, by Flora Lewis and Richard Reeves, depicted the events at Unesco as symptomatic of a change for the better in the U.N. system as a whole. Both referred to the more positive attitude toward the U.N. by the Soviet Union under Mikhail Gorbachev, and Lewis pointed out that the Soviets and their allies had been a significant factor in Mayor's nomination. In a column that ran in about 60 papers in late October, Lewis wrote that Unesco had suffered the most from "the U.N. disease of ideological log-rolling, mismanagement, verbal aggression, even corruption."[58] One reason that M'Bow's African supporters were so doggedly against Mayor was that "he can be expected to open the books, get rid of M'Bow's cronies and cut out boondoggles." Mayor, said Lewis, faced an "enormous task."

The Reeves column appeared in about 50 papers at the end of October.[59] It referred to Unesco as being managed by a "particularly nasty cabal of Africans and Asians who thought they could right the wrongs of colonialism by channeling U.N. funds into anti-Western propaganda at home and pro-Western high life around Unesco's Paris headquarters." Mayor's election, said Reeves, "may not herald the beginning of a new age, but it is progress, a welcome bit of civilization in world affairs."

In contrast to the controversy over the withdrawal in 1984, the U.S. government was not directly involved in the election of a new director general. There were no State Department briefings or press releases. As a result, relatively few American spokespersons were quoted. The State Department policy of focusing on such issues as politicization and mismanagement, rather than on personal criticism of M'Bow, no longer influenced the coverage to any great extent. Instead, the conflict was presented in terms of contrasting personalities: black and white, bad and good, M'Bow the destroyer and Mayor the potential savior. Just as M'Bow was depicted as having single-handedly destroyed Unesco, so Mayor alone could redeem it. Within the space of a single month, Unesco was transformed in the eyes of the media from being an international basket case to an organization that had at least the potential for improving the cultural and intellectual life of humankind.

Content Analysis

To quantify the direction of the coverage, a content analysis was made of all reports about the election filed by AP, UPI and the New York Times News Service, and of one-half of the 125 separate editorials that appeared, arranged chronologically and selected on a random-interval

basis. The unit of analysis was the theme. Factual statements in news reports about the mechanics of the election—who won how many votes in each round—were omitted from the calculations. But any statement or expression of opinion about the major candidates or about Unesco and its programs was counted. Coding was done by students in a senior-level college course in international communications and was checked by the author. Intercoder reliability was above 82 percent.

News Agency Reports. Just under 15 percent of the themes in agency dispatches referred to institutional aspects of Unesco (see Table 9.1). Three-quarters of these were critical of the organization—specifically, that it was mismanaged (wasteful, inefficient, corrupt); that it was politicized (anti-Western, anti-American, anti-Israel); that it favored a New World Information Order and generally was in need of reform. Pro-Unesco themes noted that the agency had a valuable role to play in promoting education, science and culture, particularly in the Third World. Many of these themes, however, suggested that Unesco's useful activities had taken place in the past, before it was taken over by the Soviet bloc and its Third World allies. About 28 percent of news agency themes had to do with the fact that the United States, Britain and Singapore had withdrawn from Unesco and that other Western countries would follow unless reforms were made.

Themes relating to M'Bow himself comprised just over 27 percent of the agency files. More than two-thirds of these were critical of the director general. He was accused of being anti-Western, anti–free press, a poor manager who appointed relatives and fellow Senegalese to high positions in Unesco, and responsible for the withdrawal from Unexco of the United States and Britain. The relatively few pro-M'Bow themes noted that he had the support of Third World nations and of France and that he was the first African director of a major international agency.

The news agency profile of Mayor was very different. Almost as many themes (25.4 percent) referred to Mayor as to M'Bow, but virtually all the references were positive. He was portrayed as being well-educated, a renowned scientist, a former minister of education and a former deputy director of Unesco. He was pro-West, pro-reform of Unesco, and a conciliatory leader who would seek the return of the United States and Britain. Were M'Bow to be re-elected, the agency reports said, it would mean the end of Unesco because other leading contributors also would withdraw. Mayor, on the other hand, would reform Unesco's profligate ways and lead the organization back to its original charter.

Editorials. Themes in newspaper editorials followed a similar pattern, with some significant variations. The proportion of pro-Unesco themes in

the editorials was higher than in the news dispatches, largely because several editorials commented favorably on Unesco's prospects after Mayor's election. But there were also proportionately more anti-Unesco themes and a far higher proportion of criticism of M'Bow's leadership. Nearly 30 percent of the editorial themes were anti-M'Bow; only 2 percent had anything good to say about him. Much stress was placed on his failings as a manager, his dictatorial ways, his opposition to a free press, and his refusal to initiate meaningful reforms.

As in the agency reports, editorial themes relating to Mayor were overwhelmingly positive. Some 24 percent of the editorial themes referred to his determination to reform Unesco, to seek the return of the United States and Britain, to restore Unesco's original mandate and its international prestige, and to his excellent qualifications for the post. The editorials made proportionately fewer references to threats by other countries to withdraw but offered more comments on the course the United States should follow. Most felt it should not rejoin immediately, but should wait and see if genuine reforms were made.

Both the agency coverage and the editorials implied that one man— M'Bow—was largely responsible for Unesco's problems, and that his successor would bring about a very different orientation. The fact that the Unesco policies that angered the West had the support of the bulk of the organization's member countries, and that no one individual was likely to change the reality of global politics overnight, was seldom mentioned.

The coverage, in short, continued the anti-Unesco tone that had characterized the reporting and commentary at the time of the U.S. withdrawal. But the media's positive response to Mayor's election suggested the possibility, at least, that future coverage of Unesco could focus on its achievements rather than on its shortcomings.

Concepts of Newsworthiness

The newspaper trade publication, *Editor & Publisher*, carried a report in December 1985 on data collected by the Unesco liaison office in New York showing that coverage had declined dramatically since the withdrawal took effect. *E&P* reporter Andrew Radlof also interviewed executives of several major news agencies, some of whom contended they had not cut down on their coverage of Unesco. Radlof quotes Ron Cohen, managing editor of UPI, as saying that "we cover what we feel needs to be covered whether the U.S. is in it or not. Sometimes there's more news than others." Nate Polowetzky, AP foreign editor, told Radlof he doubted that Unesco had become non-existent in the view of U.S. papers. "You can go through the papers and find things," he said.

Jim Hoagland, assistant managing editor for foreign news of the *Washington Post*, said that the *Post* had not been able to send a reporter

to cover the General Conference in Sofia because it had applied too late for a visa. He pointed out that the main reason the *Post* wanted to send someone to Sofia was that the Warsaw Pact heads of state were meeting there at the same time. "If we had gotten a visa, we would have tried to cover both things. Had it been only Unesco, I am not sure we would have sent a reporter," he said. Warren Hoge, foreign editor of the *New York Times*, was quoted as saying that the U.S. withdrawal was a "glitch on the screen" that warranted special attention by the media. And Alvis Shuster, foreign editor of the *Los Angeles Times*, told Radlof that his paper had never covered Unesco on a regular basis: "We pick it up when we think it's newsworthy." Shuster said there were a lot of organizations that were not newsworthy: "It depends on what the issue is. The question of U.S. withdrawal was very newsworthy. If Unesco's saying they were more newsworthy at the time of the withdrawal, they were right."[60]

NOTES

1. *New York Times*, 14 February 1985.
2. *New York Times*, 13 February 1985.
3. Letter to the *New York Times* from Alain Raffray, deputy director of the Unesco Liaison Office at the United Nations, 25 December 1985.
4. *New York Times*, 10 November 1985.
5. Associated Press, 8 November 1985.
6. *Seattle Times*, 22 August 1985.
7. *New York Times*, 5 December 1985.
8. *New York Times*, 12 December 1985.
9. United Press International, 13 December 1986.
10. *New York Times*, 12 March 1986.
11. *New York Times*, 8 June 1986.
12. United Press International, 8 May 1986.
13. Associated Press, 23 May 1986.
14. *New York Times*, 6 October 1986.
15. United Press International, 28 September 1987.
16. *New York Times*, 24 September 1987.
17. Associated Press, 7 October 1987.
18. Associated Press, 9 October 1987.
19. Diana Johnstone, "Compromise Candidate May Solve Unesco's Heritage Problems," *In These Times*, 12 (4–10 November 1987), p. 11.
20. United Press International, 9 October 1987.
21. United Press International, 16 October 1987.
22. United Press International, 7 October 1987.
23. Associated Press, 10 October 1987.
24. Associated Press, 17 October 1987.
25. Associated Press, 18 October 1987.

26. Ibid.
27. *New York Times*, 7 November 1987.
28. United Press International, 4 November 1987.
29. New York Times, 7 November 1987.
30. *New York Times*, 24 September 1987.
31. United Press International, 24 September 1987.
32. Associated Press, 18 October 1987.
33. *New York Times*, 18 October 1987.
34. London *Daily Telegraph*, 19 October 1987.
35. *Houston Post*, 28 September 1987.
36. *Chicago Tribune*, 16 October 1987.
37. *San Diego Union*, 28 September 1987.
38. *Miami Herald*, 30 September 1987.
39. Elkins, W.Va., *Inter-Mountain*, 1 October 1987.
40. *Atlanta Constitution*, 9 October 1987.
41. Cleveland *Plain Dealer*, 15 October 1987.
42. *Christian Science Monitor*, 22 October 1987.
43. *The Oregonian*, 23 October 1987.
44. Fort Lauderdale *News/Sun-Sentinel*, 24 October 1987.
45. Omaha *World-Herald*, 26 October 1987.
46. *Boston Globe*, 28 October 1987.
47. *New York Post*, 22 October 1987.
48. Santa Rosa *Press-Democrat*, 21 October 1987.
49. *Miami Herald*, 24 October 1987.
50. *Wall Street Journal*, 1 October 1987.
51. Pittsburgh *Post-Gazette*, 22 October 1987.
52. *San Diego Tribune*, 22 October 1987.
53. *Wall Street Journal*, 22 October 1987.
54. *Miami Herald*, 24 October 1987.
55. *The Oregonian*, 23 October 1987.
56. *Atlanta Constitution*, 21 October 1987.
57. *Denver Post*, 22 October 1987.
58. *New York Times*, 20 October 1987.
59. *The Houston Post,* 31 October 1987.
60. Andrew Radlof, "A Unesco Blackout?" *Editor & Publisher*, 7 December 1985, p. 11.

ORIENTATIONS: TABLE

TABLE 9.1. ORIENTATION OF THEMES IN NEWS AGENCY REPORTS AND NEWS-
PAPER EDITORIALS ABOUT UNESCO ELECTION (PERCENTAGES)

Themes	Combined news agencies n = 728	Combined editorials n = 1,274
Pro-Unesco	2.7	6.2
Anti-Unesco	11.3	14.0
Nations have/ will withdraw	27.9	16.2
Pro-M'Bow	8.1	2.4
Anti-M'Bow	19.4	29.4
Pro-Mayor	25.1	24.1
Anti-Mayor	0.3	0.2
Unesco forum for East-West or North-South conflict	0.8	1.5
U.S. should not rejoin	1.9	0.7
U.S. should wait & see	2.5	5.3
Totals	100.0	100.0

CHAPTER 10

The Antagonists

The U.S. pullout from Unesco is a conservative cause celebre, spark-plugged by the Heritage Foundation.

—*Gannett News Service*

Unesco officials, looking at the torrent of hostile coverage that threatened the universality and financial underpinnings of the organization, could be forgiven for suspecting that there was an organized media campaign against them. Director General M'Bow complained in March 1984 of a "veritable smear campaign" against him and in September said that Unesco was a victim of "systematic denigration" in distorted news dispatches. Doudou Diene, the Unesco representative in New York, charged that "the publication of false and misleading stories" was either "an international campaign to sow distortion and lies about Unesco or an abysmal ignorance of the facts." Even Leonard Sussman of Freedom House, a card-carrying critic of Unesco's shortcomings, asserted at a news conference on August 4 that the Reagan administration was manipulating the press and that, "on the Unesco question this year, the facts have indeed been distorted, relevant evidence buried and ideological dogma substituted for honest debate." There was a campaign. In fact there was more than one campaign. They were mounted by those who sought to retain U.S. membership and by those who wanted out. The latter were far more successful in getting their views across in the press, and ultimately triumphed.

The reason the United States was able to pull out of Unesco with remarkably little domestic opposition was that Unesco had managed to offend three politically powerful interest groups, who formed an effective coalition against the organization. The other potential coalition—those scientific, educational and cultural organizations that opposed the withdrawal—never did achieve an effective united front and could not command media support for their position. The campaign against Unesco was spearheaded by conservatives, both inside and outside the U.S. government. Debates and resolutions in Unesco ran directly counter to their concept of the ideal world. The most common complaint about Unesco from government and conservative sources was that it was "politicized." More specifically, it was accused of being anti-Western and anti-American. On the other hand, Unesco was alleged to be in favor of collective, rather than individual rights; of being pro-Soviet and pro-Third World, and of supporting national liberation movements. These arguments reflected the Reagan administration's fervent anti-communist foreign policy. Unesco was depicted as the worst-case model of the U.N. system as a whole: of being a forum for Soviet propaganda on peace and disarmament; of backing centrally controlled economies instead of free-market principles; of favoring the statist rights of peoples over individual rights. This ideological conflict with Soviet bloc interests extended also to the non-aligned movement and the Third World generally. Conservatives were contemptuous of the redistributive aspects of the New International Economic Order, blaming the plight of underdeveloped countries on their own domestic policies. Unesco was perceived as an enthusiastic supporter of the new economic order and a denigrator of free-market incentives to economic development. The communist bloc and the Third World were seen to have an automatic majority in Unesco votes and of using this to trample the West's cherished democratic ideals.

A second component of the anti-Unesco coalition was the Jewish lobby. A recurrent theme of Unesco's critics was that it was anti-Israel and supportive of the Palestine Liberation Organization. This was mentioned more frequently even than anti-Americanism. Influential Jewish groups in the United States were swayed by this argument to support the Reagan administration. American Jews had traditionally been strong supporters of the United Nations system, particularly since it was the U.N. that created the state of Israel in 1948. Their opposition to Unesco reflected, in part, the conversion of liberal Democrats of the 1960s to strong supporters of Ronald Reagan in the 1980s. According to one analyst, the evolution during the late 1960s of the U.S. civil rights movement into the Black Power movement alienated large sections of the Jewish community who previously had played a key role in the civil rights struggle. Their sense of rejection and betrayal deepened after the 1967

Arab-Israeli War. Much of U.S. Jewry reacted anxiously to Israel's diplomatic isolation as international public opinion swung in favor of the defeated Arabs, as reflected in hostile votes at the U.N. and Unesco, which voted to equate Zionism with racism, condemned Israeli archaeological digs in Jerusalem, excluded Israel from its European regional group in 1974 for a year, and offered comfort and support to the PLO.

The third major interest group opposed to Unesco was the U.S. media establishment. The arguments here were both ideological and economic. Unesco was identified as the major forum for promoting a New International Information Order. In the coverage of media issues, criticisms of the new information order in general were the most frequent theme. Unesco's perceived support for state control of media and for licensing of journalists were also mentioned often. As demonstrated in Chapter 1, this issue predates the Reagan administration, and in fact was a catalyst for congressional action against Unesco. Debates over Unesco's Mass Media Declaration, with its early insistence on state control of media, were particularly offensive to a nation whose press had traditionally been conceived of as a watchdog over government in the public interest. Proposals that governments be held responsible for the activities of media in the international sphere were directly contrary to U.S. constitutional guarantees of press freedom from government control. In addition, Unesco's attempts to achieve a better balance in international information flow were seen a threat to the activities of Western news agencies. And Unesco efforts to build up Third World communications infrastructures were considered an attempt to use funds contributed by the West to create government-controlled competition for the free enterprise news agencies.

ANTI-UNESCO GROUPS

The United States Government

Once the decision to withdraw had been taken, the U.S. government became a major source of anti-Unesco rhetoric. Newell's memorandum to Shultz recommending withdrawal and listing as reasons Unesco's politicization, mismanagement and hostility to the West, was leaked to the *New York Times* in mid-December 1983. This report was then picked up by the AP and UPI, and was widely published. The formal announcement of withdrawal by State Department officials was followed by press conferences and briefings that expanded on the reasons for the pullout. An example is the detailed memorandum issued to the media in February by William Harley, a communications consultant at the State Department, giving questions and answers about the withdrawal.

This campaign must be seen in the light of Newell's classified memorandum of 16 December 1983 recommending to Secretary of State George Shultz that the United States should withdraw. Newell proposed a strategy for disengagement that would include a campaign to manipulate the press to generate public support. He suggested sending articles supporting the administration's policy to the *Washington Post* and the *New York Times*. Newell also suggested that "private sector" individuals should submit "articles of support" to the press and proposed a letters-to-the-editor campaign. It is not clear whether, or how, this was implemented. But columns by Owen Harries of the Heritage Foundation giving reasons for the pullout appeared in the *New York Times* on December 21, in the *New York Tribune* on December 27, in the *Houston Chronicle* on December 28, and in the *Washington Times* a few weeks later. Even before the decision was formally announced in December 1983, four widely syndicated conservative columnists—Patrick Buchanan, Flora Lewis, William Safire and George Will—wrote articles making essentially the same arguments in favor of withdrawal. Columns by William Buckley and James Kilpatrick followed soon after the announcement.

Newell's memorandum acknowledged that there was little support for the withdrawal, and that there would be opposition to the move both in the United States and abroad. Even other branches of the State Department seemed to be taken aback. Reviews of Unesco by the State Department, as mandated by the Beard amendment, generally gave Unesco passing grades before Newell was sent from the White House in 1982 to become assistant secretary of state for international organization affairs. He clearly was a man with a mission. As Newell testified at congressional hearings, the recommendation to withdraw initially came from him and was channeled through Deputy Secretary Lawrence Eagleburger and Secretary of State Shultz to the president. But Leonard Sussman says Eagleburger and Shultz were surprised and annoyed by the recommendation. Newell didn't have the political clout to push through the withdrawal by himself. He had powerful backing in the White House, apparently in the person of presidential counselor—and later attorney general—Edwin Meese. (Newell was rewarded for his efforts by appointment as U.S. ambassador to Sweden.)

In addition to his involvement with the media, Newell pushed the case for withdrawal at several congressional hearings. He and Jean Gerard, U.S. ambassador to Unesco, were the chief spokesmen for the government's position. Others who voiced the administration line were William Harley and Edward Derwinski of the State Department, and Jeane Kirkpatrick, U.S. ambassador to the United Nations. Further instances of government efforts to manipulate public opinion concerning the

pullout abound. Copies of the draft General Accounting Office report that was highly critical of Unesco's management were leaked to the press in September—before it was made available to Unesco officials. The government ignored the recommendation of the U.S. National Commission for Unesco to retain membership, even though the commission was the official body appointed by the State Department to advise it on Unesco policy. Instead, it appointed a 13-member civilian monitoring panel, headed by James B. Holderman, who had close links with the Reagan administration. Observers noted that most of the panel members could be expected to support the withdrawal. Their report at the end of the year that there had been "no concrete change" in Unesco was then cited by the government as justification for confirming the withdrawal.

The government's position on Unesco's communications policies clearly reflected the interests of American media organizations. In 1986, the U.S. General Accounting Office, at the request of Sen. Arlen Specter, conducted a content analysis of materials produced by the U.N. Department of Public Information. Entitled *United Nations: Analysis of Selected Media Products Shows Half Oppose U.S. Interests*, the study focuses on four topic areas, including the New World Information Order. The State Department provided the GAO with criteria on these topics to define what political positions would be considered contrary to U.S. policies or interests. The criteria are totally congruent with the position of the media. With respect to communications, they include:

- Advocating imposing on the media the obligation to undertake special social tasks;
- Advocating licensing of journalists or establishing an international code of ethics;
- Advocating a policy of government control over the content of mass communications;
- Criticizing the practice of advertising;
- Promoting curbs on the independence of transnational news agencies;
- Proposing to restrict the principle of the free flow of information;
- Requiring the media to accept public participation in the management and operations of private media under the rubric of the "right to communicate";
- Advocating establishment of an international body to impose restrictions on the Western media;
- Restricting the right of journalists to gather information from private as well as public sources of information;
- Legitimizing the concept of orbital sovereignty for developing countries;
- Favoring the concept of government media over independent media;

- Stating or inferring that the Western media are distorting news and information without providing evidence;
- Criticizing the commercial basis of the media as inherently evil.[1]

Each of these criteria had previously been identified by media organizations as inimical to their interests.

The Anti-Defamation League, B'nai B'rith

Among those who advocated a withdrawal were Jewish organizations, offended by what they viewed as a pro-Arab tilt in the United Nations generally, and particularly by a series of anti-Israeli votes in Unesco over the years. Maxwell Greenberg, chairman of the Anti-Defamation League of B'nai B'rith, told a congressional hearing that the Arab bloc at Unesco, "urged on by the USSR and its clients and supported by some Third World nations, sought repeatedly to undermine Israel's legitimacy." In vote after vote, said Greenberg, "in matters ranging from geological excavations in Jerusalem to support for the terrorist PLO," Unesco had tried to discredit and defame Israel for strictly political purposes.

Burton S. Levinson, chairman of the national executive committee of the Anti-Defamation League, also expressed the organization's concern over the fact that Unesco was used by "interests who are anti-Israeli and supporters of terrorists and terrorist activities." Levinson told a House subcommittee hearing on 26 July 1984 that the Anti-Defamation League "supports the administration position on withdrawal from Unesco."

Similar views appeared in Jewish publications. In December 1983 *The Jewish News* (circulation 16,500) reprinted extracts from Owen Harries' column in the *New York Times*, and commented that hate-mongering had become "the basic activity of the United Nations, under the domination of the Arab and Soviet bloc." Nevertheless, there had been "only a minimal proposal" that the United States withdraw from the world organization. "There is one agency, however, which continues on a path of so much venom that it cannot be tolerated, even the State Department suggesting that the United States withdraw from it." Unesco was the forum for outrageous treatment of Israel, *The Jewish News* continued. The United States should begin to end its vileness with a denial of funds; "it must proceed with a total withdrawal."

In September 1984, *The Jewish Press* (circulation 209,000) reprinted an editorial by the national director of B'nai B'rith, Nathan Perlmutter, that had appeared in the Anti-Defamation League newsletter. Unesco, said Perlmutter, had "served as the U.N.'s hit-man, a contract holder stalking Western values, ganging up on Israel." It had voted to exclude Israel from membership in the European regional group—"tantamount

to expulsion for America's lone reliable ally in the Middle East." Only the pressure of U.S. purse strings got Israel reinstated. Perlmutter quotes Levinson as saying that until Unesco returned to its original mandate, the United States should withdraw.

The executive council of the American Jewish Committee, however, while critical of Unesco's involvement in "contentious political issues," recommended in November 1984 that "in the light of our traditional support for the ideals and purposes of Unesco and for institutions of genuine international cooperation," that the government postpone the decision on withdrawal for one year. This would give Unesco time to make changes. "Meanwhile, we acknowledge and support our government's decisive and firm position of withdrawing from Unesco if appropriate reform is not accomplished."

The Heritage Foundation

The most prominent advocate of a withdrawal was the Washington-based Heritage Foundation, a private, conservative research organization that claims to serve as a "key intellectual resource" for the Reagan administration. Founded in 1973, the foundation is financed by conservative individuals such as Colorado brewer Joseph Coors, Pittsburgh millionaire Richard Mellon Scaife, and industrialist John Olin. In 1984 it had an annual budget of $9.5 million. Its policy papers on a wide range of domestic and international issues are circulated to nearly 1,000 members of Congress, and mailed to 6,000 journalists, editors and academics. The foundation also has its own news service, Heritage Features, which it advertises as "America's fastest growing syndicate."

Because of the influence the Heritage Foundation had on the decision to withdraw, it is informative to examine the themes of its anti-Unesco campaign. The attack on Unesco appears to have begun in October 1982 with a foundation "backgrounder" entitled "For Unesco, a Failing Grade in Education." Written by policy analyst Thomas G. Gulick, the paper raises many of the themes that were to be repeated and developed later. Unesco, Gulick wrote, had made some valuable contributions to the world's cultural resources. Regrettably, however, it had become "biased increasingly towards socialist economies and a utopian strain of internationalism that is unsympathetic (often hostile) to the free enterprise system." Pervading programs in every Unesco sector were arguments advocating a New International Economic Order (NIEO), "a simplistic scheme to redistribute the world's wealth and resources to more than 100 underdeveloped nations, creating a global welfare state financed mainly by the U.S. and the Western industrial nations." These ideas were seeded into education systems through Unesco's educational models,

which "exhibit a dangerous drift towards a highly centralized, state-controlled educational system modeled closely after socialist-style planned economies." The NIEO concept, Gulick wrote, was being promoted in the United States under the title "Global Education" or "Global Perspectives" by a group of "radical educators." What was to be done? Americans should "demand that all U.S. tax dollars supporting Unesco NIEO-based education and social science programs be cut off" and should encourage its Western allies to follow suit.

A second backgrounder by Gulick appeared in December 1982. Entitled "Unesco, Where Culture Becomes Propaganda," it dealt primarily with the Unesco-sponsored Mondiacult '82 conference held in Mexico City that year. The conference, Gulick asserted, had "turned into the kind of three-ring political circus that is now the modus operandi" of Unesco. It had served mainly as an arena for communist and Third World political machinations, including a call for a New World Cultural Order. This order was an attack on Western culture and cultural industries, the thesis being that Western culture "lays waste to any other native culture it contacts." Written into the 1981–83 Unesco mandate for culture and communications, said Gulick, were endorsements of the new economic order "and its socialist offspring, the New World Information and Communication Order." The culture budget "helped fund attempts by the Unesco secretariat and radical members of Unesco to promote NWIO proposals to license journalists and censor Western-owned international news and information services."

Gulick argued that the United States had failed to fight back at Unesco. Rather, as at Mexico City, the U.S. strategy had been "damage control," seeking to excise offensive language from Unesco documents. Time after time American representatives had caved in to the assault of the radical NIEO political strategy of the developing countries, including the new information order debate, "a major tactic of the G-77 war on Western free enterprise." This Heritage document went further than its predecessor: Instead of merely withholding funds from Unesco, "the time had come for the U.S. and its Western allies to fight back or get out of Unesco." The organization's cultural sector had worthwhile programs, but "the few good programs serve as a convenient cover-up for what Unesco really is: a very large amphitheater for international political propaganda." Americans should insist that a firm Western voice be heard at Unesco. "If this voice is not raised, then the U.S. and the Western nations should pull their logs out of the Unesco fire and go home."

A third Heritage Foundation broadside against Unesco, "The IPDC: Unesco vs. the Free Press," appeared in March 1983. Also written by Gulick, it accused the International Program for the Development of Communications of being "the spearhead of the NWICO assault on the

Western media." The thrust of the New World Information Order (NWIO) strategy had been to "attack the commercial free press of the West, while promoting and supporting the government-controlled press and media of the Soviet bloc and the radical Third World." The IPDC had been created at the 1980 Unesco General Conference in Belgrade. At the four previous general conferences, the Soviets and the G-77 had mounted such a virulent attack on the Western media that the West "looked on the IPDC as a reason to buy peace." The West had agreed to increase foreign aid and the transfer of communications technology and training to the Third World through the IPDC. The Third World, in turn, had indicated it would cease its NWIO attacks. But the promise had not been fulfilled. "Rather than buy peace on the issue, the newly-created IPDC has simply become another battleground for the NWIO attack against Western businesses and the freedom of the press."

By October 1983, the Heritage Foundation had a new resident critic of Unesco, who built on Gulick's work and pursued a new, tougher line. Owen Harries, who had become disenchanted with Unesco during a term as Australia's ambassador to the organization from February 1982 to August 1983, joined Heritage as a policy analyst. On December 5 he issued a backgrounder entitled "The U.S. and Unesco: Time for Decision." In it, Harries argued that the United States should serve notice that it would quit Unesco at the end of 1984 unless sweeping changes were forthcoming. It should do so for two reasons:

- "Because it is morally and politically wrong for America to continue to lend authority and legitmacy—and to provide some $70 million each year (25 percent of Unesco's budget)—to an organization dedicated to attacking its fundamental American values and interests.
- Because the existing structure and ethics of Unesco make it impossible for the United States and other liberal democracies to change things from within, by debate and negotiation."[2]

Harries followed this up on December 5, 1983, just after the 22nd General Conference of Unesco in Paris, with a new backgrounder, "The U.S. and Unesco: Time for Decision." The conference, he wrote, had changed nothing. It was true that the conference was unusually low-key and muted. But this occurred only after some straight talking by Gregory Newell, who made it clear that the United States meant business. Those in control at Unesco then decided that it was prudent to be restrained— for the time being. But a tap easily turned off can just as easily be turned on; and the same hands are on that tap." The original Unesco programs, "with all their ideological biases and wastefulness," remained essentially intact. The only effective political leverage available to the United States

was a commitment "to withdraw and withhold the very substantial contribution it now makes to Unesco's budget, unless the organization puts
its house in order and dramatically changes its ways." This backgrounder
was reprinted verbatim in the *New York Tribune* on December 27. The
Houston Chronicle ran a Harries column the next day containing essentially the same arguments.

A more general attack on the U.N. system as a whole appeared in a
1984 anthology published by the foundation and called *A World without
the U.N.: What Would Happen if the United Nations Shut Down*. The
thrust was that Americans would be better off.

Once the decision to withdraw from Unesco had been announced,
the Heritage Foundation kept up the pressure. Harries put out a report
on 9 July 1984 that summarizes and comments on a letter of resignation
sent to M'Bow by Peter Lengyel, an Australian who had served as a
senior Unesco official for some 30 years before becoming disenchanted
with the managment of the organization. Harries' commentary, entitled
"An Insider Looks at Unesco's Problems," was read into the *Congressional Record* and became the basis for several newspaper editorials and
columns.

In October 1984, the *Reader's Digest* published an article by Harries
on "Why Unesco Spells Trouble." The article is significant because of the
huge circulation of the *Digest*—more than 17 million copies—and also
because it summarizes the foundation's criticisms of Unesco:

- *It was politicized*: Unesco was dominated by the Third World and
  Soviet bloc, and pervaded by anti-Western ideology. It deliberately distorted traditional Western ideas of human rights such as
  freedom of speech, religion and assembly—"rights that protect
  individuals from excessive state power."
- *It was mismanaged*: The organization had been taken over by a
  "bloated Paris headquarters staff" that was politicized and inefficient. Although generously paid, the staff were incompetent,
  key documents were often months behind schedule, conferences
  were chaotic, and job vacancies took months or even years to fill,
  while work was contracted to expensive outside consultants. In
  1983, Unesco had drafted a large budget while most other U.N.
  agencies were holding down costs.
- *It was anti–free press*: Unesco's New World Information Order
  could lead to "a licensing of newspeople and the establishment of
  state-dictated codes of conduct."
- *U.S. funds paid for all this*: Although the United States contributed 25 percent of the agency budget, it "had no more say than
  miniscule St. Christopher-Nevis-Anguilla."

- *Reforms were needed*: To avert a U.S. pullout, Unesco would have to concentrate on programs concerned with education, science and culture, and leave political, economic and military problems to the General Assembly. It would have to give more influence to major contributors, restrain its budget, and replace its director general.
- *There was support for the U.S. position*: The United Kingdom, the Netherlands and Denmark had delivered "strong letters indicating their demand for far-reaching changes. A number of other countries are thinking along the same lines."
- *The change so far was too limited*: Unesco had already missed one chance to meet demands for fundamental reforms. At its executive board meeting in May 1984, the director general merely set up a study panel. "If nothing more than promises result by the end of the year, the U.S. should leave the organization forthwith."
- *Criticism of M'Bow*: The director general ran the secretariat as if it were his personal fief. "The Dictator, as many call him, goes into a rage at the slightest criticism." A Third World militant rather than the mediator he was selected to be, M'Bow lived in luxury in a penthouse atop the Unesco headquarters building— when he was not traveling in style with a retinue of staff members.[3]

These themes are remarkably similar to those given by Newell and other State Department representatives as the reasons for the withdrawal—that Unesco had "extraneously politicized every subject it deals with," that it had "exhibited hostility toward the basic institutions of a free society," especially a free market and a free press, that it had served anti-American political ends, and that it had demonstrated "unrestricted budgetary expansion." These also were the dominant themes in news reports, editorials and columns.

To check the correspondence between Heritage Foundation views and those of the State Department, a content analysis was made of the Heritage documents on Unesco, and of State Department press releases, briefings, and statements at congressional hearings. The analysis showed that speakers for the State Department reiterated both the language and the emphasis provided by the Heritage reports. There were some differences. The Heritage Foundation criticism of M'Bow was not reflected by the State Department, apparently as a matter of policy. The State Department also paid more attention to what would happen after the pullout—usually statements that the United States would use its Unesco contribution to fund other educational, scientific and cultural projects. Apart from these changes in emphasis both the arguments and the rhetoric were almost identical.

The textual evidence that the State Department was responding to the Heritage Foundation agenda is reinforced by the perceptions of other observers. An AP Washington correspondent, Joan Mower, noted in a report on 12 December 1983 that the State Department's announcement that it was reviewing participation in Unesco because of what spokesmen called the agency's budget mismanagement and anti-Americanism "is consistent with the views" of the Heritage Foundation. The *Houston Chronicle* carried a column by Harries in December 1983 with a note to the effect that "his critique of Unesco has reportedly been an influence" on the administration's expected decision to withdraw." Fred B. Hill, writing in the *Baltimore Sun* on 9 January 1983, noted that those in favor of a withdrawal time and again "quote the same solitary expert, Owen Harries." And Elsa Dixler, writing in *The Nation* on 22 December 1984 commented that "the relationship between the Heritage Foundation and the administration has been so incestuous that it is hard to tell whose policy is whose." The *Washington Post* reported on 24 December 1983 that

> some of the impetus for a U.S. withdrawal came from a recent Heritage Foundation report by Owen Harries, a former Australian Ambassador to Unesco. This added to existing anti-United Nations views of many right-wing organizations within Reagan's core political constituency. Concern about a centrist and liberal backlash was diminished after the lead editorial in the Dec. 16 New York Times recommended U.S. withdrawal. Once that was published, official sources said, there was very little worry that the U.S. gesture might carry a domestic political price on the eve of a presidential election year.[4]

Harries himself refers to the campaign against Unesco in an article in the September 1984 issue of the journal *Commentary*. In it he offers "A Primer for Polemicists." It was surprising how lightly and casually ideological polemics were taken in the West, he wrote, and set out to offer "a few modest precepts or rules, both to help the novice and to stimulate experienced practitioners to give the matter some thought." Rule 2 stipulates that one should pay great attention to the agenda of the debate: he who defines the issues, and determines their priority, is already well on the way to winning. For example, "in the current debate over Unesco, it is essential to insist that what is at issue is the actual performance of the organization, not the worthiness of its ostensible aims as originally set out in its constitution, or the seriousness of the plight of the world's poor." Harries' constant repetition of criticisms of Unesco—in colums, backgrounders and testimony at congressional hearings—is explained in Rule 6: "When you have a good point to make keep repeating it. Success in

ideological polemics is very much a matter of staying power and will, and the same battles have to be fought over and over again." There will always be someone who is hearing you for the first time, he noted, "and even most others will really register something only when they have been exposed to it several times."

Rule 7 notes that "knowing what you can afford to give away is one of the great arts of polemic." Thus, in the debate over the withdrawal from Unesco, "it is not necessary to contest the fact that the organization does *some* good work, any more than it was once necessary to contest that Hitler built good roads or that Mussolini made the trains run on time."

The Heritage Foundation itself claimed credit for engineering the withdrawal. The *New York Times*, in a September 30, 1983, report on the occasion of the foundation's tenth anniversary, quoted Heritage Vice President Burton Pines as saying that "we are having an impact...we know that our arguments, taking a free market approach to domestic policy and a pro-national approach to international problems have at least been put on the table." In the same article, Heritage President Edwin Feulner remarked that the conservative think-tank was "serving as a key intellectual resource for the Reagan administration." Reagan was the foundation's featured guest at the anniversay celebrations.

A foundation publication, *Heritage Today*, claimed in its issue for January/February 1984 that Harries' report "The U.S. and Unesco at the Crossroads" had greatly influenced the Reagan administration's decision. *Heritage Today* said that its "carefully documented studies, which were harshly criticized by Unesco and U.N. officials, left little doubt that the organization had become so overly biased against Western values that the U.S. was wasting its money." This conclusion, said the journal, "drew support from a broad spectrum of U.S. opinion, ranging from the *Wall Street Journal* to the *New York Times* and the *Washington Post*. The same issue of *Heritage Today* reprints an editorial from the *Washington Post* that quotes the Heritage Foundation arguments. It also has a photograph of Nathan Perlmutter of the B'nai B'rith explaining the origins of anti-semitism at a Heritage roundtable discussion.

In October 1984 the foundation launched a direct-mail campaign for contributions to support the planned withdrawal, and to counter Unesco's hiring of the public relations firm Wagner & Baroody to improve its image. In the fund-raising letter dated October 8, Feulner called on Heritage members to "help stop a corrupt third-world despot from undoing one of The Heritage Foundation's most significant achievements." The withdrawal from Unesco, Feulner wrote, was "a direct result of a paper by Heritage Fellow Owen Harries that detailed a long list of shocking abuses by this United Nations agency." Now Heritage had

learned that M'Bow had launched an expensive public relations attempt to pressure the United States not to withdraw. For an international organization to "meddle in the internal affairs of the United States in this way . . . contradicts the diplomatic conventions of the civilized world." It was, said Feulner, just one more proof that Unesco was "under the control of communist and third-world diplomats whose only standard of conduct is raw power." He had asked the foundation's U.N. policy analysts to undertake an emergency effort to counteract the liberal campaign to keep the United States in Unesco. This would cost $75,000. The letter repeated the foundation's charges against Unesco, and said that the liberal and Third World lobby, including the U.S. National Commission for Unesco, was going all-out to reverse the decision to withdraw. "Because Heritage is the acknowledged expert on the U.N. among conservatives, Members of Congress have turned to us to give them the facts to refute the Commission's report." Feulner's letter included a form for people to return with their "tax-deductible contribution to help you in your emergency effort to monitor and counteract the liberal effort to keep the U.S. out of Unesco." And it included a postcard, addressed to Jeane Kirkpatrick, U.S. ambassador to the United Nations—"a good friend of the Heritage Foundation and of me personally"—urging her to stand firm in the decision to withdraw.

The foundation's compaign was not restricted to the United States. In November 1984, according to a report in the *Manchester Guardian Weekly* on 13 October 1985, Harries was sent to London to influence British cabinet ministers and news media. Harries argued the case for American-British solidarity on the issue in meetings with three cabinet ministers—Education Secretary Sir Keith Joseph and Overseas Development Ministers Timothy Raison and Timothy Renton. *The Guardian* reported that Harries and U.S. Ambassador to Unesco Jean Gerard also had a series of private meetings with influential British columnists, editors and broadcasters. "In the weeks that followed a rash of anti-Unesco articles and editorials appeared. In that way a political climate was created which made it easy" for the government to announce Britain's intention to quit Unesco unless reforms were introduced." *The Guardian* said that "Harries told an interviewer last July that he had been 'amazed' at the impact his lobbying had made on British newspapers."

The views of the Heritage Foundation influenced press coverage in several ways, finding a responsive echo in news reports, editorials and columns. Because the U.S. government had essentially adopted the foundation's agenda on Unesco, and because, as this analysis shows, the news agencies quoted government spokesmen more frequently than all other sources combined, those views naturally appeared in the news agency reports, and hence in the press. Since the themes appear though a

filter of State Department policy, they are not pure Heritage Foundation, but closely approximate its arguments.

A second, more direct way was through columns written by Heritage officials like Harries and Feulner that ran in the press under their bylines. Occasionally, newspapers also published "Heritage Editorials" from the Heritage Syndicate, or based on the foundation's background papers. More common, though, was for the editorial writers and columnists to quote Heritage arguments directly or indirectly. Nearly 5 percent of the editorials cited the Heritage Foundation as a source. An even higher proportion used the Heritage material without attribution, although at times their wording echoed it word for word. Arguments made by some of the widely published conservative columnists can also be traced to the same source.

PRO-UNESCO LOBBIES

Unesco Public Information Office

Overwhelmed by a flood of unfavorable publicity, groups who backed continued membership tried vainly to stem the tide. The most active organization in this regard was Unesco itself, working mainly through its Public Information Office at the United Nations. In the latter part of the year, Unesco hired the Washington-based public relations firm of Wagner & Baroody to improve its image.

The New York office, under Director Doudou Diene and Chief of Public Information Joseph A. Mehan, used three main strategies to get its views across: mailings to the press, special briefings for journalists, and speeches to media and other organizations.

During the "year of crisis," more than 50,000 pieces of mail were sent from the New York office to the media, to members of Congress, the U.S. National Commission for Unesco, United Nations Association chapters, and individuals. Altogether 77 mailings were sent to each of the top 100 newspapers. These included fact sheets and press releases. Many of these were routine announcements of Unesco activities: announcements of grants and prizes for educational, scientific or cultural projects; new projects, including programs to further computer science in the Third World and improve communications infrastructures, and steps to curb traffic in and use of narcotics.

Most, however, had to do with the withdrawal. In January 1984 the office mailed to the media a fact sheet that sought to demonstrate that the planned withdrawal was contradictory to the record of recent U.S. participation in Unesco. The United States had been a major participant in

the 22nd General Conference, held in October/November 1983, where more than 95 percent of the resolutions had been approved by consensus with the United States joining in. The only negative U.S. vote was cast on Unesco's budget for the two-year period. The chief of the U.S. delegation, Edmund P. Hennelly, had said that vote was based on a U.S. policy for all international organizations for zero growth, and Unesco could not be an exception. The fact sheet pointed out that U.S. Ambassador Jean Gerard said at the conclusion of the conference: "We take pride in the work and many accomplishments of this general conference . . . . I believe —I hope—that we have laid the groundwork here for greater efficiency and effectiveness in Unesco's programs." The document quotes Dana Bullen, executive director of the World Press Freedom Committee, as saying that "If anyone is looking for an assault on the media at this conference serious enough to justify United States withdrawal, they won't find it." And it quotes Leonard Sussman of Freedom House as saying that "I feel the conference generally showed that it can be responsive to Western positions. If we sever our ties, we would have still less chance of influencing policy consistent with our objectives."

The fact sheet refers also to analyses of Unesco's work by the U.S. government that generally had given the organization a clean bill of health. For example, the report to Congress in February 1983 by the Department of State, in terms of the Beard Amendment, had found that "Unesco programs for the most part contribute to broad U.S. policy goals and particular U.S. educational, scientific and cultural interests." The report found that Unesco expenditures that benefited the United States— including fellowships, procurement of U.S. equipment, and consultation fees paid to American staff—amounted to about 40 percent of the value of the U.S. contribution. And it concluded that "Unesco to date has debated but has not implemented procedures of an anti-free press nature. There are at this time no grounds to withhold funding."

The fact sheet refers also to a letter from Newell to Holderman, asking for a review of Unesco by members of the U.S. National Commission. Holderman's reply, dated 8 November 1983, stated that the commission had polled some 20 national associations and their "unanimous recommendation is that the country should remain in Unesco." These groups included the American Newspaper Publishers Association, the National Academy of Sciences, the American Library Association, the National Education Association, the League of Women Voters and the Social Science Research Council. The commission, Holderman wrote, "is convinced that the best means of serving U.S. interests in Unesco is to press for reform from within."

Other fact sheets distributed to media over the year drew attention to moves made by Unesco to improve its functioning and efficiency to

avert a U.S. withdrawal. In July, for example, a fact sheet reported on working groups that recommended reforms to improve the organization's effectiveness. It quoted M'Bow as saying that "We take seriously specific suggestions from some of our major members and will make every effort to improve where improvement is found possible." In September, a fact sheet quoted Deputy Director-General Gerard Bolla as saying that recommendations for reform by five working groups had been accepted by M'Bow. In October, Unesco put out a press release noting that the organization's outside auditor had found "nothing that could justify accusations of corruption, bad management or negligence."

The New York office also sent to news organizations a number of source documents, including the text of the National Science Foundation's memorandum to Newell recommending that the United States "take a strong leadership role and commit additional resources to specific programs of interest and benefit to the U.S." It sent out transcripts of testimony at congressional hearings, including the testimony of people not reported in the news agency accounts. It distributed reprints of articles, columns and letters opposing the withdrawal that had appeared in other publications.

Among the documents in the mailings were reprints from foreign publications, some from Third World papers that gave the perspective of the developing nations. Also included were the texts of resolutions of support for Unesco from a variety of Third World organizations like the African, Asia and Pacific groups at Unesco, the Organization of Islamic Conference, the Organization of African Unity, the Union of African Journalists and the Group of 77.

In addition to its mailings, the New York office held special briefings for newspapers and journalistic groups. These consisted of a presentation of Unesco's position on the controversial issues, followed by questions and answers. Among the briefings held were those for the *New York Times* editorial board, the *Washington Post*, the *Christian Science Monitor*, United Press International, and committees of the American Newspaper Publishers Association and the American Society of Newspaper Editors (ASNE). Members of the New York office staff also made dozens of speeches, most of them to meetings of the United Nations Association, or to journalistic groups like ASNE, Sigma Delta Chi, and the National Newspaper Association.

Wagner & Baroody

Wagner & Baroody, a Washington-based public affairs consulting firm, was retained by Unesco in August 1984 to advise and assist in disseminating information about its purposes, programs and structure. It was paid

$15,000 a month, plus expenses. According to a press release by the firm, the contract was prompted by criticism of Unesco, "some of which seemed to be based on misunderstandings and misperceptions."

Wagner & Baroody compiled a mailing list of some 1,100 individuals and groups, including 440 press representatives, 535 members of the House and Senate, and 75 non-government organizations. Over the next few months, the firm sent out about 30 mailings to these groups. These included news releases giving details of reforms undertaken by Unesco to meet U.S. demands, denials of allegations made about Unesco in the press, letters to editors setting the record straight, details of how participation in Unesco was of benefit to the United States, and news about the organization's activities that was not being reported in the media. Several mailings had to do with the issue of reforms. They pointed out that Unesco had taken action in direct response to American criticisms. These included:

- *Politicization*: Unesco's executive board had passed a resolution providing for the refocusing of some programs, especially in the areas of communications, futures studies, peace and disarmament, and human rights. The board had called for emphasis on programs with "urgency, usefulness, efficiency and support."
- *Mismanagement*: M'Bow had announced he would institute a series of administrative changes designed to improve efficiency and streamline operations. The changes would include decentralization of authority within the Unesco secretariat, and greater accountability to member nations on budget and other matters. Unesco had also undertaken reforms in line with issues raised in the GAO report.
- *Zero-Growth Budget*: The Executive Board, meeting in October, had unanimously passed a resolution calling for a zero-growth budget for a two-year period. The resolution said the budget for 1986–87 should be limited to $391 million—the same as the 1984–85 operating budget.
- *Press Issues*: While some participants in Unesco meetings had proposed governmental licensing and monitoring of journalists in return for granting assurances of personal safety, Unesco itself had never approved the licensing or censoring of journalism. Unesco had been judged on the NWIO issue on what some member states proposed rather then what it did. The position of one or two states "no more represents overall Unesco policy than would introduction of legislation to license newspapers by an individual member of the House or Senate mean that Congress or the U.S. government seeks to abridge press freedom."

Wagner & Baroody also drew attention to the benefits the United States derived from its participation in Unesco. The information was based on documents submitted to the State Department by U.S. government agencies and non-governmental organizations. The United States, in exchange for its $50 million annual contribution, received the following benefits:

- Unesco bought about $5.5 million worth of equipment in the United States a year.
- Unesco gave the United States a voice in formulating conventions and protocols affecting transborder electronic communications of all kinds. The U.S. share in the $60 billion world information industry was about $49 billion. Without the protection provided by an American presence at Unesco, it risked international regulations handicapping American interests at a potential cost of millions of dollars.
- Unesco provided a forum for the U.S. publishing industry to encourage enforcement of the Universal Copyright Convention, which protects the rights of authors and publishers.
- Unesco provided an economic forum for regular contacts with Third World trading partners. Sales of American scholarly publications were enhanced by Unesco cataloguing systems.
- American ecosystems were protected through other nations' control of their pollution, encouraged by Unesco. The agency's scientific and educational programs enhanced conservation of food, wildlife and other resources—to the benefit of the United States and all other nations.
- The United States shared in the findings of international research programs in geology, physics, resource management, informatics, the biosphere, and earthquake prediction.

In addition to these mailings to the media, Wagner & Baroody arranged for Unesco officials to meet with the editorial boards of newspapers and set up briefings. It encouraged members of non-governmental organizations to write press releases and op-ed pieces for their local newspapers.

U.S. National Commission for Unesco

Also active in promoting continued membership was the U.S. National Commission for Unesco. In December 1983, just before the United States gave notice of withdrawal, a majority of commission members at their annual meeting approved a resolution urging the United States to remain

and work for reform from within. This resolution was largely lost in the flood of reports that quoted the administration's criticisms as reasons for the withdrawal. The commission's most determined attempt to sway public opinion to the idea of continued membership came in August, when it called simultaneous press conferences in New York and Washington to release its 30-page study that sought to refute the administration's criticisms of Unesco and argued that strong U.S. leadership within the organization would lead to desired reforms. In addition to being released at the press conference, the report was sent—using private funds—to a hundred media outlets, to the news agencies, and to correspondents and columnists in New York and Washington. A New York Times News Service report of the press conference was picked up by six papers; the AP version ran in two; a report by UPI was not used at all. Freedom House, whose director Leonard Sussman was also vice chairman of the U.S. Commission for Unesco, also was active in urging that the United States retain its membership.

NOTES

1. U.S. General Accounting Office, *United Nations: Analysis of Selected Media Products Shows Half Oppose Key U.S. Interests* (Washington, D. C., April 1986), pp. 43–45.
2. Owen Harries, "The U.S. and Unesco: Time for Decision," Heritage Foundation *Backgrounder* No. 40 (5 December 1983).
3. Owen Harries, "Why Unesco Spells Trouble," *Reader's Digest*, October 1984.
4. "Shultz Will Seek Withdrawal of U.S. From Unesco," *Washington Post*, 24 December 1983, p. A1.

CHAPTER 11

Summary and Conclusions

Many people have come to believe there is something wrong with the way this country makes its foreign policy. They probably don't know how wrong.

—Robert C. McFarlane
White House national security adviser

It is apparent, then, that a wide range of opinion on the Unesco issue was available to the press, with the groups favoring withdrawal and those supporting continued membership both devoting a good deal of time, money and effort to get their views across. Yet Unesco's opponents were far more successful in gaining access to the news and editorial columns.

The Unesco story, during the year between the American announcement of intention to withdraw and its actually doing so, drew an unusual amount of attention to the organization. Yet, far from being deluged by information, most people who relied on their local media for news about the issue would barely have gotten their feet wet. Of the nation's 1,700 daily newspapers, fewer than one-half carried anything at all about Unesco. Of the 800 papers that did carry something, one-half carried only editorials with no accompanying news reports. Another 94 ran only opinion pieces—editorials and columns—with no news. Just 200 papers, or about 12 percent of the total, ran new stories plus opinion pieces, either editorials or columns or both. This apparent dearth of information was offset by the fact that the papers that did carry a comparatively large amount of news and opinion were among the largest in the country. The top 100 papers, in terms of circulation, among them accounted for one-half of all the articles published.

These papers relied heavily on just four sources for their news—the AP, UPI and the New York Times or Washington Post/L.A. Times news services.

ORIENTATION OF COVERAGE

News Agencies

As has been demonstrated, the news services portrayed the dispute in the following way:

- Taken as a whole, the agency coverage was strongly anti-Unesco and supportive of the withdrawal. About 70 percent of the themes in the reports were critical of the organization or supported a pullout.
- The pro-Unesco or anti-withdrawal themes comprised just over one-quarter of the total.
- Just 3 percent focused on what impact the withdrawal would have on Unesco, other member countries, or future U.S. participation in scientific, educational and cultural programs.
- Unesco was repeatedly portrayed as being politicized, misman-aged, anti-West, hostile to a free press, anti–free enterprise and badly in need of reform.
- Denials that the agency was guilty as charged were greatly out-numbered by accusations.
- Although there was a substantial body of opinion in the United States that withdrawal would be a mistake, these views were reported far less often than those of people or organizations that favored the pullout.
- The news-agency reports showed an overwhelming preference for government sources of information, rather than Unesco sources or American non-government organizations that stood to lose, like the scientific community. More than one-half of the themes re-ported were attributed to U.S. government spokespersons. Add spokespersons for Western governments and the figure rises to 80 percent.
- The four agencies were remarkably similar in their orientation. Far from providing competing and diverse sources of information, the general orientation of the reports, and the range of events and subjects covered, was almost identical.
- This imbalance occurred because of selective reporting of events, selective use of sources, and a style of writing that generally

relegated pro-Unesco themes to the end of reports, where they were likely to be omitted from published versions.

Published Reports

- Reports that appeared in the press were even more negative toward Unesco than the news-agency files on which they were based.
- The newspapers followed the news-agency agenda but tended to select from the agency files those reports most critical of Unesco, while ignoring those that supported the organization or opposed the withdrawal.
- When newspapers edited agency reports, they frequently cut out statements supportive of Unesco, largely because they simply trimmed stories from the bottom, which is where the pro-Unesco material often appeared.
- Once the withdrawal took effect, Unesco largely largely disappeared from view. News-agency coverage tapered off, and fewer newspapers picked up what they did report.

Editorials

Editorials and editorial columns in the press reinforced the anti-Unesco orientation of the news reports. Many newspapers carried only editorials—twice as many as carried any news reports. The editorials were far more critical of the organization than the news stories. Nearly 85 percent of the themes in the editorials criticized Unesco, or urged the administration to follow through with its intention to withdraw. A handful of large papers called for continued U.S. membership, but even they acknowledged Unesco's shortcomings. The majority saw no merit in Unesco and applauded the withdrawal.

A substantial proportion of the editorials were not written by the papers that carried them but were "canned" editorials bought from syndicates or distributed by chains. Nearly one-quarter of the 1,417 editorials recorded were duplicates. These editorials were seldom attributed to their source but appeared under such misleading headings as "In Our View" or "Our Opinion." This practice was most common among, but not confined to, smaller papers, many of which carried several editorials but no news reports. The most frequently used source of the canned editorials was the Copley News Service, followed by the Scripps-Howard News Service and the Hearst News and Feature Service.

Like the news-agency reports, the editorials were generally based on

specific news events—usually those that depicted Unesco in a negative way. Largely ignored by editorial writers were news events that could be interpreted as favorable to Unesco's cause. The editorials expressed the same themes as the news coverage, but with a stronger emphasis on themes critical of Unesco. They manifested the concern of publishers and editors over Unesco's support of a new information order. Many stated expressly that Unesco's efforts to curb the press were the major reason for the withdrawal.

Editorial Columns

Columns by a small group of syndicated conservative columnists dominated the coverage. The five most frequently used writers accounted for half of the 580 columns relating to Unesco that were published over the year. Four of the five—George Will, Flora Lewis, William Buckley and James Kilpatrick—were critical of Unesco and praised the pullout. Columnists who opposed the pullout, like Richard Reeves, Garry Wills and William Pfaff, were few in number and generally were used by fewer newspapers.

The overall orientation of the columns, like the editorials, was heavily critical of Unesco and supportive of the pullout. The themes they stressed were similar to those in the news reports and editorials—accusations of politicization, mismanagement and hostility to a free press.

Papers that attacked Unesco in their editorials reinforced this orientation by publishing anti-Unesco columnists. The half-dozen larger papers that opposed the withdrawal were less consistent. They carried a higher proportion of middle-of-the-road or pro-Unesco columns than those papers that took an anti-Unesco line. But the conservative columns still outnumbered the liberal on their pages.

Television News

Like the press coverage, reports on the network television evening news focused on a handful of events that tended to show Unesco in an unfavorable light. The commercial networks among them broadcast a total of 13 news reports on their evening news over the year. Eight of these dealt with the initial announcement that the United States planned to withdraw, and three more with confirmation of the decision a year later. Only two other events were covered: a fire at Unesco headquarters, and the United Kingdom's decision to pull out. Television presented essentially the same message as the press, and had precisely the same anti-Unesco orientation.

EVALUATION OF THE COVERAGE

The Media as Informers

Few people in the United States have any firsthand knowledge of Unesco. Although a substantial number of scientists and educators, among others, have participated in Unesco programs, almost everyone else must base their opinions about the organization on the information they get from the media. It is a fundamental tenet of the American political system that decisions ultimately lie in the hands of the people. To make those decisions they need a wide range of factual information and conflicting opinions from their media. Bernard Cohen articulates this concept in his seminal book on the press and foreign policy: "Today and every day the American people must make decisions on which their whole survival may depend. To make sound decisions, the people must be informed. For this they depend on the nation's press."[1]

As Cohen points out, however, the American people as a whole do not make foreign policy decisions in any direct sense. That function is delegated to their elected representatives. In the case of Unesco, the decision to withdraw was not even made by the Congress: it was the executive branch, the Reagan administration, that pulled the plug. There was no direct public input into the decision. Why then did both the proponents and opponents of Unesco seek to mobilize public opinion, and why would it matter if the information presented by the media was inadequate, or biased, or both? As W. Phillips Davison puts it, even though the public at large do not make foreign policy decisions, decision makers must take public opinion into account. The media can influence these decision makers by making it possible for political leaders to take certain actions or by enabling others to persuade the political leaders to behave differently.[2] The media help set the agenda for the political leaders and provide much of the information on which their decisions are based. As Davison points out, the quality of government decisions is closely related to the quality of press coverage. The Unesco saga is a good illustration of these functions. The fact that the media, for their own reasons, targeted Unesco as the worst-case example of the U.N. system and kept up a drumbeat of criticism over the years put the organization on the political agenda. Although the administration made the decision to pull out of Unesco, it had to consider both public and congressional opinion. And the media provided arguments that reinforced the decision. Congressmen or members of the general public reading accounts of the Unesco dispute would have little exposure to arguments against the withdrawal, and no reason to question it.

The Watchdog Role

The analysis raises important questions regarding the performance of the press in relation to government and special-interest groups. American journalists are wedded to the concept of objectivity, the idea that the media do not manipulate the news or slant it for partisan purposes. One might argue that it is unfair to single out for criticism the performance of American media, that coverage of the withdrawal in *Pravda* or *Isvestia* would have been equally, or more, one-sided. But that misses the point. Those papers don't make any claim to objectivity. The American media do, and should be judged by that criterion. Objectivity is generally understood to mean separation of fact from opinion, and presentation of events without shading. It implies also that news should be balanced, with an effort to give all points of view when an issue is in dispute. The idea is that the press should be a neutral conduit, providing factual, balanced information on which people can base their own judgments about policy issues. As this analysis shows, with Unesco that clearly was not the case. The media acted as a mouthpiece for those groups that criticized the organization and supported the withdrawal. There was little counter-balancing information, and an almost total neglect of groups that opposed the withdrawal.

Another shibboleth of American journalism is that journalists are skeptical of politicians and government, that it is the responsibility of the press to question whether policy decisions are soundly based. The press is thought to serve as a watchdog, as an adversary of government. In this instance, however, with the exception of a handful of papers, there was no adversarial relationship. Instead, the relationship was symbiotic. The government responded to the media's concerns about Unesco and the press in turn supported the government's action, both through its choice of news sources and topics, and its editorial stance. Rather than recommending alternative courses of action, the general effect of the coverage was to serve as an advocate for the government's policy.

REASONS FOR THE IMBALANCE

New Technology

Ironically, part of the problem lies in the very communications technologies that have speeded up the flow of information to media. Most newspapers in the United States now get their news-agency copy from satellite feeds directly into their newsroom computers. Only local copy is

keyboarded in by their own staff. It is much more time-consuming and expensive to retype material that arrives by mail than to call up news-agency copy on a computer screen for editing and automatic typesetting.

The pro-Unesco press releases by the U.S. National Commission for Unesco, by Wagner & Baroody, and by Unesco itself were—like most press releases—usually ignored by the news agencies. Because the agencies controlled the distribution channels, Unesco supporters had to mail their press releases to newspapers, which were usually not inclined to keyboard it into their computer systems. The material was not consi-dered "hard" news, as it might have been had it come across the agency distribution system. While copy that arrives in the mail may be used by local editorial writers or columnists, it is not likely to appear in the news columns. This means also that if a newspaper publishes a report from the news agencies, and it later receives in the mail a correction or clarifica-tion, that response is not considered newsworthy and may at best be used as a letter to the editor, carried in a brief "corrections" column, or be referred to in an "ombudsman" column. Most likely, this analysis shows, it will be ignored. Even when the news agency itself issues a correction to an earlier report, that is not used by anything like as many newspapers as carried the original, incorrect version. And if it is used, it is seldom given the prominence of the original. This was the case with reports on the fire at Unesco headquarters on the eve of the General Accounting Office audit in 1984. The first, widely published reports noted that the fire had been started by an arsonist and implied that the intention was to destroy incriminating documents. Later reports that nothing of consequence had been burned were used by far fewer papers. Likewise, many papers carried news reports and editorials about a large pay raise for M'Bow in 1985. But few ran an agency clarification that while his base pay had increased, his cost-of-living allowance had been cut by a corresponding amount. The result is that organizations like Unesco, wanting to get across views that are not adequately represented by the news agencies, or that want to correct errors in published reports, face an uphill battle.

Reporting Practices

Partly responsible also was the laziness of reporters, editorial writers and columnists to do their own research rather than rely on handouts from interested parties. Partly it was due to the well-documented tendency for reporters to rely on government spokesmen, rather than seek out a range of alternative views, and to report what officials say rather than to research source documents. One correspondent told the author that dead-line pressure was a contributory factor. He would cover a State Depart-ment briefing on Unesco and have to file a report for his agency as

quickly as possible before moving on to other events. This often precluded seeking the input of dissenting voices.

Yet another factor was the audiences served by the media. This influenced the line taken by papers like the *New York Times*. That newspaper has always championed the free flow of information and resisted efforts to muzzle the press. For that reason it could be expected to oppose Unesco's information policies. But, in addition to being the major national newspaper of record, the *Times* is the local daily for the largest Jewish population outside of Israel. This inevitably affects its coverage. Since Unesco was perceived as being anti-Israel, the *New York Times* was hostile toward Unesco for that reason as well. And the *New York Times* coverage in turn influenced what the news agencies reported: AP or UPI reports often quoted the *Times* as their source, or followed up on reports that first appeared in the *Times*.

Election Year

A contributing factor was that, especially in an election year, opponents of the pullout were reluctant to speak up for Unesco, which was identified as being anti-Western, anti-Israel and anti–free press. The record of congressional hearings on the Unesco issue suggests an intense awareness of its domestic political implications. Even Walter Mondale, who was running as the Democratic party candidate for president against Reagan, sensed the political folly of opposing the groups who favored the withdrawal and went along with the decision.

Media Involvement

That does not explain, however, why the news-agency copy itself tended to be one-sided, or why the press selected from the agency files mainly those reports that showed Unesco in a poor light. The answer lies partly in the media gatekeeping process. As indicated earlier, media organizations were not dispassionate observers of the debate. Representatives of the news agencies, of editors and publishers, and of the broadcast media had long been active in resisting Unesco proposals to implement a new information order. To be pro-Unesco was to be anti–free press, even anti-American. Besides, the anti-Unesco campaign now had the imprimatur of the U.S. government.

The World Press Freedom Committee (WPFC), spearhead of the campaign against Unesco's media policies, refused to take a stand on the withdrawal issue once the government had made its decision. WPFC officers met after the United States announced its plan to withdraw in December 1983 and the committee's chairman, Harold Andersen, stated

that the decision "was based on a number of considerations and was taken by the U.S. government, not the news media." Although not expressed in public, the real reason for not taking a stand was concern that the media would be seen to have a conflict of interest, of reporting and commenting on events which they themselves had to a large extent precipitated. Before the announcement, media criticism of Unesco had focused almost exclusively on its media policies. Once the government added charges of politicization and mismanagement, these were picked up by the press as the major reasons for withdrawal, and media issues were given a much lower profile.

There is no evidence of a centrally coordinated campaign by the news organizations to denigrate Unesco, although that may have happened at the newspaper-chain level. But there were campaigns run by political groups, using the press for the most part as a willing handmaiden. The result was that the news coverage displayed a systematic bias against Unesco and in favor of the withdrawal, through selective reporting of events and choice of sources. The orientation of the news reports was strongly reinforced on the opinion pages (Table 8.2, page 221). The institutional bias of the press against Unesco is demonstrated by the fact that newspaper editorials were even more critical of the organization than the news-agency reports.

Third World Concerns

This analysis does not extend to coverage of the withdrawal outside the United States. But there is no reason to think it was much different. A cursory examination of newspapers from other countries, some in the developing areas, indicates that their primary sources for news about the pullout were the international agencies. Lacking foreign correspondents of their own, the Third World media used the Western version of events as transmitted by the AP and UPI, or by Reuters and Agence France-Presse. Reuters dispatches on the withdrawal that appeared in a handful of American newspapers had a very similar content and orientation to that of the U.S. agencies. Gerald Long, managing director of Reuters, is on record as saying that "the recent activities of Unesco in the field of information, the field in which I have spent my working life, are mischievous and dangerous and must be closely observed and countered by those who value freedom of information."[3] And a previous study of Agence France-Presse's reporting of Unesco and the New International Information Order characterized it as "at best incomplete and at worst openly biased."[4] The coverage by the Big Four agencies reflected the orientation of Western media and governments. The views of Third World government leaders seldom were reported. To most readers in the

Third World, the true story of Unesco would not be the ideological conflicts and crises that sometimes rage there, but the organization's long-term projects to promote scientific, educational and cultural development. Yet it is precisely these activities that are missing in the agency coverage. The emphasis was almost entirely on Unesco's failures, not its successes. And the Third World generally was depicted as being in league with the Soviet Union in attempting create a New Information Order by restricting international news gathering rather than by building up their own communications infrastructures. The coverage was precisely the kind of thing they complain about.

ONE-SIDED PICTURE

The average reader of one of the top 100 papers in the United States— with a few notable exceptions—would have been exposed to 9 or 10 news reports on Unesco over the year. Typically they would have been that the United States had decided to withdraw because Unesco was corrupt and anti-American; that officials had tried to burn down Unesco headquarters to destroy incriminating evidence wanted by congressional investigators; that Unesco was trying illegally to withhold a refund of some $80 million that was due to the Western nations; that the United Kingdom had also become so disgusted with the organization that it would join the U.S. pullout; and that by the end of the probationary year Unesco's attempts at reform were merely cosmetic and had come too late for the United States to change its mind. The typical reader would also have been exposed to a couple of editorials and one or two conservative columnists who sharpened and intensified the negative images of the news reports. The coverage, in short, dealt with political issues, with little or no reference to the educational, scientific or cultural losses the United States might suffer if it withdrew, and even less attention to the impact of the pullout on developing countries. Those who got their news only from television would have been exposed to an even more limited perspective, since although the general orientation was similar to that of the press, the range of issues covered was narrower.

The upshot was that most Americans who relied on their local media for information about the issues involved would have received a very one-sided picture. No studies were made of changing public perceptions of Unesco over the year. However, there is evidence that the campaign did have an impact on public opinion, even if not intended. In December 1984, after a year of media attacks on Unesco, the United Nations Children's Fund (UNICEF) experienced a sharp drop in contributions from Americans, who apparently had confused Unesco with UNICEF.

The press then felt obliged to run news reports and editorials pointing out that UNICEF was a worthy cause; it was Unesco that should be shunned.

Where Unesco made its mistake was in offending three of the most articulate and influential groups in the United States—neo-conservatives, the press and the Israeli lobby. This ensured that Unesco would have difficulty finding support, especially in Congress. And the Reagan administration could proceed with a cherished neo-conservative initiative secure in the knowledge that its flank was protected from carping critics in the press.

There were voices of support for Unesco, and there were sharp critics of the American action. But these views seldom found expression in the media. The critics of Unesco were far more successful in gaining access to news and editorial columns, and the critics ultimately triumphed when the United States confirmed the withdrawal. But Americans who had no source of information other than their local media were not, for the most part, exposed to sufficient factual material or opposing viewpoints to make informed judgments as to the merits of the action.

NOTES

1. Bernard C. Cohen, *The Press and Foreign Policy* (Princeton, N. J.: Princeton University Press, 1963), p. 5.
2. W. Phillips Davison, *Mass Communication and Conflict Resolution: The Role of the Information Media in the Advancement of International Understanding* (New York: Praeger, 1974), p. 20. See also Andrew Arno and Wimal Dissanayake, eds., *The News Media in National and International Conflict* (Boulder, Colo.: Westview Press, 1984).
3. Gerald Long, "A Search for Truth . . . Or a Denial of Truth," in Leonard H. Marks, ed., *The Media Crisis* (Miami: World Press Freedom Committee, 1981), p. 51.
4. Colleen Roach, "French Press Coverage of the Belgrade Unesco Conference," *Journal of Communication*, 31 (Autumn 1981), pp. 175–186.

Index